Behind Every Hero

C. L. Neely

Behind Every Hero
Copyright © 2011 C. L. Neely

All rights reserved. No part of this publication can be reproduced, stored in a retrieval system, or transmitted in any form or by any means—electronic, mechanical, photocopy, recording or any other—except that copying permitted by U. S. Copyright Law, Section 107, "fair use" in teaching or research, or for brief quotations in printed reviews, without permission in writing from C. L. Neely.

Cover art by author

Dedicated
To my parents
Jack and Bertha Miller
Who remained an inspiration
and encouragement
all of their lives.

Acknowledgements

There are many people I wish to thank.

For help with research I would like to thank Maureen Goddard, librarian of the small town where I lived. Her encouragement and ability to order extremely out of date and never-before heard of books was a great help. I want to thank the employees at the Plumas County and Sierra County courthouse, and Bill Copren who helped me find some important missing newspapers. I would also thank the helpful people in the libraries of the Universities of Nevada and Chico, and Bowdoin College in Maine.

For all the editing help, I wish to thank Mary Olsen, Jack Bibb, Bill Powers, Arthur Rathburn and Kathy Gilman.

The major sources for the details in this book are from James Sinnott's series of books on Sierra County, and from newspaper articles from the 1940's written by Charlie Church. Credit for the bear story goes to Obediah S. Church who recounted the story in the newspapers in 1941.

I would like to extend a special thanks to Mary Olsen, and Arthur Rathburn, who picked up my book and felt it worthy to publish.

Most important, I thank Larry Neely and Kathy Gilman who have watched the progress of this book with patience and humor, and my Lord who has whispered me forward.

To the readers who choose to take this trip into California history, I hope you enjoy it, and thank you.

MAP OF SIERRA VALLEY

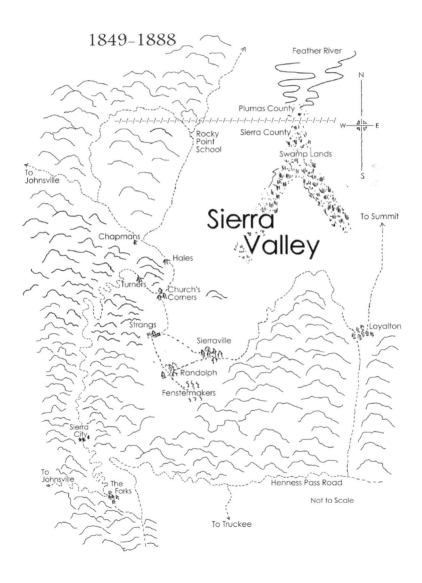

INTRODUCTION

The California gold rush of 1849 brought thousands of people clawing through the Sierra Nevada mountain range in search of its wealth and luster. This is the true story of a few of those men and women who settled in Downieville, Ca, and later moved down to Sierra Valley, where they struggled through the challenges of pioneer life in a forgotten corner of that world.

The only fictitious names in this story are Buffalo Mike and Spuds. All other characters bare the true names of the individuals they play, although some may be altered a little for clarification, such as Hartwell Franklin Turner, who was always called Frank, and is referred to as Hart in this story.

The conversations in this book are fictitious, and never took place (as far as the author knows), and the feelings people had for each other is purely conjecture. Also, all letters documented in this story are purely a figment of the author's imagination. How James Galloway voted at any time in this story is also speculation.

All dates of births and deaths recorded here are taken from public documents; and newspaper quotations are directly from the newspapers mentioned.

I hope you enjoy this little trip into the past, and realize how often our lives intertwine, and how those we push to the front to become our leaders are held there by the support of their families, who fill in the blanks spaces they leave behind.

C. L. Neely

CHAPTER ONE - 1888

Mirrors and calendars reflect the image of an old man, but the mind that turns beneath this snow capped dome rejects the tell-tale passage of time. And the vows I made in the arrogance of my youth seem unimportant now, as I anxiously await the result of the election.

I am a Democrat. If I should die tomorrow and the coroner examined my remains, he would find inside democratic bones—for that is how deep my party allegiance goes. So, how is it that I should come to vote for a Republican?

That is a question I have asked myself a thousand times during the last few weeks.

"Old Fire Eater", that's what they called me—the roaring editor of the *Downieville Democrat*. Faithfully I voted the party ticket . . . until now.

I pace the floor like an ignorant old fool, and my heart pounds with the same hot anxiety it felt when I, James Galloway, was the honored candidate for State Senator in 1861—for the great party. And now where is my hope? With a danged Republican!

With each anxious step from wall to wall, my mind returns to those early innocent days on the beautiful Yuba River.

CHAPTER TWO - 1850

It was a warm spring but none of us knew it then, as we were all newcomers to this place we called The Forks.

I sat quietly on a bolder, washed smooth from the thousands of years it rested undisturbed on the shore of the transparent, emerald green Yuba River. The anxiety in my heart matched the swirling, demanding water that raced madly downstream away from its frozen confinement on the snowcapped peaks that towered above us.

In my hand I held the tool of the gold miner's trade, a large flat gold pan that still had the brilliance of being new. Relentlessly I clawed at the small piece of river bed I claimed. I let the water sort out the light weight particles, while heavier bits of sand and gravel remained at the bottom of the pan. Once and a while I dropped its hopeful contents into a second pan I held between my tall leather boots. My feet shivered beneath the ice cold water.

My eyes seldom strayed from my work, as I watched for a sign of golden metallic sparkle. Occasionally, curiosity would nudge me to glance over at my nearest neighbor, old Tom Turner, to see if his luck might be better than mine. My legs ached from the cold, and my head pounded from the concentration.

I stood up, and set my pan down on the dry ground, and stretched. My luck was terrible. There was nothing but a couple of minute gold specks and a lot of ugly black sand to show for all my effort.

A hat swirled down the middle of the river. It dipped out of sight when a rapid grabbed it, then reappeared just as quickly. I looked up stream, and expected to see its owner waving madly. Instead I observed the common site of miners bent over the water like herds of thirsty animals. It was that way up and down stream, as far as I could see. I watched hungrily as a thin redheaded fellow shouted, "I've got color! Beautiful gold color!" His legs flew in a rhythmic laughter as he danced a jig—careful not to spill the precious contents of his metal pan. I noticed he was not wearing a hat.

Gold: It seemed always to be in someone else's pan.

I tried to stomp off some of the water that made those rough canvass pants cling to my legs. The mid-day sun played tag with drifting clouds, unconcerned with our madness, and reluctant to spread its warmth.

I left my comfortable home in Pennsylvania, and traveled thousands of treacherous miles to search for this gold. Now, where was it?

From a wellspring deep within me, I felt laughter begin to bubble. It burst forth unrestrained, and old Tom looked my way. He kept his chin down so his hat shaded his eyes from the sun.

"You got an itch?" he asked.

I waved my hand at him, and shook my head as I tried to gain composure. "I'm blind! Stupid and blind!" I shouted.

"The sun will do that to ya." The old man started to hobble over in my direction. "Ya gotta sit so your body shades the water, or it'll blind ya."

I shook my head madly. "It's not the water. It's Rachel!"

Old Tom's head cocked to one side. I could almost see his ears twitch. "Rachel? Who in tarnation is Rachel?"

Tom Turner. He was a lonely old man, and I hated to drag him into a conversation. He could talk for hours, and in his own magical way, he could take any topic and head it straight for Maine, southern Maine to be exact. The final resting place for the wife he dearly loved, and the home of children he left behind in the care of his sister Mary. I never guessed then, that I would ever meet these off-springs of old Tom, but my future would be closely linked with theirs by that invisible Weaver's thread.

I shook my head at the old miner who now stood in front of me with gleaming eyes. Carefully I scraped the black sand from my gold pan into a tin cup. Later I would sort out the gold. But now I had news! News that overwhelmed me, as my mind interpreted the signals from my heart.

Tom poked at my arm. "You ain't got a gal on your mind, have you Son?"

"Rachel Daugherty!" The rhythm of her name felt good on my tongue.

Tom's puzzled look, and shaking head, made me explain, "You know—the lady everyone is talking about!"

"That white gal?" Tom raised his bushy eyebrows, and

grinned—a toothless grin. "Now ain't she somthin'! Yep, she can make a fella blind all right!"

In those days, the forest grew all the way down to the water. I walked over to a large tree where I had dropped my coat. Tom stumbled along beside me. I guess I really did want to talk to someone about her. "You know, I traveled in the same wagon train with Rachel—all the way from Pennsylvania."

"Pennsylvania!" He pulled at his ear. "I can't figger out why a fine lady like her would be comin' to a God-forsaken place like this!"

"Same reason the rest of us came: For gold!"

". . . But a white woman! I tell ya it don't make sense. The trip alone would kill most white women. They ain't built for it. They're spoilt: Too soft . . . Used to fine dainty things."

"Not Rachel. She's tough!" I picked up a round stone, examined it for color, and then threw it into the river.

The truth was, on my journey West, I never took much notice of Rachel, because my mind churned with only one idea—making a fortune. When the ice cold reality of wet feet and empty stomach became the cost of fortune hunting, my heart searched for a more substantial idol to worship. It was then I saw the beauty of Miss Daugherty, reflected in the eyes of the other lonely miners. She suddenly became a treasure of rare quality—and desire engulfed me.

Tom watched where my rock hit the water. He removed his hat, and exposed a shiny sunburned head that sprouted only a few gray strands of hair.

"I hear tell, that gal came in from Volcano," he said, in a tone that suggested that he doubted my honesty.

"We all came in from Volcano." I sat down on a boulder next to the tree, and scraped in the mud with the heel of my boot, pushing up small rocks. "That is as far as the wagon train got, last fall, before the storms set in."

An unfamiliar heaviness rested on my heart as I looked up the river toward the little tent village that lined the bank. I knew where Rachel pitched her tent, not far from my own. For the first time, I began to wonder where she was.

That trip from Volcano was a treacherous adventure. Like blind men, we felt our way through dense forest land, with no road, not even a marked trail to guide us. We were a small band of gold crazy men who agreed to stick together, and watch after the independent, headstrong woman in our group—Rachel. She insisted she did not need our help, but we shoved it on her anyway. I've yet to know for sure if maybe it was because she was such a good cook.

The only intelligent ones on the journey were the mules. We overloaded the poor animals with all of our supplies, and they balked every step of the way! We whacked, cussed, swatted and shouted across every mile of those Sierra Nevada Mountains, up the Yuba River, and constantly heard the echo thundering back from the deep canyon walls. Oaks and evergreens surrounded us—often blocking our view of the rugged rock cliffs that adorned the high ridge above.

We were obsessed men chasing a rainbow's end, caught up in a mirage. As soon as we reached the place where the river forked, we dashed to mark our claims, and Rachel's welfare was forgotten.

I picked up my gold pan, and the old wool jacket that held fond memories of back home. I nodded to old Tom, and began to walk upstream toward the tent village.

Behind me I heard his coarse voice. "Ya know Sonny, if you're gonna let that gal Rachel run wild in your mind, you ought'a try and stake a claim. The ways I hear tell, there ain't no man got a claim on her!"

The old man's words grabbed at my heels, and I couldn't move. He was right. No one owned Rachel, and my chances of winning her now were pretty slim. You don't ignore a woman for several months, then when thousands of men suddenly swarm her for attention, just step in and expect her to . . .

Slowly I walked back to my place on the river.

"What's the matter Sonny? Are ye afraid?" Tom asked.

I could feel the hot red blush rise above my collar. I was *not* afraid.

"Well, that's all right. She's probably too old for ya anyway."

I always looked a good deal younger than my age, and it was of great embarrassment to me when I was young. Boldly I said, "I am thirty two!"

Tom raised his eyebrows. "Hmmm . . . thirty two? I figured you to be younger—about the same age as my middle boy. You remember me tellin' ya 'bout Henry? He speaks pretty like you do."

"I know. You told me about Henry."

"He's in school ya know: Medical School. What did you say you trained for?"

"I'm a lawyer."

"That's right." He sounded disappointed. "There ain't much use for a lawyer here. No law! But it ought to impress a gal, just the same. Ya ain't bad lookin' either. You ought to give it a try."

My heart and mind wanted to believe him. "You think so?" I asked.

"'Course I think so. Said so, didn't I?"

Sometimes just a word of encouragement is all a man needs. I felt my heart flutter as it sent gushing sounds past my ears. It took only seconds for my feet to respond. Back up the river I raced, as I shouted over my shoulder, "Thanks Tom!"

I stumbled over boulders, and pulled myself up. One miner looked up at me and smiled—another scowled. I suppose, they though my excitement was the result of finding the golden treasure we all sought.

Where would I find her? She worked the river like everyone else, and she dressed like a man, in an oversized shirt, dungarees, and a floppy hat. Bent over their gold pans, they all looked the same.

My eyes searched the rocky bank. The only areas void of trees were littered with tents. A beam of sunlight filtered down through the clouds, and rested on a small stream that trickled down the side of the mountain. A flash of inspiration traveled with that heavenly light. For, there along that giggling brook grew a small grove of wildflowers.

A pleasant memory nuzzled my mind. During that long journey from Pennsylvania, Rachel picked wild flowers from meadows and pastures, and draped them in her apron. I remembered the pleasant, simple satisfaction upon her face.

Within seconds I stood among the flowers. I picked the biggest and most beautiful bouquet I could manage from poppies, wild violets, lupine and some white flowers that I could not identify. I added green leafy ferns, and when I thought it looked impressive I turned, and with the flushed cheeks of a young school boy, I went on up the river to deliver this bouquet of love to the object of my heart's desire—Rachel Daugherty, the first white woman who ever set her dainty foot in The Forks.

I found her a few tents upstream from my own. She was spreading a newly washed shirt across a bush to dry. She turned, and saw me standing there. "James!" she said.

She reached to her hair, and quickly pushed a few loose strands back in place. Her plaid shirt hung outside of her canvass pants, and her face was smudged with dirt—but I thought she looked beautiful!

"These are for you," I said, as I held the bouquet between us.

As she stepped close, and took her gift from my hands, she blushed, and from that moment I knew she was mine.

The wildflowers got Rachel's attention, but I like to think it was my charm, and not the flowers, that won the lady's heart.

CHAPTER THREE – 1850

I look back now, and know that we were fortunate to witness the birth of a town; although, at the time, the frustrations of isolation from the rest of the world seemed to plague us on a daily basis. There was no preacher, or Justice of the Peace, to marry us, and this caused a lot of pre-marital friction. So, during an extraordinary long and rocky courtship, I built our future home: a small log cabin in the forest, a mile and a half up the mountain above The Forks.

While tramping across this vast country of ours, I envisioned my first year as a young '49er, kneeling beside the bank of a river that sparkled with brilliant gold, instead of blue. In my dreams I picked out nuggets as large as my fist, and stacked them in the corner of my tent. But instead of counting bags full of gathered wealth, that year of 1850, I became a home builder. I debarked logs, and used our mules to drag them into a square frame, where I filled in the gaps with mud. Rachel helped. She worked hard and diligently by my side, and that is exactly where I wanted her—away from the other miners. I took her wherever I went, and spread the word that I, James Galloway, had a claim on Rachel Daugherty . . . and cautiously I watched for claim jumpers.

A combination of the world's most industrious men filtered into the mining camp, and their minds never rested from discovering inventive ways to fill their pockets with gold. A man named Dugan built our first industry: a sawmill—on one of the flats where the river branched. Dugan charged an extravagant $80 in gold for 1000 foot of lumber, and the customer had to lash the boards onto the back of their own mule, and drag them to their destination. Dugan did not deliver. Greed ran rampant, and because of our isolation, we had to pay the price.

If I had the luck of some, whose hungry eyes searched the river and found fortune, I would have bought lumber from Dugan. And I'd have paid the $16 to $20 a day the carpenters were asking, to have them build my house.

We weren't very understanding of the hardships these pioneer merchants went through to supply us with our needs. Cut-Eye Foster opened the first store, and with his inflationary prices, he quickly became a villain in our new little community. A pound of potatoes at Foster's Grocery and Grog cost three dollars. Butter and flour cost the same. When the coolness of spring was replaced by summer's heat, supplies ran short. The three dollar potatoes became a luxury, and men gladly parted with their hard earned gold. But the same prospector's tongues began to wag with unforgiving venom when the rumor circulated that Cut-Eye Foster watered down the liquor!

* * *

The thundering roar of men tunneling their way into the side of the mountain accompanied every hour of those warm summer days. The echo of their excavation sounded like the cymbal crash in an orchestra, with the background rhythm of an ax penetrating the base of a tree. The soft, subtle melody of chirping birds, and chattering squirrels rose and set with the sun.

With each tree that fell, the edge of the forest slowly crept away from the river, and men proudly displayed their new lodgings—built intermittently between rows of tents.

Occasionally a miner gave up in exasperation, and someone else quickly gobbled up his claim. New claims were in great demand. One couldn't go anywhere without tripping over a stake someone drove in the ground to show ownership. Some of those stakes were mine. I kept my original spot on the river, next to old Tom Turner—and my future was invested in the little mountain hideaway above the village. However, my favorite place to work was Rachel's claim, located where the river forked, not far from the new sawmill, and right next door to one of The Forks' liveliest characters, Major William Downie.

In my mind I visualized The Forks as becoming an active, healthy community, and I mentioned it one day to the Major. He quickly answered, "Could be, but I won't be around to see it."

"Where are you going?" I asked, and Downie began one of his many soliloquies about moving on to the next big strike. "It could be anywhere," he said. "But, as long as men keep burrowing in the ground, they will strike gold! And wherever they find it, I want to be there and get my fair share." His eyes sparkled when he talked, and he often would blend a joke or two with his stories. He wasn't a big man in stature, but his outgoing personality rubbed off on those around him, and his presence could monopolize a room or conversation.

The Major accompanied the first group of prospectors who found gold at The Forks. And he was there on that ordinary day when I accidentally took the first step that would change the direction of my life. I wanted to be nothing but a prospector, but destiny had other plans.

We were chatting—the Major, myself, and a small group of miners. One of the men pointed out a row of cabins near the river's fork. "Did you fellows notice anything unusual about the way those houses are built?" he asked.

Like birds with bulging eyes, we craned necks. No... Nothing unusual... Our heads shook in unison.

"They are all facing the same direction!" ... came the obvious answer from our inquisitor.

We shrugged. "So what?"

"We don't have roads, and we don't have wagons—yet, everyone built their cabins facing the same direction. And... they left enough room in front for a road!"

There were others who had a vision like mine. "We have progressive thinking citizens here," I said smugly.

"Well, don't you think it's strange that this new fellow hasn't followed suit?" our observant friend said. He pointed to a new claim (close in distance to my own) and marked with common stakes driven into the ground.

"Let's go over and take a look at this," I said. Our little troupe moved closer to research the situation.

The name Vineyard, printed in smeared ink on the claim paper, meant nothing to me then. The ornery cuss appeared to have a building of some sort staked out, totally out of line with the others that were being built nearby. "Seems might peculiar," I said.

"Do you think it would be fittin' to measure out another man's claim?" Downie asked.

"I can't see how it would hurt anything," I said, and began to pace out the distance with my three foot stride. "Only seventeen feet: The man left only seventeen feet for a road!" I took off my hat and wiped my brow. The sun's heat intensified my disgust.

"That ain't right," someone finally said. "Everyone else left plenty of room for a roadway. If this fella... what's his name?

"Vineyard."

"If this Vineyard fellow wants to put up some kind of building, he should have to keep it in line with the rest of us. What happens if we do decide to put in a road some day? Why he'd have a house right in the middle of the street!"

"There is no law which states that a man has to set aside part of his land for a road," I reminded my friends.

"It still ain't right!"

We all agreed that Vineyard was wrong.

"There is one way we can solve this," I said. "We can hold a town meeting."

Major Downie groaned.

"It is the only way to give everyone a chance to vote on the matter."

Those in our group less reluctant than the Major spread the word about the first town meeting held at The Forks. We attracted a curious crowd. They gathered at the only building large enough to accommodate more than a handful of men: Cut-Eye Foster's Grocery and Grog.

The place reeked with the pungent odor of a back room still, and the low ceiling made it uncomfortable for anyone over six foot tall. We worked our way between an assortment of axe handles, canvass pants, candles, lanterns, rope and a variety of supplies that a miner would need in an emergency. Lumber was a premium, and Foster didn't use it for shelves. Instead he just piled good up against walls, and behind a rustic counter that looked like it was made from weathered old wagon wood, which Foster probably hauled up the river on the back of a mule.

I moved over behind the bar, which seemed to be the center of everyone's attention . . . not because of its beauty. It was nothing more than a couple of planks laid between two overturned barrels, but the liquid refreshment served there, was of interest to all.

As the miner's arrived, and pushed their way inside, they blocked off most of the light that came from the small windows which Foster carved out of the rustic walls. Cut-Eye sauntered over, and lit the oil lamp hanging over the bar.

I pounded on the counter with an empty tin cup. When the noise of the crowd dimmed, I shouted loudly, "Gentlemen. . ."

"There ain't no gentlemen here!" someone yelled from the back of the store. This was accompanied by waves of laughter.

When the men quieted down, I explained the purpose of the meeting.

Loud and angry opinions flew around the room.

"Seventeen feet . . . Why that ain't enough room for two wagons to pass."

"We ain't got no road into The Forks anyway, so where ya gonna get two wagons?"

"Why this town might be just like a lot of others: A future ghost town!"

"Yeah! Why should we give up valuable gold land for a road?"

"We have to think of the future, men. We have to consider progress."

"What if this did become a town—even a city. Why we'd be in a heck of a mess with narrow, impassable streets."

On and on the discussion went until most of us had enough talk, and demanded a decision. We took a vote, and set the width of our streets at twenty six feet.

With that order of business taken care of, I banged the tin cup against the bar once more, and gave a little speech, which I remember well. "Fellow citizens . . . I have listened patiently, and with some amusement to the lengthy discussion on the correct width of a street in our little community. I would now like to remind you that while we have been making plans for the proper development of this town, we failed to approach the problem of a name. Where we have always referred to this area as The Forks, I am reminded of an eating utensil! In my opinion we should have a more fitting name: A name we can say with pride—a name which complements the town. I therefore submit to you the suggestion of 'Downieville'. It is the worthy name of one of our founding fathers, one of its first, and well loved citizens—Major William Downie!"

This was the moment I finally met the man whose name instigated the meeting: Mr. Vineyard. He jumped forward. His eyes blazed in anger. With teeth held together in a tight grip, he sputtered out the words, "I object!"

The room became uncomfortable silent as he tried to express his feelings in a civilized tone. "Sure, we all know Major Downie. But, if we want to name a town for someone, I think we should name it after Cut-Eye Foster."

Moans and groans echoed around the room.

Vineyard held up his hand. "Wait. Listen to me. Downie doesn't even care enough about this place to attend the meeting. Isn't that right? Major, if you're here, defend your reputation!"

There were a lot of shuffling-of-feet, while men looked from one to another. Of course, the Major didn't appear, because it was true: He wasn't there.

"Now," Vineyard continued, "Over in the corner there, is a man who has always cared for this community. Foster brought in the first provisions—opened the first store and grog. Why if it weren't for him, we would have all given up long ago! I suggest 'Foster' as the new name for our town!"

The room began to pulsate with argument as the men talked among themselves. Vineyard pushed his way to the end of the bar, and stood beside Cut-Eye, smug and defiant. Our eyes met and froze in an icy cold stare.

I felt a trickle of sweat dribble down the side of my face. Body pressed against body in that dark crowded room almost overpowered the smell of fermenting berries. My tin cup hit the plank wood bar once more. "We have two ideas for the name of this town!" I shouted. "If there are no more suggestions we will bring the question to a vote."

I tried to read the faces of the now silent men. "Those in favor of 'Downieville', signify by saying 'Aye'."

"AYE!" The deafening sound ricocheted against the walls of the grog, as miners raised their hands with clasped fists.

I couldn't withhold a smile as I continued, "Now, those in favor of 'Foster', signify by saying 'Aye'."

Vineyard stepped forward. With both hands clasped in fists above his head, and with all the volume he could muster, he shouted "AYE!" His eyes, black with intention, penetrated mine like a knife, daring me to announce that *his* voice did not carry the same weight as the rest of the men.

My smile didn't fade. It was genuine. It amused me that this arrogant man could think he could overpower the majority vote!

"Well gentlemen, it looks as if we have a new name for our town—Downieville! And, I think that concludes the business at hand. It's time to celebrate!"

As if his entrance was announced, Major Downie arrived at that moment. His eyes bugged out when friends slapped him on the back and told him the news. They pushed him forward to the bar, and I shook his hand. If Cut-Eye were disappointed, it didn't show. He moved along the bar, and smiled at the customers, placing his home-made brew on the dull counter, and holding out his small greedy hand for the gold piece it cost.

Vineyard stood in the shadows and watched. I now think he could have had his way at this first dramatic confutation, if there had not already been another town, only 25 miles downriver, named Cut-Eye Foster's Bar. I misjudged the demanding power of Vineyard's voice, and his persuasive tactics. On that day, which I considered triumphant, I encountered my first political enemy.

CHAPTER FOUR - 1850

Politics: Men fight, steal, and kill, just to feel a touch of its glory. I don't think mankind is born to such a base desire. Until I felt the Sierra Nevada mud under my feet, I had no inclination in that direction.

I clawed away at the gold dusted soil at The Forks, while others succeeded in getting statehood for California. We celebrated with shouting and drinking, and I felt a stir within my soul. It was a democratic stir. And it nudged me to participate in my choice of favorite parties. Nothing exceptional, but I decided to take an active role in molding this new country. I visualized myself as an election board officer, or even a delegate to the local Democratic Convention.

I was in this frame of mind when Major Downie leaned on my vanity. "You're a natural born leader," he said. His motivation for such a remark was the upcoming First Territorial Election. He felt my training as a lawyer qualified me for the position of Justice of the Peace. He and Rachel mixed the perfect combination of compliments and pleading, until I agreed to run.

My opponent that Election Day, June 1850, was none other than the angry man with the greed driven claim stakes—Mr. Vineyard. Once again the fine citizens of Downieville had to side with either me, or Cut-Eye Foster's close friend.

In reality, there was no competition. Our newly named town was entitled to *two* justices, so despite the outcome of the vote, we would both be elected. However, as in all contests for political gain, we fought with all the cunning of two foxes after the same rabbit. We flexed our muscle at the naming of the town, and fortune found my favor that day. Now, once more, we battled for popularity.

Election Day I sat in the depths of our mining pit sorting out rocks and examining them for gold. I strutted to the poles early in the morning, and was one of the first to cast my vote. The rest of the day moved along like a turtle in the shade, and I accumulated quite a pile of rocks to take back to my tent. Actually I would take the rocks to Rachel's tent, where we had a make-shift table, a sledge hammer, pick and other things to make it more comfortable.

When the sun slowly crept behind the mountain peaks, I walked with other miners away from our claims—tired and hungry. Rachel already had a pot of beans simmering on the coals of the campfire, and the smell brightened my spirit. As I stumbled into camp from one side of the fire, Major Downie popped up from the other. "Beans again?" he asked.

Rachel smiled, and said, "We had biscuits and beans last night. Tonight we're having beans and biscuits! Sit down and sup with us, Major."

"Pleased to . . ." Downie said, and sat on an old log we had placed near the fire. I dropped my bag of rocks inside the flap of Rachel's tent, and then plopped down beside him.

Rachel dished the beans onto tin plates, placed a biscuit on the edge, and handed us each a serving.

"I just took a walk over to the polls, and the votes are counted," Downie said.

Rachel's eyes widened and her ears seemed to stand at attention. She had her hair piled on top of her head, anchored with pins, and a few locks hung down beside her face where they had come loose during the day, and she hadn't pinned them back up.

"I know the result. I won," I said, grim faced. "You can't lose when there are only two candidates to fill two positions."

"Hang the positions!" Downie protested. "You and I, and Vineyard, all know that this was a race between *you* and *him*!"

I dipped my biscuit in the bean juice. Even over a campfire, Rachel made fine biscuits. "All right . . . Give it to me. Who won?"

"You did!" The major grinned, sitting straight up, holding the tin plate on his lap.

Rachel sat across the campfire from us, on a rustic old chair, made from a round of wood, and a few straight branches. The smoke seemed to constantly drift in her direction, and she tried aimlessly to brush it away like a pesky fly. Through the haze I could see the proud twinkle in her eyes.

"All right, what was the score?" I asked.

"496 to 492."

My spoonful of beans stopped in mid air somewhere between the plate and my mouth. *Four votes*? It would seem on the surface that I won the election by four votes, but it was much more complicated than that. This was my first lesson in practical politics. No matter how unpopular an opponent may be, during the heat of the battle, tables can turn. Lying words sway votes—at least long enough for the election to pass.

Every Downieville voter had the opportunity to cast two votes for Justice of the Peace, as we were electing two justices. I refused to vote for Vineyard, and I believe the Major did the same. It looked as if only two other voters declined to cast that second vote, although they knew the other candidate was a scoundrel!

* * *

I assumed my new position as justice of the peace, with a winner's smile; while Vineyard, (the poor looser that he was), continued to sharpen his claws. On each writ he signed, he carefully scrawled the location as "The Forks". I, in turn, carefully penned "Downieville" on all my writs. The people voted for this new name, and as far as I was concerned it was official. This third battle was a petty affair, but I won it also. "The Forks" faded into history, and "Downieville" took its place.

My popularity in the diggings, I contributed to my friendship with Major Downie. But with this new position of prestige, I began my new identity as Downieville's Justice of the Peace. Our little community held the only court for miles in every direction, and our jurisdiction took in all the mines including all the miner's squabbles. Before the first autumn storm, that year of 1850, I tried 325 cases, and served fines that ranged from ½ to 6 ounces in gold each.

CHAPTER FIVE - 1850

I am a pioneer: A vagabond. I left the home of my birth and traveled the span from the Atlantic to the Pacific. It seemed natural and easy for me. I welcomed the prospector's life as one welcomes spring. These first small political battles were simple triumphs—something a man does with finesse, then sits back and reaps the rewards. But confronting a woman is compared to death itself. It is not natural. And when my turn came, I think I would have welcomed more, a six foot hole beneath the ground.

I dressed fit for any funeral, in my best, cleanest shirt and pants. I parted with a fine piece of gold for a perfect haircut and shave—then put on enough fancy water to scare off an entire herd of deer. I wore out a pathway across the dirt floor of my tent, pacing back and forth to the small square of tin which offered a distorted view of my reflection. I knew Rachel would marry me, she had promised. But I was going to demand that my freedom be sacrificed immediately. I felt like an absolute fool.

With shy awkwardness I approached her tent. I could hear her inside moving things around. "Rachel I want to talk to you," I said, lowering my voice an octave, trying to sound like a strong man with authority.

The tent flap opened and she peered out at me.

I stood with my feet spread wide, and my sweaty hands placed firmly on my hips. "We're getting married!" I said.

She stepped outside, and folded her arms across the front of her dirty plaid miner's shirt. She examined me from head to toe with those questioning eyes of hers, and pulled her lower lip between her teeth.

"No more courting. No more waiting. We're getting married now!" The pitch of my voice steadily climbed until it sounded unnatural, even to myself.

A smile crept up the corner of her lips. "Do I have time to change my clothes?"

My well practiced speech drummed on my mind, totally closing off my ears. "This courting business has gone on long enough. Now that I am justice of the peace, I don't have the time anymore. I can't watch out for you like I used to, and I don't like you spending time down at the river without me."

"All right," Rachel said.

"Besides—the way I see it is, you either love me or you don't!"

Rachel held out her hand, and touched the sleeves of my shirt. "I love you James."

The gentleness of this woman confused me. I cleared my throat. "You do?"

She took my rough hands in hers, and nodded slowly.

"Can we get married now?" I asked, not sure if I had won or lost the argument.

She nodded again.

I pulled her into my arms. I wanted to kiss her, embrace her, and drag her into the tent.

Gently she pushed me away, and I realized that we had attracted quite a curious crowd of lonely men, who cheered, clapped and hooted. Rachel's cheeks bloomed violet, and she asked, "Who will marry us? Vineyard?"

"Vineyard?" I repeated her ridiculous conclusion.

"He *is* the only other justice of the peace," she reminded me.

Vineyard. It looked like that serpent managed to crawl his way into my personal life. If he knew how desperately I wanted to get married, he would probably refuse to do it.

We should always be thankful for our friends. They have the ability to take over when it is celebration time. While Rachel magically produced a lovely blue dress, and transformed herself into the most beautiful bride I've ever seen, these friends of mine searched both river and mountain until they found a preacher. On that warm summer day, along the shore of the Yuba River, in God's natural chapel of evergreens, with birds that sang as sweetly as angels, we were wed. Rachel wore wildflowers in her hair, and held in her hands a pretty bouquet. Her eyes glowed with excitement, and her cheeks blushed a pretty rose shade over her naturally tanned skin.

Many of those rough and eager miners put down their gold pans long enough to witness this historic event. We had hundreds of best men, and not a single maid of honor.

* * *

The rush of autumn combined scramble, bustle, and color in a combination no painter has ever captured. With the slightest breath of wind, the oak tree loosened its grip on the yellow-gold leaves. They gathered together again like old friends, and floated lazily down the river. Their golden hue mocked the prospectors, who still lined the muddy banks.

The daylight hours were shorter, and miners spent every bright moment at their claims, digging out that "one last nugget" of gold. Tempers flared, and I spent more time as judge, and less time at my claims.

The cold snap vanished after it turned many of the trees on the lofty green mountain into shades of yellow and orange. Once again the evenings were pleasant and warm. The weather could have fooled us, but other signs warned that winter waited impatiently. Drifting fog greeted us each morning, rising like waking clouds. High above, the sound of honking geese made us look skyward, and marvel at their large V formations steadily moving toward a milder climate. The old gray squirrel and the friendly chipmunk that lived near our cabin, no longer had the patience to approach us for treats. Frantically they gathered acorns, and buried them all along the mule's corral. It was time to make the decision we deliberately postponed.

"We have to leave here," I sadly told Rachel, one evening as we sat on the porch of our little honeymoon cottage, and watched the moon dart behind anxious clouds, that gathered and separated into pictures in the sky.

Rachel nodded sadly. One couldn't ignore the small exodus beginning down at the river. Winters in the Sierra Nevada Mountains could be treacherous, and with supplies already insufficient, starvation would be certain if all of us miners chose to stay.

"We will come back in the spring," I said. Her lips turned upward in a forced smile.

Downieville . . . In such a short time, it captured our hearts—the fork of the Yuba River—birthplace of our love.

Rachel's waistline pressed against her clothing, and she searcher through her scant wardrobe finding pants and shirts with seams that could be let out. I worried about her, and shuddered at the idea of her giving birth to our first child deep in the wilderness. When friends learned that Rachel was pregnant, they told horror stories of women who waited until their mid-thirties before having their first child. I wanted her to be in the city, in a clean room, when our baby was born. The winter's chill did not frighten me; nor the mysterious grizzly that roamed the mountain's ridge. But I can still remember the icy fear that clung to my spine, when I envisioned being alone with Rachel, in the isolation of winter, while she experienced the complications my friends predicted.

And so it was. We left the little tent village behind, with all its unpolished character, and spent the long winter months hundreds of miles west, beside the Pacific Ocean, in San Francisco.

When spring signaled the jubilant pilgrims back to the gold mines, we stayed. Our arms surrounded the tiniest little bundle of charm I'd ever seen—our new little daughter, Agnes Galloway. All the gold in the world could not have tempted us away at that moment.

We did not leave the city until we were sure that both mother and child could make the long exhausting trip safely. The moment came at Rachel's suggestion, far before I thought they were ready. In late June, we began our delayed trek back home.

My face flushed with anticipation as the flat land of the great Sacramento Valley rolled into the soft waves of red foothills, dotted with oaks. Another day past, and we entered evergreen forests, and the rocky retreat of the hawk, mountain lion, and coyote. The crisp air of this high elevation scratched at my lungs, and invaded my senses with a wild taste of green moss and molding pine needles.

A well beaten trail wound along the ridge of the steep mountains, quite different from the follow-the-stream navigation we used on our first trip to The Forks. We finally reached a point where I recognized my surroundings. The trail dipped over the edge of the canyon, and became narrow and treacherous as it dropped toward the Yuba River at the point of Downieville.

We rode quietly over the crest, and leaned back on the rocking mules as they trudged downward. The village below came into view and my heart fluttered. I stopped in the trail, twisted around in the saddle, and glanced back at Rachel. She held our precious bundle, wrapped in soft blankets, and a vision of the Madonna and Child flashed through my mind.

"Look!" I said, pointing to the fork in the river—our long awaited destination.

"The river is brown!" Rachel cried. The once crystal blue-green water was muddy now, from all the excavations. Brown, and snake like, it twisted its way through the canyon. "And the tents—where are all the tents?"

Our industrious neighbors had transformed the little tent village into a town.

Organ music drifted upwards to where we watched, and it was not church music we heard. Men scurried toward saloons, pushed their way through swinging doors, and bumped into others that staggered out. A mule train unloaded baggage in front of a large two story hotel. Down the street from this grand establishment, other hotels sported fresh paint, and new signs; and along the side roads there were neat rows of new homes. Stacks of hay, piled high behind newly built stables, awaited the work-horse of the mining camp—mules. Across the rapid river we counted two bridges connecting the three flat areas which made up the boundaries of the town.

"Look at that!" I said, and pointed to a giant circus tent which rose out of the center of all the activity. It grabbed my attention with a colorful flag which waved from its peak. I squinted and could barely read the words "Orleans" painted crudely on a large sign which hung above the front entrance.

A group of men came down the trail behind us. I used my boot to encourage our mules along.

The braying of another mule greeted us as we rode into town, to which my beast lifted his neck and returned an obnoxious, "Hawww!" Mules were everywhere: enclosed in sturdy corrals, burdened down with packs along the river, and tied to railings and posts. Except for the welcoming bray, it looked as if we entered the town unnoticed, as the miners rushed here and there trying to make the most of daylight hours.

Then it came—a spark of recognition. "It's Galloway! Judge Galloway! And he's got a baby!"

The announcement bounced down the street like a rock skipping across a pond.

"It's Galloway!"

"He's got a baby!"

"A what?"

"A baby! You know—diapers and stuff."

"A baby?"

"Who has a baby?"

"It's Galloway!"

Murmurs and exclamations echoed through the swinging saloon doors in both directions along the river, and finally faded into the distant hills, where I am sure they captivated the attention of the lonely miners long enough to contemplate this historic event. The first sign of civilization arrived at the river's fork—a real flesh-and-blood baby!

* * *

All of my senses rebelled at the changes in Downieville. The look of the town of course was different, but my ears twitched in memory of the wind blowing through the branches of the trees—or the Blue Jay's cry as it screamed its annoyance at the human invasion. These sounds (that previously sang to us as we silently panned along the river bank) were but whispers above the rattle of mule teams, and the crash of rocks being dumped from one location to another, as prospectors developed more sophisticated ways of mining. I always thought the blue jay made an irritating noise, until I heard the constant brawling of disillusioned gold seekers, who drown their failures in whiskey brewed in the back room of every saloon, and sold to these pitiful souls for 50¢ in gold coin.

I suppose my position as justice of the peace, made me more aware of the repetitious problems in our community. Once more I sat at the judgment bench to reconcile the disputes that broke out among the miners. Each case I tried made me more relieved that my cabin sat in the peaceful forest above the town, away from the noise and bickering, now part of Downieville's new personality.

As a sober judge, I listened with all the seriousness I could muster, but as a miner my ears tingled in pure amusement to the stories that circulated among the men. Storytelling became a major form of recreation—the bigger the story, the greater the sport. In dark saloons, that smelled of stale cigars and fermenting fruit, newcomers would drool as they listened to an account of the forty foot ledge of pure gold that cashed in at $30,000. Like fishermen discovering a ripe hole, the other players joined in—always serious—no matter how many times the story had been told.

"That ain't nothin'. We take 20 to 60 pounds of gold every day from our claim!" came the proclamation of the Jersey Company crowd.

One of the boys from Tin Cup Diggings would lean back in a chair and ask, "Do you know how our mine got its name?"

A wide eyed stranger would shake his head.

The miner would let the front two legs of his chair slam back on the floor, as he answered, "Because we never stop for the day until our tin cup is full of gold!"

The prospectors from Gold Bluff were big fellows. They always joined in the fun by standing, flexing their muscles, and saying, "All the mines put out enough color. But, it's not the amount that is important; it's the size of the nuggets. Why at our claim, we found a perfectly round ball of pure gold that weighed out at 25 pounds!"

Law and order brought this braggart security to the gold fields. Men no longer hid their findings under a veil of evasive behavior. But who could tell fact from fiction? Gold was pouring out of the mountains into the miner's purse, but to what extent? No one knew for sure. But the stories netted their own profit. They opened a greenhorn's pocketbook, and bought drinks for the storyteller.

These newcomers suffered daily from pranks and practical jokes. By following another's advice, they were found digging in privies, and climbing trees in their lust for gold. Some bought established worn out claims, and often struck it rich there. Frequently a seller marched angrily into court, and complained that some lying rascal tricked him into selling out his mine, and now he wanted it back. I am ashamed to say that those first courts were quite uncivilized—but they seemed fitting to the town. Seated in one of the public shelters—usually a saloon, the brandy bottle became the hub of the proceedings. Lawyer's struggled for the eloquent words that flow so freely now, and the brandy loosened their tongues, and it often pacified the complaining party! I soon put a stop to the sweet beverage during court, and I confess that it was not conscience that brought on this verdict, but the fact that our necessary papers were always splotched with unsightly spills.

The town increased daily in population. In my estimation, by the first of July, 1851, over three thousand men roamed the streets of our village, and at least 2,000 more clung to the sides of the mountains, reforming it into a rock pile that resembled Swiss cheese.

The quest for entertainment became everyone's preoccupation.

As a result of its powerful cry, the men constructed a plaza on one of the flat plateaus, and there they raised a theater. Often rude, always lacking culture, two local men adorned the stage, and we thought they were delightful. The sound of music and laughter stirred our tired feet, and men danced with other men. The lonely sang, danced, laughed, drank heavily, and lied; but the longing that imagination could not fill was created by man's own lustful heart. For the comfort and pleasure of 5,000 residents, there were only 11 women. Actually this total was 12, counting Rachel, but her presence fulfilled no one's pleasure but mine!

    I'm sure this shortage of women caused Rachel some heartache, but within me it created an unnatural preoccupation. I began inventing believable, original, fabricated excuses to relate to my sweet bride, to convince her to stay behind, as I rode into town; and to pacify her loneliness we held dinner parties in our home. We sent invitations to Major Downie and a few other hand-picked guests. At these parties I noticed that Rachel began her own campaign to balance nature's call. She made a special point of encouraging every one of our friends to send for wives and families they left behind on their pilgrimage west.

CHAPTER SIX - 1851

California was a spanking new state, and Downieville planned a bang-up jubilation to celebrate America's Independence Day that year, 1851. We decorated the plaza with red, white and blue streamers, and built a small elevated stage for speeches, and recruited men with fine voices to sing our patriotic songs.

Enthusiastically I pitched in to help the local Democrats organize a convention to be held on that memorable holiday. Nothing could be more patriotic than practicing our right to nominate Sierra County's first lawmakers, and representatives to the new state of California.

As the day approached, miners put aside their gold pans, and flooded the town like water oozing from the blue-white snow during the first spring rain. The saloons felt the strain, as thirsty miners pushed their way inside. I sensed a stirring at the base of my neck. It traveled down my spine, and settled in the pit of my stomach like an unwelcome heavy lump.

Was it possible? In my vigor to serve the party, had I forgotten about Rachel? I spent every day in town, ignored the hints she dropped, and during my absentmindedness I brushed aside her suggestions for a dinner party for some of our friends on the Fourth.

Silently I untied the mule from a pole next to the Plaza. The animal looked to me with dark somber eyes, and flipped its head in annoyance at being disturbed. I patted the wiry hair along its neck, and put the reins over the saddle horn before I mounted. I turned the beast toward the bridge which led to the lower plane, where the steep trail to Galloway Ridge began. Slowly I rode up the hill. My mind uncontrollably roared with arguments, as I silently witnessed the struggle between my two great loves—Rachel and the Democratic Party.

As I entered the little clearing where our log cabin sat nestled safely between giant pines, I noticed the branches of all the trees had a natural inclination to point upwards. Like knowing fingers they reminded me of answered prayers—a good wife, a healthy baby, a safe home. It was then I knew who won the struggle with my heart.

* * *

On the morning of the fifth, the sun glared down through the trees promising to be hot and uncomfortable all day. I wasted hours just poking around the house and corrals, and when I finally saddled the mule, and headed for town, the sun leaned toward the west, and the noon hour was spent.

I guided my mule through shade spots cast by the trees, and when there were no more shadows to protect us, the sun seemed to burn right through my shirt. As I passed over the bridge, the glare from the swirling water below blinded me for an instant. I squinted, and pulled my hat lower on my head.

Crowds of men, who I thought should be back at their mines, were gathered everywhere. When I reached the plaza, one of my friends waved me over and shouted, as I came closer, "How come you're never around when the fireworks go off? You missed all the excitement!"

"I'll bet I did!" I said. My mind imagined a celebration instigated by 5,000 lonely, drunken miners.

"I'm not joking! You should have been here this morning! Didn't you hear the news?"

A few men gathered around as I dismounted and tied my mule next to half a dozen others on a hitching rail. "What news?" I asked. I knew they would tell me anyway. No one could stop a wild fire, or a juicy piece of gossip.

"They hung that Mexican gal—the one that does the washing!"

We stood in the shade of the theater. I took of my hat, and blinked my eyes, trying to adjust my vision after coming away from the bright sunshine. Positive I hadn't heard him right, I asked, "What did you say?"

"You know—the pretty one—the young gal that lives with that Mexican gambler who deals Monte in the saloon across the way."

"Jose? ...the fancy dresser?"

"Yeah! That's the one! You know his woman—they called her Juanita..."

"What do you mean they *hung* her?" I asked. My eyes finally dilated, and the serious faces of the men around me came into focus—yet the words they spoke were still distorted in my mind. I could think of several things a pack of inebriated gold miners might do to a pretty young thing like Juanita, as they celebrated Independence Day, but hanging was not one of them!

"Yeah, they hung her!" shouted a tall fellow named Buffalo Mike. His muscles bulged and glowed with perspiration as he pushed his way through the crowd, until he stood in front of me. "A couple of hours ago ... They hung her from the bridge. You missed the whole thing. You should have been here. I ain't never seen nothin' like it!"

My mind buzzed. Had the world gone crazy? The entire idea was insane! "Why did they hang her?" I asked.

"Why? Well, she killed Joe Cannon, that's why!"

"Joe Cannon?" I visualized the tall, young, blond man. He was a nice fellow when he was sober; A little rowdy and loud when drunk—but nothing that would…

The air was still, and yesterday's colorful banners hung like laundry forgotten on the line. Sierra County's Democratic Convention was history. I missed the political speeches, and apparently I missed a call to duty as the local justice of the peace.

I closed my eyes for a minute, and tried to shield myself from the unwelcome news several men were trying to relate to me at the same time. I tried to visualize Cannon: a mammoth of a man, over six feet tall. He weighted close to 240 pounds.

How could a petite little thing, like Juanita, kill a powerful man like that? . . . and why?

I held up my hand. "One at a time! Why did she kill him?"

With nudging from the others, Buffalo Mike said, "Nobody knows for sure, except she wasn't sorry she did it. She said she'd do it again. She said he called her some ugly names."

I squeezed out the rest of the story.

It seemed that Cannon wanted to party all night on the Fourth. He went door to door, woke people up, and insisted they have a drink with him. When he got to the flimsy tent-shack where Jose and Juanita lived, there was no response. When he pounded and kicked on the flimsy door, held loosely to the door jam with leather hinges, it gave way to the onslaught, throwing the intoxicated Cannon onto the cabin floor. His friends quickly picked him up and drug him out to the street, as he muttered and sputtered some very select and derogatory Spanish words. He laughed boldly and staggered off between the rows of shacks, accompanied by his merry friends.

The Australian born Englishman, Joe Cannon, had lived in

China for nine years. When confronted by a coolie, he could rattle off complements or insults in their sing-song dialect. Foreign words slipped of his tongue easier than most men speak English My mind totally accepted the idea that Joe could express himself clearly to the local Mexicans in their own native language.

On the morning of the fifth, Cannon's stomach sent him messages of rejection, and the memory of the previous night pounded painfully in his head. He sprinkled his face with Yuba River water, which he kept in a wooden bucket; and as he gazed into the distorted tin mirror, which hung from a nail on the wall of his drafty cabin, his conscience nagged him. He put on a clean shirt, and walked over to Jose's place to apologize.

The cabin door stood ajar, hanging loosely from one hinge. Cannon stepped over the threshold and knocked softly. In the darkness of the unlighted shanty he heard whispers in Spanish, and Jose stepped up to him. Jose's dark eyes glared with anger, and through the gap of his open shirt, his hairy chest expanded, as he pointed a waving finger in Cannon's face, and began to degrade him.

Those who knew Cannon usually avoided a confrontation, not only because of his powerful size, but because of his spitfire tongue that hurled foul abuse when angered.

As Jose stood in front of him, waving a finger in his face, Joe Cannon responded with some choice Spanish words, picked from the negative side of his vocabulary, insulting not only Jose, but also his family, his nationality, and his woman Juanita, as well.

Soft—like the movement of a ghost, Cannon realized motion as his side. Smooth—like a boat slipping through a mirror lake, a knife slid into his chest. Quiet—like the last star to come out at night, Cannon slipped into everlasting sleep.

Juanita stood above his crumpled body like a triumphant matador, a bloody knife at her side, and red traces of Cannon's life dripping down the folds of her skirt.

The story continued to unravel, and I sorted out the facts that most interested me as a lawyer-judge. Downieville had no jail, so Jose and Juanita were placed in two heavily guarded log cabins. A sneering group of men, with a lynch rope in their hands volunteered to be the jury. The blundering crowd drafted, as their magistrate, "*Judge*" Rose, from Rose's Bar! And another volunteer named

Thayer, defended Juanita, while the charges against Jose were dismissed.

The platform which I so carefully helped build for the Fourth's celebration was used to stage this mockery.

One hero emerged from the midst of the sheep who performed this charade—young Doc Aiken. He told the jury that Juanita was pregnant. The guardian wolves grabbed the young doctor, placed him on the back of a mule, and drove him out of town. But the seed of doubt he planted diverted a swift conclusion to the trial and after a couple of hours in argument, a committee of *"doctors"* were appointed to see if Juanita was indeed expecting a baby.

These men took the wash woman into the jail-cabin where they poked and prodded her young body. Her screams of indignation were heard up and down the river. Convinced that Doc Aiken's report was untrue, they returned her to the inquest.

When Juanita's physical condition was no longer in question, the jury found her guilty. The vengeful crowd escorted the condemned woman to one of the new bridges, where thousands of entertainment-starved men watched the hangman do his duty.

"You should have been there," Buffalo Mike repeated for about the fifth time. "She put the noose around her own neck, and borrowed a man's hat, which she threw out to the crowd as she shouted, 'Audios Senores!'. I ain't never seen nothin' like it!"

I made no comment to this remark. Uncontrollably my teeth ground together. Heat radiated on my cheeks, and I didn't need a mirror to know I was flushed. I could not believe this misguided justice. Those pitiless miners, with no regard for common decency, infringed on Juanita's right to a fair trial. It was a cold-hearted lynching!

I looked up toward Galloway Ridge, and remembered how I lingered there in the warmth of my family's love. I knew Juanita would still be alive, if I had only come into town a few hours earlier.

A welcome breeze drifted through the plaza, and sent shuddering waves through the red, white, and blue banners. In the cemetery above the town, the scraping sound of the shovels that dug a pit for Juanita's rough, wooden casket became only a part of the melody played by other picks and shovels digging up fortune along the Yuba River.

CHAPTER SEVEN - 1860-1867

Where do the years of youthful bliss go? It seemed that in the blink of an eye, our sweet, babbling baby in leaky diapers was suddenly being fitted with school shoes. Then instantly, those precious expensive shoes were too small! Agnes—our little native California child . . . although she was born by the bay, she was Downieville's first baby, and she grew up with the town.

By the time she reached school age, Downieville had introduced civilized behavior to its citizens. Yes, we build not only a school, but a couple of churches as well.

As a mother, my wife shined. She guided our daughter through those childhood years as a gentle shepherd leads a lamb.

Agnes did not excel in school, as I hoped she would. We both encouraged her, but it was Rachel who sat with her and helped her. In my mind I see them yet, sitting in the light of that old oil lamp. Their two chairs pulled close together at the table, and the family Bible as the text. My ears moaned at the combinations that girl could imagine from simple words. It was like listening to a poor musician on a badly tuned violin. I bit my lip in impatience as she stumbled from sentence to sentence.

1860—our tenth wedding anniversary came and went. What Rachel and Agnes did during the first part of that decade is a bit fuzzy in my mind. The destructive War Between the States obsessed our country, and Lincoln's policies outraged me. I spared no words expressing my bitter opinions, and my big mouth was rewarded with a Democratic nomination for Sierra County's seat in the State Senate.

Of those turbulent years I only remember the party—with its desires and needs—the great Democratic Party. It pampered me, swayed me, and finally seduced me.

I know I lived in that little cottage up on Galloway Ridge, and I shared Rachel's bed. I must have watched Agnes, petal by petal, blossom into a young lady. However, I knew none of her youthful appetites, dreams, and ambitions, as she stumbled through those caterpillar years.

It took loosing the election to bring my feet back on solid ground. Suddenly Agnes was fourteen years old, fresh out of the cocoon with still-wet wings; a wisp of a girl, who swung back and forth from sullen lonely child to vivacious exciting young woman. I never knew from day to day, which Agnes I would encounter. And I didn't know how to handle either one!

After my unsuccessful bid for the big political seat at the capitol, I settled down to practicing law, and doing a bit of mining on the side. *Gold Fever* no longer triggered the hysteria of '49, and a new interesting prospect popped its head up across the state border, in Virginia City—silver! With its own fascination and magnetic pull, it uprooted many of our neighbors. We sadly watched as old friends moved their homes, businesses, and dreams to the silver land—eastward, over the mountains.

With each burdened mule that passed along the trail, headed out of town, I saw Agnes' heart growl with envy. She pleaded and cried, "Why can't we move to Virginia City like the rest? You can be a lawyer there! Please, please, please!"

Her young spirit longed for new friends and adventure. Then one cold February afternoon in 1864, we witnessed one of the most dramatic events of our lives.

The word, "*FIRE!*" screamed up Galloway Ridge. No other word (except maybe WAR) can cause the spine to tingle in that same fearful way. From childhood we are taught *never* to shout this word in vain. So when it is heard, echoing through a town, village, or forest, it is a word to be reckoned with. I grabbed my shovel, and didn't stop to saddle the mule—just hopped on bareback. I didn't know where the fire was, but the cry of panic came from the direction of Downieville. Every second counted, and every man would be needed to extinguish the flames.

Without looking back, I knew Rachel and Agnes followed, as I galloped down the steep mountain trail. When the town came into sight between the trees, I gasped for breath. Beneath dark boiling clouds, flames totally engulfed the small butcher shop, and shot angry tongues of red and orange toward the magnificent four-story International Hotel.

As hotel patrons raced out into the chaotic street, they clutched their rumpled bags, and shouted fearfully as they pointed to places on the porch that were already ablaze.

By the time my mule clattered over the wooden bridge, firemen in black raincoats were braced, four and five together. Their faces strained as they hung desperately on to the hoses, and aimed streams of water at the billowing flames which devoured the hotel in a dramatic 20 foot fire wall—fanned by its own energy.

I left my mule with others, far from the action, and raced to help the men who were already hard at work—Downieville's proud Volunteer Fire Department with its two well trained hose companies. I could hear Mr. Cocran's voice boom directions, "Pull back! Pull back! We have a wild fire here!" Flames leaped in every direction, like demons determined to destroy everything in their path.

Water, ejected toward the blinding fury, disappeared in hissing steam, vapor, and smoke. Our efforts were better spent evacuating the storekeepers and their families, from the devil's path.

To the backdrop of a feverish orange sky, and suffocating mountains of smoke, our grand hose companies performed at their best. They were indeed heroes. When the battle ended, and the fire exhausted all of the fuel in its path, my eyes rested on the once glittering gold stripes, spangles and silver letters of the town's magnificent new hose carriages. Now they stood abandoned and covered with bitter ash. Dr. Aiken kneeled on his haunches, and gave first aid to one of the firefighters who peered upward with sad eyes, through a soot covered face.

The rest of us just stood in small groups, staring—hardly talking. The little town we all depended on for our worldly provisions, lay charred and fallen. Murky streams of black water oozed from the waste, and emitted an offensive odor of sulfur and mud. From underneath piles of indistinguishable debris, an occasional dying ember coughed up final puffs of smoke.

Through the heat and destruction, four stone buildings stood complete. Like Shadrack, Meshach, and Abednego, they survived the blazing fire. These immortal fortresses were the Craycroft Building, two smaller stone structures, and Charlie Gilbert's Tin Shop and Hardware Store.

A clean line marked a trail down Charlie Gilbert's soot covered face, where beads of perspiration escaped from beneath the sweatband of his hat. His head moved back and forth in disbelief, and his teeth gleamed like white pearls between smudged lips, turned upward. He kept repeating the words, "Thank God. Thank God." His gratitude, aimed at Heaven, fell on the deaf ears of his neighbors, who lost everything.

In the days that followed, expressions of sympathy and brotherhood played their healing role and the homeless were also thanking God for loving neighbors and friends.

A few days after the fire I visited Charlie in his store. He pushed a broom gently against the ash-dust, which settled on everything.

"As soon as I sweep it up, it reappears again!" he said.

I don't remember now exactly what I was looking for that day, but the shelves were practically bare. It is good business for the survivor, when a town burns down.

"I'm a lucky man," Charlie said. "Yes indeed. And you know what? It's really got me to thinking."

He leaned the broom against the counter, and placed both hands on his hips as he spoke, "I've got a daughter back in Illinois. She's just about the same age as your little girl, Judge."

In all the years I'd known Charlie, he never mentioned this before. Fourteen year old girls are a puzzle to everyone, and sometimes so obstinate that you'd like to send them away to live with relatives, but in reality I knew my heart would ache if I had to be separated from my daughter by such a distance. I shook my head in sympathy.

"Well, I think it is time I sent for her," Charlie said, and he picked up the broom and began to whisk more white powder toward the door. "I only hope it is not too late! Why she's practically grown!"

A teenage girl from Illinois—a perfect little charmer; I never dreamed this tin-maker's daughter would play such an important role in our destiny.

* * *

Agnes skipped home from school one day all smiles and chatter. Charlie Gilbert's daughter arrived, and instantly they were best friends.

"Her name is Ottie! She came all the way from Illinois! She told me all about it. She knows everything! She's got real nice clothes from back East! Just imagine . . . she traveled clear across the country all by herself! She's seen everything too! And, Papa you'll like this, she's smart. I guess they've got better schools back East. She knows more than anyone in our school, except for the teacher, of course. And she can play the piano and sing. I guess she has a pretty voice, I haven't exactly heard her sing . . . but she said she could."

"Agnes, how could you learn so much about your new friend in such a short time? I hope you weren't whispering in class," Rachel said.

"No Mother. We talked during recess, and I walked home with her—it was right along the way . . ." She looked at me with wide innocent eyes. I had forbid her to dally on the way home from school.

I gave her a reassuring smile. It was impossible not to share her joy. Agnes seldom displayed a happy face over friendship.

"Her middle name is Temperance—can you imagine that?" Agnes giggled. "I teased her about it. And she said my name sounded dull. So, she is going to call me Aggie! I like that! . . . Aggie."

"I don't think 'Agnes' sounds dull. I've always liked your name," I said.

"Oh Papa... Just listen . . . 'Aggie'. Now, doesn't that sound better? It's more alive! . . . More modern!"

I lost that argument. Soon even I called her Aggie.

During the next two years the girls shared everything. Their giggle became as familiar in Downieville as the babbling of the Yuba River. They found a joke in just about everything and everybody. When the two were together, Aggie's eyes shined like the ripples in the water as they caught the rays of the sun. It was love. The kind of love most of us are blessed with at least once in childhood—love for our closest friend.

* * *

It was autumn, 1867, and the wind blew down the canyon ripping the leaves from the trees. I stood and enjoyed the warmth of the old pot-bellied stove that stood on bricks in the corner of Charlie Gilbert's Hardware Store. I came to fetch Aggie, who lingered on, and found one excuse after another to stay just a few more minutes. I didn't mind. Let her enjoy her friend a little longer. As long as there was wood to stoke the fire, and the wind continued to blow, I was in no hurry.

The two girls dusted shelves, with short handled feather dusters, and whispered secrets to each other. A slender, dark haired man appeared at the door, pushed his way inside, and then a gust of wind caught the door, and closed it with a slam. The man took two steps forward, and then stood with his feet apart and his hands on his hips. He smiled broadly at Charlie.

With instant recognition, the storekeeper slipped around the front of the counter, and said, "Henry! You old grizzly bear . . . Where've you been hiding out?"

The visitor, Henry, grasped Charlie's hand with a firm grip, and said, "Same old place—God's gift to the world, Sierra Valley!"

"Oh come now, you know you miss this civilization," Charlie said. "That's why you keep coming back here to pester us!"

Feather dusters stopped in mid air, as our two young ladies stared at the stranger. He noticed them, removed his hat, and said, "Well, I see you've finally got some good help around here!"

Charlie walked over to where the girls stood gawking. He put his arm around Ottie's shoulder, and said, "You mean you haven't met my daughter? Ottie, this is a friend of mine, Henry Turner."

Henry's eyebrows lifted suddenly. "Well I'll be! You sure do keep secrets, Charlie." He reached over and took Ottie's hand, and said in a softer, deeper voice, "I'm pleased to meet you Miss Gilbert."

Ottie's face turned crimson. Henry smiled.

"And you know Judge Galloway's daughter?"

Aggie stood there, with eyes as large as saucers, when Henry said, "I knew the judge had a little girl, but my-oh-my, you've become a young lady, Miss Galloway." He tipped his hat, and the girls giggled.

I felt a hankering to step forward and put a stop to this man's boldness, when Charlie raised one hand, and said, "Whoa Turner. Pick on someone your own age!"

The girls giggled again.

"That's why I'm in Downieville," Henry said.

Charlie leaned backward against the counter, with his hands folded across his chest. He asked, "You came to pick on someone your own age?"

"No. I'm looking for a school teacher."

Charlie laughed. "To marry—or did you finally find out you need to learn a few things?"

The girls pretended to resume their dusting. They glanced from Charlie to Henry as the two men joked.

"We need a teacher in the valley, if we're going to become as civilized as you," Turner said.

"How do you get stuck with these odd jobs? You don't even have kids."

"You know me. I've got a finger in every pie. I'm trustee for the new school we're building at Rocky Point."

"Hmmm . . . I don't know what luck you'll have finding a teacher here." Charlie scratched his head.

Aggie stepped away from her friend's side, and said boldly, "Ottie could do it!"

Ottie grabbed Aggie's arm, and pulled her backward, whispering, "Hush Aggie!"

Aggie jerked away. "Ottie could do it. She is almost seventeen, and she's the best student in our school."

Henry faced the girls squarely, and placed his hands on his hips again. Without smiling, his eyes scrutinized Ottie, from the tip of her shoes to the top of her lovely brown hair. Then he looked directly in her eyes and asked gently, "Is this true?"

"Well . . . I . . ." Ottie could not return his inquisitive stare, and quickly turned her eyes toward her father for help.

Henry also looked to Mr. Gilbert. "What about it, Charlie? Do you think your daughter could handle the job of teacher at Rocky Point School?"

I don't know what protective thought drifted through Charlie's mind as he stared at his daughter. Her stay with him totaled barely two years. I wondered if he could actually let her go so soon. I looked at the hopeful anticipation on Ottie's smooth face, and then wondered if he could ever say no.

"She can do it, if anyone can," he said sadly.

"Don't I need a teacher's certificate?" Ottie asked.

"If you are the student your friend and your father say you are, it shouldn't be too difficult to get the papers you need. I'll make arrangements with Rev. Fish for you to take the exam. And, if you pass, Rocky Point is yours."

I huddled beside the stove, thinking I could remain invisible, but Charlie pulled a jug out from underneath the counter, and said, "Come over here Judge. We're going to toast Ottie's future."

Only the warmth captivated inside the bottle could have budged me from the hot stove. While Charlie uncorked the jug, and poured its liquid into three tin cups, he asked his friend, "You remember

Judge Galloway, don't you?"

"I don't believe I've had the pleasure," Henry smiled widely, and extended his hand. His firm handshake revealed the confident competition I usually found in the political arena. "I know you Judge, but by reputation only!"

I smiled. "Well, I hope you don't believe everything you hear."

"I hear you are a man to keep an eye on—politically speaking."

I raised an eyebrow in Henry's direction, and said, "You talk like a Republican, Mr. Turner."

With a sly grin, Henry raised his glass in the air, "You found me out!"

It became uncomfortably quiet for a minute, as we mentally weighed each other's political strength. We raised our cups toward Ottie, and wished her luck. My mind wandered, and a memory stirred up the face of old Tom Turner—the lonely old man who used to bore me for hours with tales of his family, and they always began with the words, "I've got a son named Henry goin' to school back in Maine." Was it a coincidence? Old Tom died years ago, two miles downstream from Downieville at a place called Snake Bar.

But the eyes, the strength of character . . . There was a strong resemblance. I dismissed the idea as preposterous, and regarded Henry Turner as just another danged Republican.

* * *

Rev. I. B. Fish, minister of Downieville's Methodist Church, and Sierra County's Superintendent of Schools, believed in honesty and justice. As he met with the other members of the Board of Education to prepare the questions for the teacher's exam, someone mentioned Sierra Valley's desperation to fill the void. "Immaterial and irrelevant," Rev. Fish said.

On the day of the examination, Ottie walked to school as usual. However, as she entered the classroom, all eyes were upon her. Word about her elevation in status rumbled from ear to ear. The teacher told her to sit at the small wooden table at the back of the classroom.

"Good luck!" Aggie whispered, as Ottie passed down the aisle, on her way to begin the long series of tests.

Ottie struggled through the questions. Occasionally she

switched the long quill pen from one hand to the other, careful not to spill drops of ink on her paper. She wiped her sweating hands on her dress. Neatness counted. Hour after hour she calculated her answers for every subject imaginable: U.S. history; geography; English grammar; arithmetic, which included difficult trigonometry. There were even questions on the theory and practice of teaching, and school law.

After two days of extensive testing, Ottie set down her pen. Exhausted, she capped the bottle of ink. She did not think she passed, and she hardly cared.

However, Ottie did pass, and with a second grade teacher's certificate in her hand, she soon stood in the center of Downieville at the Plaza Livery Stable, watching her father strap her small leather trunk to the back of a mule.

Aggie rose before dawn on that day, and she was down the hill at about the time the sleepy old sun began to project its light. Aggie watched her best-friend-in-the-whole-world ride off with Mr. Garnosette, and his long mule train. Ottie's destination: Hale's Ranch in Sierra Valley.

"You make sure you write to me, Ottie Gilbert!" Aggie yelled, before the train disappeared out of sight.

"I will!"

Aggie's trembling lips turned upward when she heard the promise echo back. A tear rolled down her face, and she used the back of her hand to brush it away. It left a dirty smudge on her cheek, from the dust stirred up by the mules.

CHAPTER EIGHT - 1867-1868

The letters came, just as Ottie promised. And, Aggie grabbed each one from my hand, and raced to the fireplace, where by its flickering light, she absolutely devoured each precious word.

Dear Aggie,
You should see my new home. It is a hotel, of sorts. Very rustic! It's built on the outskirts of a little village called Church's Corners. No, this is not a little town built around a church, as you would expect. It was dubbed thus, for its founding fathers, the Church family. Actually three brothers with that name reside here.

The hotel is owned by an older couple, George and Rachel Hale. George is Irish, and very funny, but his wife seems a bit stuffy, and rather strict. My meals are provided in the small hotel dining room, and the waitresses are widows who live in the hotel. They are older, probably in their thirties and much too worldly wise for me! I stay in my room . . ."

One after another the letters came, and told of Ottie's latest adventure:

". . . remember Mr. Turner, the trustee who offered me this position? He took me to see the school, which hasn't been built yet! However, he showed me the site. It will rest on the side of a hill, overlooking Sierra Valley—a green and luscious valley, completely enclosed by mountains. New people are taking up land here all the time. The school is named for some large granite boulders that rest on the end of a little finger of land which points southward toward Church's Corners. Until the school is built, we will hold classes in the hotel. That should be interesting! There are not many children of school age here, but I think there will be enough to keep me very busy preparing lessons . . ."

And then:

". . . In my last letter I wrote you about Mr. Turner, and my trip to the new school grounds. You will never believe this, but he is Mr. Hale's brother-in-law! He comes around the ranch a lot to see Mr. Hale . . ."

And then:

". . . Mr. Turner, the school trustee, came by the hotel today to check on my class accommodations. He is so considerate . . ."

And then:

". . . It has been such a long time now since I was in Downieville. I miss you so much Aggie. I don't really have any friends here, as the school work keeps me busy. My only friend seems to be Henry (the Mr. Turner I've written

to you about). He isn't as old as we thought. Anyway, age doesn't really matter in friendship, does it . . . ?"

Not long after that, Aggie received the letter she half-way expected:

"Dearest Aggie,

I think I'm in love! You've probably guessed by now. Who else do I write about? Yes. It is Henry Turner!"

Letters Ottie sent after that were filled with tales of her romance with Henry:

". . . He is such a gentleman, not at all like the rustic Downieville type. More like your father, Aggie. But definitely not a Democrat! He is a very intelligent man with strong opinions, and good ideas for the improvement of our valley . . ."

And then:

". . . it snows much deeper here than in Downieville. When the snow gets deep, people park their wagons and take to sleighs. It is a very novel idea, and lots of fun. Henry and I went for a sleigh ride alone one evening, and watched the stars in the crisp, clear sky . . ."

And then:

". . . Great news!—the best news ever, dearest Aggie. Henry has asked me to be his wife! You will never guess my answer. Ha! We plan to get married as soon as this school term ends, in the spring. Imagine me as Mrs. Henry Turner! It sounds
divine . . ."

The happiness Aggie felt for her friend bordered on envy. I heard her tell her mother one day, "Ottie is right about the Downieville type of men. They are not only rustic, most of them are antique! The younger ones have only one thing on their brain—GOLD! And, I think gold fever has made them senseless."

Another letter came:

". . . remember Aggie, I am counting on you to be my bridesmaid. Henry's brother Hart is going to be the best man. You two will have to meet. He is a fine man, but I don't think he likes me too much. He is more your type! Ha! Sorry to say, he is a confirmed bachelor. But then, so was Henry!"

* * *

On Tuesday, May 19, 1868, after the trail was reopened over the mountain passes, and the Darling & Garnosette's Mule Train was running for the summer, Henry Kennedy Turner and Ottie

Temperance Gilbert were married.

I watched with amazement the confusion this event caused in our household. Rachel and I decided to accompany our daughter to the wedding, and as those two Galloway women prepared for the magical day, they were like little girls set loose with their grandmother's trunk. It wasn't only the *dressing up* that caused excitement, I kept hearing the words, "We're going on a trip! A real trip!", and I realized that, although I traveled around from village to village in my official position, Rachel's two feet remained within the boundary of the Upper Yuba River, ever since our arrival here when our daughter was an infant. And, Aggie's memory held visions of no other place.

I believe the wedding took second chair to the journey. The adventure! The trip!

Aggie stood beside her friend at the Methodist Episcopal Church, a few miles south of Church's Corners, in Sierraville, and this heart of mine squeezed with pride. I suppose most people admire the bride. I worshipped the bridesmaid! There she stood before me—a woman. What happened to my little girl? Proud confusion—something only fathers know.

As I witnessed this formal affair, I soon became aware that one other person, besides me, did not approve. My objection came because the bridegroom proclaimed to be a Republican. I would prefer my daughter's best friend marry a fine young Democrat. But, I noticed that the best man, Henry Turner's brother, Hart, seemed a little too solemn for one whose job it is to cheer up the groom.

I never did care much for weddings, and sighed with relief when Rev. Hinkle finished reading the vows, and the party adjourned to the reception area.

I lost Rachel in the crowd, and then spotted Aggie happily chatting with some other women. I worked my way over to the punch bowl, where Hart Turner had quietly planted himself.

"Fine wedding," I said, trying to stir up conversation.

"I suppose, if you like that sort of thing," Hart replied.

"You don't act like you're in a celebrating spirit," I said, as I dipped out a cup of punch from the large ornamental bowl—apparently I struck a nerve.

"I don't see why, when they went up to Downieville, a couple of weeks ago, for their marriage license, they didn't just get married by the justice of the peace, instead of putting everyone through all this misery," Hart said. He stuck his finger behind the stiff, white, newly starched collar of his shirt, and gave it a tug, loosening and disarranging his tie.

I laughed. "You have a point there!"

Hart finished his cup of punch, picked up the dipper, and dipped more out of the bowl.

With our backs to the wall we faced the jolly crowd, and looked straight across the room toward the happy couple. "The bride is a lovely girl," I said.

"I suppose so. But I can't understand why Henry wants her. She's too young, and too fancy. What good is an uppity female school teacher going to be on a ranch? If Henry had to get married, why didn't he find a good cook? A better wife would be a local girl. Someone raised in the mountains, and familiar with pioneer people and their ways." I saw him glance over at Aggie, and felt another uncomfortable tug at my chest. I guess he didn't realize I was her father.

He took a sip from his cup, and continued with his complaint, "Someone pretty, and bubbly, like that girl over there." He nodded in Aggie's direction. "And strong . . . yeah, strong!—someone who could help with the work."

I turned to the table and refilled my cup. It made me uncomfortable to see this young man looking at my daughter. I felt perspiration against my own collar, when I noticed my shy little girl return his attention, with coy, flirtatious glances.

The father of the bride walked over our way. "Congratulations Charlie," I said. "She's a beautiful bride."

Hart remained silent. Then George Hale joined us. I remembered him from several years back, when he had a hotel outside of Downieville, along the trail to Sierra City.

"Hello George," I said. Our hands met in a tight grip. "It's been a long time. I understand you have a new hotel in this valley."

"I not only have a new hotel," George said, "but, I have a new wife also!" He nodded across the room toward a slender woman in a dark green dress. She wore spectacles, and had graying dark brown hair, which she wore knotted at the top of her head.. "We've been married, coming on two years now."

I made introductions all around.

"You've got a beautiful daughter, Mr. Gilbert," George said. "You'll have to meet my wife Rachel. She'll brag on her for sure."

Charlie smiled and said, "It's the best thing I ever did—sending for Ottie. She has been the joy of my life these last few years. I don't know why I let so much time pass without her."

George squinted. "I have a daughter back East, myself—Harriet. We call her Hattie. I've got a picture taken of her a few years back. She's a pretty little lass. Guess she got that from her mother!" He laughed, took a sip of punch, and then frowned. "This stuff ain't fit for a baby! Don't they have anything stronger?" Then he noticed someone in the corner with a bottle, and we all four began to drift in that direction, while George continued to talk, as if the conversation had not been interrupted. "She must be about the same age as your Ottie—maybe a little younger. Let's see . . . she'd be fifteen now. I haven't laid my eyes on her since she was a wee babe. Her poor mother died, and I came out west. I left little Hattie with an old aunt—had to. The West is no place for a lass without a mother. Besides, what could I teach a girl?"

While the man with the bottle generously added spice to our cups, the truth about the Turner family dawned on me like the rising of the sun. This *was* old Tom Turner's family! . . . That old miner who worked his fingers raw on the claim next to me, on the Yuba, during my introduction to the Sierra Nevada Mountains. Standing before me, in flesh and blood, were the players in the stories he told. I knew them all, from the old man's memories: The son-in-law, George Hale; the new little granddaughter Hattie; his sons Henry and Hart. There was a third son, Merrick. I wondered what fate brought them all back into my life.

Charlie's eyes glowed and the words sputtered out of his mouth in excitement, "You ought to send for her, Mr. Hale, before it's too late! Why she's almost grown, like my Ottie. I tell you, it is the best thing I ever did sending for my girl. Just look at her . . ."

While Charlie and George admired the bride, I studied Hart for some resemblance to his father, old Tom. His strong shoulders maybe, and large rough hands. That was about all.

"A man needs a family," Charlie continued. "I am so proud today! I walked down the aisle with that pretty little lady, and gave her over to one of the finest men in the country. That is what you are going to miss if you don't send for your daughter, Mr. Hale."

George took a sip from his cup and sighed. Only then did he look with renewed interest at Ottie. "I never thought of her as someone's daughter before—the little school teacher. Maybe I *should* send for Hattie."

For the first time since the wedding began, I noticed a spark of excitement in Hart's voice, as he said, "Rachel will help you. Talk to her about it! Wouldn't it be great to have Hattie here with us?"

Charlie nodded, and held his cup toward the man with the bottle. I noticed George shudder and frown. I wondered what he feared. A reunion? Or, possibly a rejection?

CHAPTER NINE - 1868

The trip to the wedding opened a whole new world for Aggie. She began to daydream about leaving Downieville, and finding her own little corner of the world—someplace like Church's Corners; of getting married and having her own ranch—something like Ottie's.

She pleaded with me to let her go down to the valley to visit, and I found it hard to resist those large, sad, puppy dog eyes of hers. I kept myself busy those days, dividing my time between the Kentucky Mine, where I was principal owner, and my law office—I had become a prominent attorney in Downieville. But, I confess, Aggie could manipulate me, and I soon found myself at her side, riding over the top of the steep mountains, past clear lakes, on a trail that led to Mohawk Valley, then on to Sierra Valley. This round-about journey exhausted even an expert traveler, but short cuts invited danger from a wilderness where the mountain lion and grizzly roamed. A wise man stayed trail bound.

I claimed the journey was a business trip, and told Aggie that I needed to talk with some influential democrats that lived near Church's Corners. I never knew for sure if she believed me.

When I dropped her off at the Turner Ranch, her sparkle and joy convinced me that I did the right thing. Henry Turner attempted to invite me to stay with them, but I declined, and moseyed on over to George Hale's Hotel.

The following day I rode south of the Corners to the twin towns of Randolph and Sierraville. I called on a few of the local democrats, and returned to Hales in time for dinner.

George and Rachel sat at a table in the front corner of the hotel's dining room, close to the kitchen. Light filtered in through a window that overlooked the valley.

They encouraged me to join them, and I did. The aroma of fried chicken teased my appetite, and my stomach sent forth embarrassing little growls. Rachel placed a plate and silver on the linen draped table, while George filled a beautiful crystal goblet to the brim with sparkling red wine. I ate with such a relish that I didn't notice Hart Turner when he came into the hotel, and walked over to where we sat.

"Hello Lad!" I heard George say, and I looked up into the sad blue eyes of Ottie's brother-in-law.

George swallowed a large bite of bread, and washed it down with wine, as he said, "Well, come on here and sit down. It's a fine evening, with all this company! You remember Judge Galloway?" Hart nodded in my direction. "Of course you do."

I smiled, and Hart tried to return the smile, but lifted only one corner of his mouth into a grin, as if his lip were as heavy as lead.

"Would you like some dinner Hart?" Rachel asked, as she rose from the table, and began to clear off her and George's plates.

"No thank you, I've eaten."

He dropped into a chair, letting his whole body fall limp. He looked as if the burden of the world's problems were on his shoulders.

As Rachel walked toward the kitchen with the dirty plates, George said, "Darlin' would you bring Hart, here, a glass of wine? And you can bring me some more too."

Rachel nodded to a waitress, who stood and stacked dishes on a small table near the kitchen door. The woman pulled a heavy crystal glass from the cupboard, and in a minute stood over our table with a fresh bottle of red burgundy. George smiled, and winked at her as she poured a glass full for Hart, and then set the remainder down on the table next to her boss.

"Here you are brother, take a sip of that," George said.

The waitress returned to her position near the kitchen door, and the smooth sway of her dark skirt, as she walked, drew my attention and that of my host. It startled me to look up and see Rachel staring at us, from the kitchen door. She shook her head as she peered over the top of her small wire glasses.

George took no notice of his wife, and said to Hart, "You look like you lost your best friend."

"It's just Henry—and that wife of his," Hart said, as he fingered the sharp edge of the crystal.

"The girl does have a name," George said. "It's Ottie."

"Yeah, I know."

Hart lifted the glass to his lips, but didn't drink. He just held it in front of him, then set it down again, and said, "It's just that I feel out of place on my own ranch! Henry doesn't have time to spend . . . Well, to do anything anymore."

"You mean they are still on their honeymoon!" George chuckled.

"Yeah..."

"That's a shame, Hart!" George continued to grin. He lifted his glass in a mock toast, and said, "They're young and in love! You should be so lucky."

Hart slammed his glass down on the table. "No I shouldn't! Never! I will never let a woman come in and take over my life. I'd rather be dead!"

"Whoa lad . . ." George lifted his hand. He seemed as concerned for his wine glass and table as he was for Hart's mood. "Calm yourself lad! You're taking it all too seriously. You know that love and marriage are like grapes and good wine."

Hart glared at him.

George lifted his hand, palm outward, and added, ". . . but, it's not for everyone. Maybe it's not for you. But, look at Rachel and me . . ." George smiled as his eyes darted toward the kitchen, where his wife scurried about. "Why we're as happy as two hummingbirds in a garden of roses. And, from what I've seen of Henry lately, he's not complaining either. He looks mighty content to me."

"Yeah, I guess so." Heart lifted his glass of wine, and sipped slowly. He still gave off vibrations of a cloudy day, brewing up a thunderstorm.

Double doors with glass inserts divided the dining room from the lobby. They swung open, and a slender young man, with dark wavy hair, walked through. His pleasant smile grew larger when he spotted Hart sitting at our table.

"I thought I'd find you here," he said. I was just heading for your ranch, and saw that old roan of yours tied out front."

George started to call the waitress, but Rachel, who stood at the kitchen door, raised her hand to stop him. "Frank would you like a glass of wine?" she asked.

"No thank you, Mrs. Hale." His eyes rested on me with a glint of curiosity. "Have you met Judge Galloway, from Downieville?" George asked.

I rose, scooted my chair backward in the effort, and shook the young man's hand. "I don't believe I've had the pleasure," I said.

"I'm Frank Campbell. Pleased to meet ya."

George smiled, and said, "Frank here, is an old Indian

fighter—rode with the Calvary. He's been working at Fletcher's Sawmill for the past two years, but don't let that fool you. He's got better things in his mind, for his life."

The flush that crossed Frank's face contradicted the tough outward appearance. "I'm on my way to Fenstermakers," he said. "And I stopped to see if Hart wants to join me.

"Fenstermakers! That's just what you two bachelors need on an August night—a trip to the hot springs," George said. He smiled at Frank Campbell, and nodded toward his forlorn brother-in-law.

Campbell quickly caught the unspoken message in George's nod. "Come on Hart," he said. "It will cheer you up. I heard those Pike County girls are visiting again."

Fenstermakers sat on the edge of a hill on the far end of Sierra Valley, about five miles south of Church's Corners, where its owner, of the same name, marketed one of the most fantastic natural wonders known to man: mineral water bubbling out of the ground at an abnormally hot temperature. Rumors circulated that the spring contained healing minerals that could cure the sick. So, Fenstermaker built healing pools, and the hot springs became a favorite vacation spot for people from all over the north section of our state—and also Nevada. Local boys liked to go there for a good time, and all I can say about the Pike County girls, is, whenever they showed up, parties lasted late into the night, and wine flowed like dew from the vine.

Hart's expression softened and he pushed his chair away from the table as he stood to leave with his friend. He thanked George for the drink, and asked, "Did you ever write to Hattie about coming west?"

George winced. It was obvious he had not written.

Hart continued, "You left her when she was just a baby, George. I remember. I was left behind too. I helped Aunt Mary watch Hattie for you, and that little girl is like a sister to me. She's an angel, George. Believe me. If you don't hurry up and ask her to come out west, I will do it!"

George held up his hand in a defensive manner. "Okay. I'll write."

Hart rested his hand on George's shoulder, and gave it a pat. Then he turned and walked out of the dining room with Frank, letting the door swing shut behind him. We watched through the distorted glass window, as the two men mounted their horses, and rode off down the trail that led to the south end of the valley.

George lifted the half empty bottle of wine, and refilled both of our glasses. He frowned, and said, "I'll write—when I darn well get around to it!"

CHAPTER TEN - 1868

That trip to Sierra Valley in August, to see Ottie, kept our young Aggie satisfied through the blustery days of September. But soon October's frost nipped at the trees, and every trace of summer's warm green disappeared. A chill entered Aggie's heart, and helplessly I watched the joy of youth fade.

November was cold. What might be welcomed in summer as refreshing rain is considered a threat in late autumn. Cumulus clouds clashed together, growling and snarling—then the rain came. A slow dribble or a down pour—in November it doesn't matter, they both resulted in dripping trees and sloppy, muddy trails. When the rain stopped, ice formed. Long threads hung from the roof tops, pointing downward. The fence sparkled with its new lacy white coat, which grabbed at my wool gloves, and held them tight. Invisible covers over the puddles sent one crashing to the ground with the first careless step.

We struggled then, as one does now, preparing for the long treacherous winters. We harvested our gardens, and packed the food away in cellars. We cut firewood, and stacked it in long rows along the side of the house. Although we sometimes felt like hibernating bears, it made us feel good to know we were prepared.

In bad weather I took fewer trips down the hill to Downieville. It was too darn cold for troublemakers to stir up much trouble. But occasionally they managed, and demanded my service as an attorney. On these trips to town, I always checked to see if we had mail. A letter from Sierra Valley, carried over the mountain on the back of a mule, brought a rare smile to Aggie's face.

One late November afternoon, I trudged up the trail toward home. The frozen ground allowed my mule to make it without slipping in the mud. The temperature remained on the borderline of freezing, and icicles grew at least an inch that day.

As I walked through the front door of my little cabin the familiar warmth of home greeted me with sweet apple pie smells, and a crackling glow from the fireplace, where Aggie stood rearranging the days wash, which had no chance of drying outside, and needed to be turned every hour or so—to face the heat of the fire.

Smiling, I removed my hat, gloves and coat; hung them on a

peg by the door; and slipped a letter from my coat pocket. I watched Aggie for a minute before I told her the good news.

Shadows that painted mysterious and sad expressions on her face instantly began to dance around the room as she smiled, and raced over to claim her prize: a letter from Ottie!

"Oh Papa, thank you!" she said, and kissed my cold round cheek. Swiftly she moved back to the flickering light of the fireplace, where she carefully opened the envelope. She did not rip it, like a man would do, but tenderly peeled back the flap, and removed its treasured contents.

As I pulled the wool scarf from around my neck, and called out to Rachel, Aggie began to read:

"Dear Aggie,

We have wonderful news, and I want you to be the first to know. We are going to have a baby! It will not be until next summer. You can not tell by looking at me, but I have felt so ill lately, and I believe it would not be premature to predict the diagnoses of my illness! Henry is as happy as I am, and of course he wants a son. The baby is due at a bad time for us. Summer on the ranch is so busy, because of the short season. I have suggested to Henry that you should come and stay with us when the time comes. How would you like to be a housekeeper for Mr. & Mrs. Turner? Our cabin is small, as you know, but I will need help after the baby arrives.

If you are being courted—some secret romance that you are hiding from me, I will understand. But, I will accept no other excuse! You have lots of time to think about it.

Your dear friend, Ottie

Aggie gently set the letter down. Her entire body went limp, as she buried her head in her arms and began to cry.

Rachel and I were in the kitchen when we heard her sobs. We went to her quickly, and I asked, "Aggie, what is it? Has something happened to Ottie?"

I'll never forget her answer. She looked up, still sobbing, and said, "Yes Papa. Something has happened to Ottie. She is expecting a baby!"

Now this is a part of the mystery that always puzzled me about women. You would think that Aggie would be happy for her friend. Having a baby is something to rejoice over—not cry! I looked into Rachel's deep set eyes for some kind of clue, and she just flipped her hand at me in a backward wave, which meant I could quietly leave the room.

Reluctantly I departed, as Mother moved to the fireplace, put her long strong arms around Aggie's shoulders, and said, "What's the matter dear?"

Like a little pet rabbit, Aggie buried her head in Rachel's broad shoulder. She hadn't done this since she was a little girl, and the corner of Rachel's lips turned upward. If maternal instinct were visible, I saw it then, and it reminded me of the day we descended the mountain into Downieville with Aggie a small infant in her mother's arms.

I stood in a silent shadow of the room, mesmerized as I watched the two people I loved most in this world—such a tender scene.

"Mother, have you ever been lonely—real lonely?" Aggie asked.

"Of course I have honey. I'm sure everyone is lonely at times."

"But you've always had Papa."

"Oh, no I haven't! In fact, I traveled clear across the states in the same wagon train with your father, and he never even knew I was alive!"

"Really?" This story perked an interest in Aggie that instantly dried her tears. She used her finger to wipe the wetness from her cheek. "But you're so beautiful! He loves you so much. He must have been blind!"

"In matters of love, Aggie darling, all men are blind. They are so busy with one project or another that sometimes they see nothing else. You have to be patient. There is someone special out there for you. One of these days he will turn around, and open his eyes, and know he can't possibly go on living without you."

Aggie smiled. Rachel's words, however prejudiced they may have been, seemed to make the girl feel better.

"I got a letter from Ottie."

"I see that."

"Did I tell you she is going to have a baby?"

"Yes, you did."

"It just doesn't seem fair, Mother. She is *so* happy."

"You will be just as happy, one day. Be patient and it will come to you."

"I know," Aggie sighed, and then remembered, "Oh, she wants

me to come and help her next summer, when the baby is born. What do you think? Should I go?"

Rachel gave me a secret glance. "You will have to discuss this with your father, but you have talked our ears off about leaving Downieville someday, and once you get over this mood you're in, you will be begging us to let you go."

A cold draft suddenly drifted into my dark corner. Until that moment, Aggie's threats about leaving our home were just that—empty threats! The chilling fact gripped me. I could not fulfill my daughter's dream. To gain happiness, she would need to step away from our protective arms. Although everything I loved in life sat directly across the room, I suddenly felt sad, as my glance at the future shot its cold arrows into my paternal heart.

CHAPTER ELEVEN - 1869

When the ground thawed enough to till, the potatoes needed to be planted, and spring calves began to drop, ushering in the milking season. It is often the busiest time of the year for the dairy man—and it was the most uncomfortable time for Ottie, whose tummy swelled to capacity, making it almost impossible for her to bend over and button her own shoes. Her letters begged Aggie to come early. And so Aggie left home, and moved on to the Turner Ranch.

A child leaving home is often compared to a bird flying from the nest for the first time—but we who have children know this is untrue. Birds don't cry. Strong leaders of the Democratic Party don't cry either, nor superintendents of gold mines, nor brilliant attorneys. Every pore in my body fought off the tears—Rachel cried for both of us.

Depression plagued her for weeks, and then one day she walked out the front door and began to pull weeds. She removed every unwanted plant in the yard, wheeled over barrels of manure from the corral, and tenderly cultivated a beautiful flower garden with wildflowers that grew from seeds she randomly scattered the previous fall. Beneath the golden and violet blossoms she buried all of her frustrations. Flowers truly played a mysterious role in the strange workings of Rachel's heart.

Ottie had no mother around to help her, but she certainly wasn't alone. Henry exercised his persuasive abilities on old Doc Schubert, and somehow manipulated the old fellow into building a cabin on the Turner Ranch. All he really needed for persuasion was a bottle of whiskey. The man's doctoring ability could measure up to any other pioneer doctor around, and I'm sure he'd come up equal—but he would not settle down. He would build a cabin in one location, and live there awhile. Then when his drinking became a real problem, he'd move on, sober up, and build another cabin. He lived in almost every corner of Sierra Valley. Old Doc was almost as good a carpenter as he was a doctor.

Mr. Fletcher, of Fletcher's sawmill, lived up the road a bit. When a woman's time came, this man's wife filled in as a midwife. She was a friendly woman, and her nearness made me feel better about sending Aggie over the mountain. I did not expect our innocent eighteen year old daughter would be much help in the area of birthing, however she had a strong back, and could lighten Ottie's chore load until the baby was born.

Everything about Aggie's move seemed right. Everything, that is, except the close proximity of Henry Turner's brother, Hart, whose bachelorhood made me nervous. The man built his own cabin up the hill, and moved out of the original ranch house, when Henry married. However, he still lived too close to suit me! I knew he would be around the ranch every day, and a young girl might possibly find Hart's rugged charm attractive.

Hart professed to be a Republican, and I objected strongly. I definitely did not want my daughter getting tangled up with a danged Republican! Hart could have been a prince, or a president—it wouldn't have mattered. My daughter would marry a Democrat, and I didn't even want her to look at a man who wouldn't show his political colors first!

I watched carefully for any indication that Aggie might be interest in him. At the first sign, I would yank her back home! I examined the letters she wrote to us, remembering how Ottie used to mention Henry in every letter. But our Aggie wrote about the weather, her chores, Ottie, and very little else. If Hart were around, apparently Aggie didn't notice him.

Aggie's letter writing displayed her lack of attention in school. Besides an occasional misspelled word, the girl did not waste time constructing long sentences. But, we treasured every letter, and Rachel tied them with a ribbon, and kept them in her cedar chest. One month after Aggie left home we received the simple birth notice, dated June 1, 1869:

"Dear Mama and Papa,
Today the baby was born. It is a boy. He is very small, and they named him Franklin Hurd Turner. The weather is nice. There is lots of work to do. I miss you
Love, Aggie"

Although her letter showed very little emotion, that June day became a milestone in our Aggie's young life. She felt new joy ripen in her heart as she stood and gazed upon the baby while he slept soundly in a cradle Henry built and polished during the long winter months. Aggie's love for her friend Ottie, created a special bond with this new life, and I am sure Aggie would have laid down her own life for him. Little Frank knitted their lives together, and the Turners began to call my daughter, "Aunt Aggie".

The second miracle born on June 1st, that year, happened in Hart Turner's cold heart. Until that day, he measured a person's worth by how they put a hand to the shovel. When Henry forced the squirming little bundle into his brother's unsuspecting arms, Hart's opinion of mankind instantly changed. The tiny, little hand reached out and clasped onto Hart's finger, and held tightly. Henry insisted that Hart look at the feet, which were smaller than two joints on the smallest finger on Hart's rough hands. Beads of sweat formed on the new uncle's forehead as the baby's coal black eyes looked blankly into his. But, the giant fell, when Ottie mentioned the fact the baby was his namesake. Little Franklin Hurd Turner, was named for his uncle, Hartwell Franklin Turner.

If I had seen the Weaver's plan then, I am sure I would have insisted that Aggie return home. As the Turner family began to knot together, they pulled Aggie into it like a blending thread.

* * *

Some folks can look backward in time, and easily sift through years of memories—picking out a single incident, or maybe a word or two that, at the time, seemed unimportant, but changed the momentum and direction of one's life.

Hart can do just that. He not only remembers conversations, but also smells and melodies that played their part.

In the summer of 1869, a lullaby sung by a new mother, sweetly and gently floated past the cradle where little Frank slept. It danced its way through an open window, and caught a current of air, meant only for birds and angels. It transformed nature's song into a masterpiece of praise.

Down the hill, Hart stood at the door of the large cow barn. He hesitated to step inside, as the faint sound of Ottie's voice reached his ear—a sound that, until recently had no part in farm life. Each note swept his heart with forgotten memories of childhood days in Maine, and a mother buried there.

Outside the kitchen door, Henry stacked freshly cut firewood. He smiled at the pure angelic sound of Ottie's voice, and felt his heart stir deep within. Intermittently the song stopped—interrupted by chattering sounds, easily identified as talking women, followed by giggles—then the lullaby would begin once more.

Henry pulled off his floppy work hat, which left a dirty ring across his forehead, and he walked over to the shade cast by a huge pine tree, which grew near the back door.

On those hot summer days, an old wooden bucket, filled with cool, clear drinking water, always sat on the back porch. A ladle hung above it on a nail. Henry took the ladle, dipped it into the bucket, and poured some cool water over his head, letting it drip down over his face and neck. Then he filled the ladle again, and brought it to his lips, not once, but twice.

Through the open kitchen door, he overheard Ottie say, "Do you know what I really miss from Downieville?"

"Your father," Aggie said.

"Besides that!"

"I can't imagine."

"My piano! But I guess that is impossible. Can you imagine bringing my piano over the trail from Downieville on the back of a mule?"

Aggie giggled, and Ottie joined her. And, although their conversation had been meaningless small talk, their laughter stung Henry's ears.

He let the ladle drop into the bucket, plopped the hat back on his head, and stormed down the hill to the cow barn where he found Hart with a shovel in his hands, getting ready to muck out the cow stalls.

Henry stood with straight legs—his feet flat on the ground. He pulled off his hat again, and held it tightly in his fist—both fists on his hips, elbows out. He clamped his jaw tightly shut, as if to keep his unspoken words from spilling out. "What's the matter with you?" Hart asked.

"I'll tell you what's the matter with me," Henry exploded. "It's this darn county! Do you know there are roads that connect Sierra Valley with every place in the world, except its own county seat in Downieville?"

Hart lifted one side of his mouth into a half-smile, and nodded, as he leaned against his shovel.

"We can't even take a wagon up the hill. I tried to figure out once how we could get a wagon load of hay to Downieville; and, as close as I can guess, we would have to take a road across the south end of the valley—south to Sierraville, then east to Loyalton. From Loyalton we could head south again over the toll road to Sardine Valley, then travel west on the old Henness Pass road. It would almost be a complete circle! You know, Hart, once we reach Henness Pass Road, it would probably be easier to haul a wagon load to Virginia City, Nevada!"

Hart scraped the floor of the barn with the heel of his boot. He peered through the slats, and then into the stalls, at the piles of manure that awaited him. Politics, and all it represented, made Hart nervous. The voice of experience warned that Henry's hot-under-the-collar attitude was leading into something political.

"Downieville is our County Seat!" Henry said, and Hart noticed his brother's cheeks begin to blush in anger.

Hart picked up a harness that drooped carelessly over a rail.

Henry continued to rage. "The new settlers in this valley are screaming—and I don't blame them! It seems as if time is standing still in our antiquated county, and the supervisors don't seem to care!"

"Look at this harness," Hart said, as he twisted the stiff leather in his calloused hands, and pointed to a worn spot held together by a thread.

"Hmmm..." With glazed over eyes, Henry looked at the harness, and said, "If our neighbor, Jared Strang, hadn't been wise enough to cut his own trail over Yuba Gap, we would still be trudging along the old route that wound through Plumas County—just to get to the Sierra County Courthouse."

Hart pulled at the leather, and it snapped in his hand. "Do you think we ought to try and repair this one more time?"

"... as it is, the trail Jared found is still nothing but an old mule trail."

"... or do you think we should make a new one?"

"A new what?"

"... A new harness. Or should we repair it one more time?"

Henry shrugged, and continued on with his singular thought, "Hart, do you know there is a lot of talk about making Loyalton our County Seat?"

Hart looked at the harness and sighed.

"Do you know what an expense that would be for us taxpayers?"

Hart put his hands on his hips and shook his head.

"We have a good courthouse, and a fine jail in Downieville. The cost of building new ones would be staggering! Besides, if Loyalton should become our County Seat, we will never see a road cut through the pass from this end of the valley."

Hart dropped the harness back over the rail. The idea of a road dominated Henry's mind, and Hart could not distract him even if he lit fire to the barn!

Henry leaned against the same rail, next to the failing harness. He squinted, as if peering into the past, and said, "Years ago there was talk about building a road over Yuba Gab—back when Merrick owned the ranch. Men got together in Sierraville to discuss the possibilities. I think it was the summer of '62. They came from all over the valley to attend the meeting. If I remember right George went, and our distinguished Assemblyman T. S. Battle. Sierraville's founding father, William Arms attended that meeting, and old Doc Webber came over from Loyalton . . . and Chapman. These are all progressive men, Hart. I don't understand why they never followed through and built the road. That was over seven years ago!"

Hart walked in to one of the cow stalls, and began to scrape the manure up with his shovel, and pitch it outside through a small window-type opening nearby. He did not want to participate in this conversation at all; however he could not help but offer what he knew. "George told me once that they did start to build the road, but they ran out of money."

"That's just it!" Henry said, encouraged by his brother's comment. "Every bill the county presented to the voters since has been turned down. Hart, if we don't get a road built to Downieville soon, we will have to find another way to make a living."

Hart stopped shoveling. Farming. The ranch. Take away the ranch, and you take his heart. Not so long ago he tenderly transplanted his roots in this California soil, and nobody better try to uproot him!

Henry looked directly into Hart's worried eyes. "Other farmers in this valley ship their butter and hay to Virginia City. Those on the north side take wagons on the Beckwourth Pass Road, and those on the south-east (around Loyalton) use the Henness Pass road. But we are stuck over here on the south-west side, with a stupid mule trail! We still have to tamp our hay into bales, load them onto the back of mules—150 pounds per mule—and pack them over the mountain to Downieville!"

Hart leaned against his shovel, and said, "I guess you heard the news about the railroads. Any day now they will be joined together, and we can travel from the Pacific Ocean to the Atlantic—by rail. Coast to coast! We will be able to go to Maine by train."

"Yeah, and we could probably get there faster than we can get to the Sierra County Seat!" This image brought a smile to Henry's face as he spoke.

Hart relaxed and grinned too. "So, what can we do about it? Build the road ourselves?" The minute these words crossed his lips, Hart knew he made a mistake.

"We may have to," Henry said with enthusiasm. "The voters turned down the Yuba Pass Road project twice now, and the county doesn't have the gumption to get the job done without a push from someone."

Hart clamped his teeth together, and scooped up some more manure. He guessed who that *someone* would be.

"Sierra Valley folks are losing patience with their leaders. If something isn't done soon, Downieville may lose its position as County Seat—or worse, we may end up with a divided county."

Henry glanced at the harness draped over the rail, and suddenly felt a tug of guilt. "I'm sorry Hart. Here you are, trying to keep the ranch running smoothly, and doing more than your share of chores. It is your effort that keeps us going. I don't know what I'd do without you!"

Hart looked up from his work, and raised his left eyebrow slightly. His brother usually followed a compliment with a request.

Henry rubbed his hands together. "If we don't get that road built, we will probably go under. The way things are now, we can't stay abreast with the rest of the ranchers in the valley."

A gleam twinkled in Henry's eyes, and his lips turned upward in a calculated smile. He said, "I'll do what I can. Meanwhile, brother, I can't thank you enough for being here!"

With these words, Henry reached out and slapped Hart on the back, then quickly walked out of the barn before Hart could express how he felt about another excuse added to the already long list of reasons for Henry's habitual absence.

Not long after this conversation with Hart, Henry threw his hat into the ring and ran for California State Senator, on the Republican Ticket.

* * *

Henry's campaign brought him up through Downieville, all the way to the north boundary of our county. Try as I might, I can't even remember his crusade to gain office. He belonged to the wrong party, and my efforts contradicted his. I do recollect hearing his name everywhere I turned—H. K. Turner.

The republicans liked Henry. He often represented Sierra Valley at the local Republican Convention. He worked hard, and built a good reputation.

Henry rode the campaign trail like a champion. When he dressed in the morning, he donned a carefree attitude, which carried him through receptions that dripped with the smell of cigars, and brought him home at night exhausted and ill tempered.

While Henry plotted, and performed for the party, Hart kept the ranch going. The battle for office did not end until Election Day in November—after Hart sent the butter off to market; harvested the onions, potatoes, and other root vegetables, and put them in cold storage; and cut, split and stacked the winter firewood.

Hay profits slid downward that year, because of a nasty little insect—the grasshopper. It ate its way through much of the valley's crop. What the tobacco spitting creatures left behind was then damaged by untimely hail storms. The meager remnant crop sold for the big price of $12 to $14 a ton.

From the time Henry began the campaign until its conclusion, Hart's moans, groans, grumbles, and mild cursing kept everyone at a distance. Henry tried to appease his brother by taking on a hired hand. The man was good, and strong, and probably accomplished a lot more around the place than the absent Henry would have done, had he been there. Nevertheless, Hart did not seem truly happy unless he was mumbling his opinion about his brother's absence.

My democratic blood ran thick back then; and I fought with pride, our party's struggle to win that one senatorial seat the state allowed Sierra County. We wanted our man in office. We wanted a democratic senator—but we lost. Henry won. I am not a good looser—never have been. This new-comer came off some back trail, and seized our prize—an office he would hold for a two year term. Anger replaced good sportsmanship, and I bit my lip at the thought that chance had supplanted fairness.

Oh, Henry was jubilant! His greatest hope had come true. However, he had not planned the intimate little details necessary to claim the victory. The legislative session would begin on December sixth—hardly enough time to get a home-away-from-home established for Ottie and the baby.

Winning united pride and guilt—and the turmoil of one to possess the other. This proud, sick feeling troubled Henry as he faced his wife at the crackling warm kitchen stove. Steam swirled upward from the heavy iron kettle, and the room was filled with that delicious smell of newly baked bread, which Ottie had carefully removed from the oven, and was placing on wooden racks to cool.

"I hate to leave you behind," Henry said, looking deeply into his wife's eyes.

As if she felt the tension suddenly fill the room, Aggie wiped her hands on the apron tied around her waist, and took her wool coat and Frank's bonnet, from a peg by the back door. She picked up the baby, blanket and all, from where he played on the kitchen floor. She plopped him into the empty laundry tub, which sat by the back door, just as Ottie said, "It's all right," to Henry's silence.

The early winter sun had moved behind the edge of the forest, and cast crisp, cold shadows on the yard where the morning wash hung, frozen and stiff on the line. Aggie set the laundry tub, and little Frank, down next to her on the ground while she unpinned the clothes. They were not dry, but had absorbed all the warmth they would from the sun that day. The job would be finished inside by the fire.

Hart came up behind, and asked, "Is Henry inside?"

Aggie's hand flew to her chest, and she dropped the clothes pins. "Hart! Never sneak up behind someone like that! You scared me half to death! Yes, Henry is inside."

Hart bent to pick up the clothes pins, and began to play with little Frank. Soon, all three of them tromped up the back stairs, shuffled across the porch, and burst through the back door. Aggie carried the wiggling, squirming baby, while Hart came behind with the basket full of clothes. His cheeks blushed when he noticed the questioning smile on Henry's face, and in an irritated tone he said, "I'm helping Aggie. Actually, I was looking for you, and could see that she needed a little help."

"Burrr . . ." Aggie said. She set Frank down on the kitchen floor, pulled away the blanket, which was tucked up tightly under his chin, and loosened the tie that held his bonnet. "It's colder outside than I thought! The clothes aren't totally dry, but we can hang them by the fire."

Ottie crossed the room to help and Henry picked up the baby.

"When do you have to be down there—in Sacramento?" Hart asked.

"Actually, right away . . . The session starts December 6th. The new state capitol building should be completed enough for us to meet there." A spark of excitement glowed in Henry's eyes. "Can you imagine it, Hart? It cost the taxpayers close to $2,600,000. What a mansion it must be! And ours will be the first Legislative Senate to meet there!"

"Well, I hope it's worth it," Hart said.

"I'm not doing this for free," Henry said. "When you think about the price we get for hay, $14 a ton, and realize I will make $16 per diem, plus another $16 for every twenty miles I have to travel to get there . . . That's a lot of hay, wouldn't you say?"

Hart whistled. "You should have told me that sooner, maybe I'd have voted for you!"

Henry shook his head and smiled.

"There is only one problem," he said, "and it's a big one."

"What's that?"

"I'll have to leave Ottie and the baby behind. There just isn't time to make arrangements. We haven't asked Aggie yet, but we hope she will stay for the winter, and help out around here, and keep Ottie company."

Aggie did not even have to answer. Her smile told all. Her eyes twinkled with excitement as she said, "Oh, you know I'd love to!"

Henry placed his hand on his brother's shoulder, and walked him over to the wood stove. He used a rag to pick up the hot kettle and pour Hart a cup of coffee. Handing it to him, he said, "You don't know what a relief it is having you around in case of an emergency—you know, someone I can rely on."

Hart raised his hand in protest. "Now wait a minute Henry!

You're not planning to leave me alone on this ranch with these two chatterboxes, are you?"

"They won't be any trouble, Hart. They have each other to talk to, and the baby to look after. That will keep them out of your hair."

Hart grunted, and peered at the woman through the steam than now rose from his cup. He felt strangely warmed and relieved that Aggie would not be returning home.

"First thing I am going to do," Henry said, "is push to get that road built to Downieville. You'll see. It will make a huge difference for us! Having the leverage of a senator will be worth the time spent. It is just the muscle we need!"

CHAPTER TWELVE - 1870

No politician worth his salt missed taking a trip to Sacramento that year to see the new State Capitol building, and of course, at the first opportunity, I made my visit also.

I never, in my entire life, encountered such a structure. They said it was modeled after the nation's capitol, in Washington, and it towered majestically over the city of Sacramento, taking up an entire city block! The builders could indeed be proud of its Roman Corinthian style, intricate in detail. It stood four stories high, with a dome that projected light to the rotunda below, illuminating a large gold statue of Columbus kneeling before Queen Isabella of Spain. Wide cement stairways spread outward from the magnificent building, and sidewalks branched down to the street, with lawns and newly planted trees—the beginning of a beautiful park.

My heart longed to be part of the proceedings that took place inside those solemn walls, and my teeth clamped in regret of the election I lost back in 1861. If I had visited during the time when Henry was there, I'm sure I would have called on him, even though I considered him a political enemy. He not only stole the coveted seat from our party, his doing so kept Aggie in Sierra Valley for the winter. However, my visit to the Capitol came after Henry returned home.

I will say one thing for Henry, he not only had a motive—he also had a plan to carry it out. In January, when the days are short, but the hours are long and cold, he had Sierra Valley canvassed. Then, as a newcomer, he stood on the floor of the Senate armed with petitions, signed by angry settlers, demanding the formation of a new county.

Those petitions gave Henry the ammunition he needed. He used them to demonstrate the discontent of citizens stuck on the east end of Sierra County, totally cut off from their County Seat; and then he introduced a bill that required the Sierra County Board of Supervisors to hold an election, and give the people a chance to vote on a $20,000 bond to build a wagon road from Downieville to Sierra Valley.

In March the bill moved on to the State Assembly, where B J. Sammons, and John Koutz represented Sierra County. They were North County boys who didn't give a hoot whether Sierra County ever got their wagon road. They insisted it was wrong to tax the entire county for a road the Northern folks would never use. The Assembly drew up a compromise, in the form of an amendment, stating that if the construction exceeded the $20,000 amount, then the county could not be taxed for the balance. However, those townships encompassing Sierra Valley and Downieville could tax themselves if the project exceeded the $20,000.

True to his campaign promise, Henry succeeded getting the matter on the ballot, and he returned home that spring, a happy and successful man.

In April we held the bond election. The project won, 868 yes votes to 365 no votes. The road would be built!

The prospect of a new road tickled me. Both Rachel and Aggie hated the slow dusty mule train, and letters hardly replaced warm hugs. I looked forward to the day Aggie would come home to visit, riding on a stage! Only one thing could hold up progress of the road—county bureaucracy. And, that is exactly what happened.

Exhausting debates began over *which* Yuba Gap route would be best: one that wound straight down Turner Canyon, and entered Sierra Valley at the Turner Ranch, or a lower pass that terminated father north, at Chapman's Ranch.

Surveyors prowled the mountain ridges and canyons, and determined that although the lower elevation of the Chapman route seemed advantageous, impassable snow drifts lingered until the month of May—when snow of the higher route (down Turner Canyon) had melted.

Our hopes remained high through April. We considered the delays merely part of the pain that accompanied the birth of a new idea, or project. Meanwhile the mule trails opened and traffic grew steadily worse as the weather warmed.

* * *

The dairy herd on the Turner Ranch presented new calves daily, and the milking season began. Milking started earlier and earlier each morning, with the introduction of new cows to the dairy. Hart, Henry, and the hired man complained of the sore, stiff fingers associated with exercising the milking muscles—a ritual of every spring.

I believe Ottie could have handled all of her chores alone, that year, but she kept Aggie on—and, of course, Aggie loved every minute of it. She worked hard. The girls served the main big meal in the middle of the day, when the men took a rest from their labor, ate heartily, and sat on the porch for a while to let the food settle.

One warm afternoon Aggie stood at the kitchen door, looking out onto the porch where Henry played with the baby—now an energetic little toddler. The remains of dinner sat in buckets ready to be fed to the chickens and pigs, and the dishes were washed, wiped, and returned to the cupboard. Ottie took the wet dish towels out on the porch to dry, and Hart scooted over a bit where he sat on the porch rail. The hired hand sauntered down the steps and headed off toward the new bunk house.

"Think of it Ottie," Henry said, as he lifted Frank onto his knee. "We will finally have a wagon road to Downieville—right down Turner Canyon! No more loading hay, butter, and potatoes onto the back of mules!"

Ottie smiled proudly. She often bragged to Aggie that if they got a new road built, people could thank her husband for it.

Henry lifted the baby over his head and shook giggles out of him. "One of the first things I am going to have delivered to our door by wagon is your piano!"

"My piano...?" Ottie gasped. "Oh Henry, that would be wonderful. I miss my music so much."

Henry put Frank down. The baby immediately toddled over to Uncle Hart and began tugging on his pant leg, wanting to be picked up and wrestled with.

"I want all of our children to learn to play the piano," Ottie said, "both Frank *and* little Mary."

Now, Ottie had only one child, everyone knew that. Hart looked at Aggie for an explanation. Aggie just raised her eyebrows, and shrugged.

Henry pulled Ottie into his arms, and Hart, feeling much like a third big toe, stood up, stretched, and headed down toward the barn. Frank stumbled down the steps, and chased after him. Aggie scooted after little Frank, who ran faster and giggled. Hart grabbed him, lifted him up, and asked Aggie, "Who is Mary?"

Together they walked down the hill toward the barn, dodging mules that crossed through the ranch on the Yuba Pass Trail.

Aggie's eyebrows went skyward as she answered, "How should

I know?"

Hart smiled. "You know everything that goes on around here. Come on now, who is Mary?"

Aggie never could keep a secret, and she said, "Mary Calista Turner."

Hart stopped. He stared into Aggie's eyes for some kind of hidden explanation. Finding none, he said, "That's a bad joke, Aggie. That's my sister's name, and she's been dead for a long time now."

"I know that. But it is also someone else's name."

"Who else?"

Aggie clamped her lips tight and shrugged her shoulders.

Hart grabbed her wrist. "Come on Aggie, you know you'll tell me!"

"Can't you guess?"

Hart let go of her wrist, and scowled. "Mary Calista Turner, my sister, married George Hale—you know, good old George. They had a baby girl—Hattie. Then Mary died. She is buried back home in Maine. And *that* is the only Mary Calista Turner *I* know."

Aggie's eyes shined with delight. She relished the idea that she knew something that Hart didn't.

"All right, don't tell me," Hart grumbled. He set Frank down on the ground, and started for the barn once more.

Aggie grabbed Frank's hand. "Ottie is going to have another baby," she said.

Hart spun around and stared at her.

"Are you sure?" he asked.

"Pretty sure. She's been sick in the mornings, and I've had to do the chores myself. She says she knows it for sure, and that it will be a girl."

"Nobody can know that," Hart said, frowning.

Aggie shrugged again. "She says so. Anyway, she wants to name the baby Mary Calista, after your sister."

"Why?" Hart crossed his arms. "She didn't even know Mary."

"She knows you got a letter from Hattie, which explained that she was going to stay in Maine, and finish school."

Hart nodded. "Yeah. I took it over and read it to George."

"Well, the news almost broke George's heart. Ottie loves George, and hates to see him so despondent. She thought that if she named the baby after Hattie's mother, it may be just the encouragement the girl needs. Maybe she will get the message that some folks out here in California care about her. Your letters don't seem to get that message across."

"She'd do that for Hattie?" Hart's arms dropped to his sides.

"Yes, she would," Aggie said quietly.

Hart looked toward the house, where Henry and Ottie had disappeared from the porch. He hesitated a moment, and looked Aggie squarely in the eye. A smile formed at the corner of his mouth, and then he said, "she better be right about it being a girl. Mary would be a terrible name for a boy!"

Aggie laughed, and Hart waved his hand at her. "Come on down to the barn, and see the new calves." He picked Frank up and smiled, "You want to see the calves, don't you partner?"

CHAPTER THIRTEEN - 1870

July came and it was hot. My patience with the Board of Supervisors became thread-bare by the time they accepted the plans for the Yuba Pass Road, and met to review construction bids.

I attended the meeting, and found it hard to speak to Henry when I saw him there. I wanted to know about Aggie—how she was doing. But my colleagues recognized H. K. Turner as, not only our Senator, but also the flag bearer of the local Republican Party, and that bothered me. When I did bolster up the courage to ask about my daughter, he kindly said nothing more than: she was fine, and helped out a lot at the ranch. He seemed preoccupied. Of course, he worried about the road. I noticed he relaxed around a fellow named Dan Cole, and found a lot to talk with him about. Dan was one of the supervisors—also an avid Republican.

When the business began, Supervisor C. W. Hendel gave his report, and finally acknowledged the bids. He read them, one by one, and for once the supervisors unanimously agreed on something. The slam of the hammer on the polished wooden table sent their answer pulsating around the room.

They found none of the bids adequate. None were accepted.

Henry stood. A red, rash-like blush started around his neckline, and rose to the top of his head. He did not say a word, as he paused for a moment and looked at the table where the supervisors sat. Then he turned and stormed out of the room.

The impression he made could not be measured with words. His authority as state senator filled everyone with apprehension. I alone shared his desperation. I wanted the road built almost as badly as he, and the irony of it was, I probably would not have cared one way or another, if Aggie were not living with the senator's family.

* * *

At the Turner Ranch, in Sierra Valley, everyone expected to hear good news about the road. So, to celebrate, Ottie and Aggie planned a special dinner that night. The women spent the afternoon fixing fried chicken, Henry's favorite, and biscuits, with potatoes and gravy, and a summer salad, fresh from the garden. Early in the day they tramped to the edge of the mountain and picked some wild strawberries for desert.

As the last ray of the sun drifted through the tall trees, the women paced, trying to keep dinner warm.

Years later Hart related the detail of that evening. The celebration the ladies planned to welcome home the victorious senator obviously fell through, but something about that warm sultry night—a simple and otherwise unimportant event—carved the memory deeply into Hart's mind. His life consisted of hard work. He was a man more suited to soil than to books, and his extraordinary memory always fascinated me.

Hart said he waited rather impatiently on the porch of Henry's house, with the hired hand, named Spuds. The men washed their hands and faces, and their cheeks now sparkled above their dirty, dusty work clothes. The rumpled towels lay on the bench next to a bowl full of soapy gray water.

Spuds sat patiently, with his legs hanging over the side of the porch. He never demanded much from life. Like many of the men who hired on, at the south-east end of the valley, he was a trapper. The small amount of money he made, addressed only a portion of his salary. The Turners built a cabin, to serve as a bunk house, for the man, and provided him with meals. This sustained Spud through the summer, until trapping season began.

Dusk crept upon them in its usual colorless way, as the last mule team of the day scurried down the hill past the house. Dust swirled around their hooves, and drifted in the direction of the Henry Turner home. It settled on the sills of the windows that Ottie kept closed, even though the kitchen pleaded for fresh air, and a cool breeze.

In the dim light Hart counted sixteen mules, as he listened to the thud of their hooves on the hard path, accompanied by the squeak of leather, and an occasional "Move on there!" from the muleskinner.

Hart's stomach growled. He couldn't understand why they had to hold dinner. He wanted to know the results of the road bid, same as everyone else, but . . .

From the side of the house, a rider burst out of the woods—Frank Campbell, on his coal black mare!

"Over here Frank," Hart waved. His friend dismounted quickly, flipped the reins over the horse's head, and flung them around the porch rail.

The kitchen door flew open, and Aggie stepped out, and yelled, "Get that horse away from the porch, Frank Campbell! Don't you see that we have flowers planted there?"

Immediately, Frank removed his hat—and his horse. "Sorry Aggie . . ."

He tied the horse to the low branch of a pine tree.

Aggie went back into the house. Hart raised his eyes skyward, and shook his head.

Frank sauntered over like a cowboy who had been too long on his horse. He let his hands fall to the side, palm outward, and asked, "How do I look?"

Hart surveyed him intently, noting the clean, white, starched shirt, and the dark tie, tucked neatly beneath the black vest. With his whiskers shaved off, his smile seemed wider. He even smelled of fancy water!

Hart grunted. "I'd say you don't look like any lumberman I know. Wherever you're going, I can tell you now, I'm too tired to join you."

"I'm not going anywhere special. Just thought I'd drop by and visit awhile."

Hart raised an eyebrow. He never knew Frank to lie before.

Ottie came to the screen door, and asked, "Any sign of Henry yet?"

"Nope . . . When are we going to eat? I'm starving!" Hart said.

"Where is Henry off to now?" Frank asked.

"He rode to Downieville yesterday, and we expect him home any minute," Ottie said, as she squinted in the dim light looking for movement on the dark trail. "Well, dinner is ready. You might as well stay, Frank, and eat with us."

"I'd never turn down one of your fine meals!"

"Look! Over there . . ." Ottie pointed to the silhouette of a rider on the trail. It was Henry. He waved to them, but did not stop, as he slowly moved toward the barn.

Ottie knew by her husband's posture that he was not in a good mood. "Aggie, look after things, will you?" she said to the shadow behind the screen door. Then she stepped off the porch, and walked quickly down to the barn.

* * *

I may not have been there that night, but I know what a wonderful meal those two women could serve. With everyone seated around the simple pine wood table, beneath the glow of the shaded oil lamp, which hung from a hook in the ceiling, Henry gave the blessing, and conversation melted away while everyone filled their plates. Oh yes. Those were wonderful meals.

As I said before, the conversation of the evening was later told to me by Hart himself, who grew very impatient with his brother and he broke the silence with the words, "Well, aren't you going to tell us how it went?"

"No good. They rejected every bid."

Forks stopped in mid-air, and the only sound came from the baby, who sat in a tall chair and banged a spoon on the table.

"Rejected them *all*?" Hart asked. Can they do that?"

"They did it. Most of the bids were totally unreasonable. With the state chomping down the county's back, I guess the contractors decided that our supervisors would be desperate enough to choose a bid at any cost."

For the first time in years—possibly the first time ever, Hart told me that he heard a note of discouragement in his brother's voice—the sound of defeat. All the time Henry neglected the farm, while off on one political escapade or another—all those years of feeling put-upon by his older brother—they seemed unimportant now. Hearing the sound of defeat in Henry's voice just didn't set well.

"I don't know," Henry said. "Last February, I stood before the Senate with my hands full of petitions from the residents of this fair valley, requesting the division of Sierra County. There I was, a brand-spanking-new Republican senator, pleading with a democratic Senate to help us get this road built. Because I am Republican, I'm surprised they even listened to me—but they did. Our supervisors don't seem to understand the seriousness of the matter. If these county leaders fail to build the road, the next senatorial session will have to take more drastic steps."

Henry cut a piece of the meat on his plate, and lifted it to his mouth. "But for us, Hart, I just don't know."

Hart lost his appetite.

While Henry chewed, he pointed his empty fork at his brother, and said, "We need to introduce something new to the valley. Hay, butter, and potatoes, are not going to buy beans, without a wagon road to take them to market. Besides, even with the road, the mines around Downieville are beginning to shut down, and the population drops off daily. I just can't see us depending on them for many more years. We need to find a local need and fill it."

Frank Campbell took a bite of his biscuit, and said, "You should ride over and take a look at the new mill we're building." He realized he was talking with his mouth full, and swallowed. "No foolin', it will be sixty feet long, and forty feet wide! Fletcher is installing a totally new system—steam power."

"Steam power!" Hart exclaimed. "That will cost him plenty."

Frank wiped his mouth with his napkin. "It should be faster, and more efficient. No one can keep up with the orders for lumber in this valley. You might consider building a mill yourselves. Look around—there is enough timber for everyone."

Hart thought of the sawmills in Maine. It was hard, dirty work, and it would take a major investment to get an operation started. "We'd be grabbing the bull by the tail if we tried that. I can barely keep the ranch above water now! Can you imagine me trying to run a sawmill, too?"

Frank nodded toward the end of the table, where Spuds sat bent over his plate. "You hire people—like Spuds . . ."

Spuds nodded. His cheeks bulged with food, and he continued to eat without looking up.

". . . or better yet, like me," Frank said, "someone to run the mill for you."

"You always say you're going to quit the mill work, and buy your own ranch," Hart reminded him.

Frank winked across the table at Aggie, and smiled. "That's true. I *am* going to settle down, when I get enough saved to buy my own place. I'm just suggesting how well things can be run, if you hire the right people."

Henry used a biscuit to dab up the last bit of gravy on his plate. "You have the right idea, Frank. But a sawmill would be a big financial investment, and like Hart said, I am gone so much of the time now. What we need is something we can do using the facilities we already have here on the ranch—with as few improvements as possible."

Henry learned the blacksmith trade, when he was a young man, back in Maine. The knowledge came in useful, especially during those pioneer days, with all its isolation. And, the Turners built a blacksmith shop on the ranch, where Henry fixed their wagons and tools. Hart couldn't resist a little poke at his brother. "We could start a blacksmith shop, but the resident blacksmith has gone into politics."

Henry raised an eyebrow, but made no comment.

"How about bricks?" Campbell asked. "Nobody around here makes bricks."

Henry looked in his brother's eyes, as this new concept took form in his mind.

"There's a lot of clay down by the meadow," Hart said.

Henry placed his silverware on his plate. "That's not a bad idea. Not bad at all. We'll have to think about it, Hart."

Everyone finished their dinner, and the conversation returned to the changes Fletcher made in the new mill; and the possibilities of a sawmill, compared to the idea of making bricks. When the conversation dwindled off, Spuds exited out of the back door and the rest of the men drifted into the small front room. Frank pulled over a woven-cane-seat chair, while Hart stood by the cold wood stove, consciously aware of his dirty clothing.

Henry set baby Frank down in the old rocker, while he lit the oil lamp. The dimness of the lamp dwarfed the normally cheerful room, which the Turners decorated with crisp blue flowered wall paper, softened by white curtains hanging at the front windows. The quietness of the night hung heavily on Hart's shoulders, interrupted only by rattling sounds from the kitchen, and the gentle sleepy-time talk by Henry, as he held the baby on his lap.

Hart stretched and said, "I think I'll mosey on up to my cabin. Are you coming, Frank?"

"What's your hurry?" Frank asked. He pulled his chair over to where he could see Aggie and Ottie, illuminated by the oil lamp which hung from a hook in the kitchen ceiling.

"Maybe you'd like to go and help the women," Hart said. He frowned, and shifted uncomfortably as he watched his friend.

Campbell sighed. "You know, you Turner men have a gold mine here. Two beautiful women to serve you hot cooked meals, three times a day. Now I'd be as happy as a lumberjack on Saturday night, if I had that."

Henry smiled, but the lines in Hart's face got deeper, and he folded his arms across his chest.

Aggie came in from the kitchen with a lit candle and placed it in a holder on the small table inside the adjoining bedroom door. When she turned, the light outlined her dark hair with a golden halo. She walked toward Henry and said, "Ottie asked me to put Frank to bed now."

Frank Campbell quickly rose from his chair, threw his chest forward, and said, "Surely you don't mean me, Aggie!"

Aggie's cheeks turned beet red, and Frank's eyes danced at his own rude joke. Henry smothered a laugh, and Hart's face, unnoticed by the others, turned almost as red as Aggie's.

Ottie pranced in from the kitchen, and faced Campbell with her hands firmly on her hips. "Now listen gentlemen, I am beginning to think there are just too many Franks around here." Unaccustomed to such forward behavior from a young man as handsome as Frank Campbell, Aggie could not make the blush in her cheeks fade.

Frank stepped across the room, took her hand, and said, "I'm sorry Aggie. If you weren't so sweet, I wouldn't be so tempted to tease you."

Her scarlet cheeks darkened, as she silently pulled her hand away from Frank's tender grasp. Then, with the grace of an actress stumbling across the stage for the first time, she took the baby from his father, and made a quick retreat to the bedroom.

Hart sealed his lips tight, as he grabbed his friends elbow a little too tightly, and said, in a hoarse whisper, "Come on Frank . . . let's go!"

As they walked out onto the porch, Hart carefully caught the screen door before it slammed. Frank untied his horse, and the two friends turned up the hill together, finding their way along the hushed trail, lit by the glow of a bright moon.

"What in tarnation has gotten into you, Frank?" Hart finally asked. "You're not getting' sweet on Aggie, are you?"

Dark shadows hid Frank's expression as he said, "Well, why not? I'm not getting any younger, and, I'm sick of sleeping alone. You tell me where a man will find a finer woman than Aggie Galloway, and I'll court her!"

Sometime later, Hart slumped in a chair on the porch of his little cabin, listening to the crickets chirp, watching the mystery of the night sky, and waiting until sleepiness outweighed the empty feeling in his heart. Sore muscles ached for rest, but his mind teased him with vague questions about the future; and his bed, which he always welcomed before, now held little comfort.

A half an hour passed since Frank rode away through the trees, and disappeared like a rock cast into a lake, swallowed up by the deep, dark shadow of the unknown, leaving nothing but an empty void. Hart looked down the hill toward his brother's house. He watched as the last flicker of light was snuffed out, behind the window where Aggie slept.

He did not like the way Frank talked to her. Even though Campbell was a good friend, Hart clenched his teeth at the thought of Aggie being married to him, and having to live at the sawmill. The tenderness she showed to Ottie's baby, danced through Hart's mind. Things would be rough for Ottie without Aggie around to help. Aggie was family!

Hart stood up and stretched. His eyelids felt heavy. As he walked across the porch, he was sure of one thing—Aggie would *never* leave Ottie and the baby . . . well, he was *almost* sure.

Of course, it was many years later before I knew anything about the events that were happening on the Turner Ranch, or the mysterious workings of these young men's hearts.

CHAPTER FOURTEEN - 1870

When the Board of Supervisors turned down the bids I thought Henry would give up the fight. Sadly, my mind retreated. "We will have to be satisfied with the mule trail," I told Rachel; and I wondered if Sierra Valley would indeed secede from the county. Little did I know that Henry had other plans.

When the rooster crowed from the top of the old hen house, on the Turner ranch, and the sun began to make its presence known, Henry left his brother and the hired hand in the dairy barn; saddled his midnight black gelding, and rode down the trail toward Sierraville. Aggie told me how Ottie stood on the porch that morning and watched as he paced his horse along the base of the hill that jutted outward like a finger pointing toward the south end of the valley. The first mule train of the day was already headed up the trail toward the mountain, plodding along, stirring up dust, packed to the limit with tamped down hay. Henry waved his hat to the mule-skinner, and looked back toward his own fields that waited for the harvester's sickle.

Two friendly chipmunks played near the wood pile, and a silly squirrel chirped protest from high in the top of a tall Sugar Pine. The sky blazed blue, without a single wisp of a cloud, and no sign of a breeze. It promised to be another hot day.

Late that afternoon Henry returned. He sat tall and sure in the saddle—quite a contrast from the night he returned from Downieville with the bad news about the Yuba Gap Wagon Road.

Hart told me that he was sitting at the round stone, sharpening a sickle bar, when Henry came into the blacksmith shop, and said, "We're going to do it Hart. We're going to build the road!"

Hart stopped the wheel, and set his work aside. "You've lost your mind, Henry. I've already got a full time job, remember?"

"Not you Hart . . . me! I talked with Sackett and Spencer, and they agreed to be partners, and I'm convinced we can get Sam Davidson to join us. I talked to him yesterday." Henry's mind seemed to turn faster than his tongue could move. "Yep, we're going to build the road."

Hart removed his hat, and wiped his brow, while he considered the men his brother named. Henry obviously exercised his instinctive talent for picking a team with experience, knowledge, and political pull. Hart flipped the hat back on his head, and examined the teeth of the sickle bar. He ran his finger carefully along the sharp teeth. "Isaac Church wants to start his cutting tomorrow, and then we will cut Abram's, then ours."

Beneath his well trimmed dark hair, Henry's ears stood at sharp attention—but they were turned inward, and apparently he did not hear a word his brother spoke. "We have a plan the county cannot turn down," he said. "We are going to make a bid for $20,000. The Supervisors cannot reject it! The vote has already been passed for that amount."

Hart wanted the road built as much as the next man, but the harvest was important too, and all the local ranchers worked together to get in the hay. "Our neighbors are expecting you to help with the harvest, Henry. You know how it is when the field is ready—everyone pitches in and helps."

Henry eyes twitched slightly, but Hart's message still didn't get through. "It will be risky, Hart. We are not even sure we can do it for $20,000. We could lose a lot of money. But, we're all in agreement that someone will have to take that risk. The road will open up this end of the valley, and just imagine the boost to the economy—not only for Sierra Valley, but for Downieville as well." He put his hand on the silent sharpening wheel. "I've been a blacksmith, a gold miner, a farmer, and a politician . . . Why not try my hand as a construction worker, and a road builder?"

Hart lifted the sickle directly in front of Henry's eyes, and asked with slight irritation, "What about the harvest?"

"The harvest?" Henry asked and his eyes widened in surprise. "Oh... Well, I guess you will have to get Spuds to take my place."

Hart tightened his grip on the long sickle bar, while his other hand unconsciously formed a fist. "That means we will have to double up on the other chores!"

"We all have to make *some* sacrifices, Hart."

Henry's eyes gleamed—evidence that his mind was off again, making plans for the road. If it weren't for the fact that his innocent act seemed so genuine, and the Senator's new crusade directly affected the future of the ranch, Hart might have stood his ground, and insist that Henry pitch in and help. Instead, Hart rubbed his bristly chin, and wondered if H. K. Turner had *ever* really been a farmer!

* * *

The swishing sounds of long handled saws, and the hypnotic chopping of ax against wood, ushered in the birth of the Yuba Gap Wagon Road. Tall Lodge Pole and Sugar Pines crashed to the ground like giants, dying to the deep throated shout of "Timber!" The earth trembled at the deafening roar of dynamite blasting its way through solid granite rock, as Henry with his partners and crew, mile after mile, cleared the roadway

Turner set the goal of October first, and with good reason. The Sierra Buttes Quartz Mining Company offered to pay $4,000 if they could open the road to Sierra City by that date. There was no way the men could complete this incredible undertaking by that deadline without dividing up the work.

Turner and friends tackled the section from Sierra City to Sierra Valley, and they contracted out the road from Sierra City to Downieville. The boss of that job was Jack Crossman, and he hired Chinese labor to do the work. With Sierra City as the hub, the road inched forward, day by day, as men pounded their way through granite boulders, vast forests, and along cliffs that would make a man dizzy.

Our daughter Aggie remained in the Turner household throughout that fall, while Henry slaved away up at the top of Turner Canyon. I'm sure the senator developed some uncomfortable blisters on his hands, as he worked side by side the other construction men, from the first ray of dawn until the lazy summer sun slowly disappeared over the mountains. He worked there, he ate there, and he slept there, until the new wagon road, narrow and snake-like in design, neared the bottom of the canyon.

When the valley came into sight, Henry could ride home at night, after the dust settled, and the sun set. He drug himself to bed exhausted, and fell into a deep sleep as soon as his head hit the pillow. Then, as the rooster crowed the next morning, he saddled his horse, and rode off to the construction site.

When the first frost of autumn nipped at the leaves on the Scrub Oak trees, the end of the road could almost be seen by the women at the Turner Ranch. Then, one day, Henry came home early. Far in the distance, beyond the customary noise of the mule trains, that new irritating background sound was missing. The scraping of the old wagon grader had come to a stop, and the familiar cloud of dust no longer rose from Turner Canyon.

* * *

Henry threw his dusty hat down on the kitchen table. Aggie described that day to me. Dirt smudged his face, and crusted on his pants. He ran his rough hands through unfamiliar dirty hair that hadn't seen a barber's scissors for a long time. His chin hid behind a thick beard, and he spoke from chapped lips, "We ran out of money."

From the hand pump at the sink, Ottie filled a large porcelain bowl with water, placed it on the table, then warmed it with hot water from the kettle on the stove, and set a bar of homemade soap beside it.

"We were so close..." Henry said, as he dipped water from the basin, and splashed his face. "So close. Now we will have to go back to the Supervisors. More evasive discussions—more trips to Downieville."

The loss of funds, combined with exhaustion, should have discouraged Henry, but it only seemed to add fire to his political blood. I'm sure his leverage as Senator helped, as he pried the funds he needed, from those penny-pinching bureaucrats: $2,580 in wagon road script, which would be paid back with a 15¢ tax.

Construction resumed, and by the end of November, Aggie and Ottie could stand on their porch and actually see the grader scraping away on the hill above Hart's cabin. The end of the road was insight! So was the Legislative Session of 1870.

On December third, the entire Turner family cheered and waved as a neighbor from Church's Corner's, Jim Miller, took the first wagon over Yuba Gap. Jim gladly paid a toll of $1.50 to haul butter and eggs up the hill to market. Every cow, sheep, hog, horse and rider were taxed to use the road—when it was new, and most of them did so without argument. This exciting link with the County Seat, and a chance for a better future, filled Henry with pride, relief, and fatigue.

For the first time in three months he looked at Ottie—really looked at her. Her waistline pressed tightly against the material of her dress, even though she let the seams out as far as they would go. There was no doubt about her pregnancy now.

They had, had no time to talk.

They had, had no time to plan.

They had not rented a place to live in Sacramento. Once more, Henry would leave his wife and child behind.

Years later, Aggie confided in me the relief she felt that day. All summer her mind tormented her with threats of the coming winter when Ottie would join Henry, and leave her behind. She knew I would never allow her to stay on the ranch alone. There would be no need for her there. So, as Henry said, "I'm sorry," to Ottie, who unsuccessfully fought the tears that streamed down her face, Aggie shed her own happy tears of joy and relief.

"It will kill me to be gone when the baby is born," Henry said. He used the back of his finger to wipe away the moist drops that fell from Ottie's eyes. "I'll try to get back. If I can get away, I will."

Neither woman expected Henry to fulfill this wish, but to Aggie, it didn't matter. The Turners welcomed her at their ranch for one more winter.

CHAPTER FIFTEEN - 1870-1871

When the mothers of some of Aggie's school friends bragged about their grandchildren, I watched Rachel's back stiffen. I would remind her that Aggie was only nineteen years old, and Rachel would sigh as she muttered, "If a daughter is not going to live at home with her parents, she should at least be married and have children of her own."

I had my own fears. Aggie was too content with her "new family", and much too satisfied with being called "Aunt". I saw no indication that she was even looking for a husband. I also longed for a grandchild, but reminded myself that what mattered was Aggie's obvious happiness.

With Henry away, the ranch fell into the capable hands of his brother Hart, who had become so accustomed to Henry's absences that things went on as usual. As soon as the cows stopped giving milk, Spuds moved into a trapper's cabin in the mountains—his home.

When the temperature dropped, and two feet of snow covered the valley floor, a day's work, at the Turner's, consisted of getting food and water to the cattle, shoveling snow, and bringing in wood. Hart found time to play with his nephew, in the white winter blanket that covered the yard.

Aggie told me many years later, that one of her fondest memories was watching little Frank and his Uncle Hart roll and pack the cold white balls, and stack them one on top of the other. Then with small round pebbles, they outlined lips, used a stick for a nose, and for the eyes they found two larger stones which they dug out from under the porch, and which Frank pounded tight with his small mitten covered hands. She remembered every small detail of that day. She remembered the red noses and cold toes, and how they stomped across the porch and into the house; and the smell of newly baked oatmeal cookies.

She watched as Hart used a straw broom to whisk the snow from his boots and pant legs. He took off his heavy wool jacket, scarf, and hat, and dropped them in the corner by the wood stove. With cupped hands raised to his face he blew hot breath between his cold fingers then quickly rubbed them together. He helped

Frank remove his boots, pants, coat, hat, scarf, and mittens, until the child stood in only a diaper and long shirt that reached below his knees. As simple as this chore might sound, it wasn't. Little Frank wiggled, squirmed, and cried. He waved his tiny red fingers, and cried, "Cold, Cold!" between his tears, while he hopped from one foot to the other.

Hart rubbed the baby's hands together, trying to warm them. He started to pick the boy up, and discovered the shirt was wet too. So he pulled it off, while Frank continued to whimper. Aggie brought over a patchwork quilt and wrapped it around the almost naked baby, changing infant tears to giggles of joy. Hart whisked him up in his arms, and carried him to a chair at the kitchen table.

"Look at this Frank," Hart said, as he discovered the plate of cookies, still warm from the oven.

From a pan on the stove, Aggie poured four cups of warm milk. One she took to Ottie, who was knitting a sweater for the new baby, as she sat in a rocker that had been moved into the kitchen and placed by the warm stove. Frank took a bite from his cookie, and held it in the air with a beaming smile, as Aggie carefully placed his half-full cup in front of him.

"Careful there young man," Hart said, as he quickly reached for Frank's cup. "It's HOT, Frank, be careful!"

Aggie sat down at the table and smiled at Hart, as she slid his cup over to him.

Hart returned her smile, and said, "I can think of only one thing that might be nicer."

With a look of surprise, Aggie started to get up. "What is that?" she asked.

"A sleigh ride—with you."

Aggie fell back in her chair.

". . . tonight," Hart continued.

Aggie blushed slightly. "Well . . . ah . . ." She quickly glanced at her friend, Ottie.

The rocking chair continued its quiet rhythm, and Ottie never dropped one stitch in her knitting. "Go with him," she said. "It will do you good. You've been cabin-bound much too much, lately."

"But . . . what about you?"

"I'll be fine. The baby isn't due for a few more weeks, and I feel wonderful."

"Well then I guess it's settled," Hart said, as he smiled and sipped his milk.

Aggie silently set her cup on the table. Her lips tightened. "Now just a minute, I haven't said I'll go."

Hart's blue eyes narrowed into thin slits. He cleared his throat. "Why won't you go? You went for a sleigh ride last week with Frank Campbell, when he asked you."

"What I did with Frank Campbell is none of your business. Besides, I didn't exactly say I *wouldn't* go with you."

Hart gritted his teeth together. He had no patience with women, and began to regret having brought the subject up. "Well, will you or won't you?" he asked.

"Maybe I will, maybe I won't. First I have to know why you are asking me. You never even knew I was alive until Frank took me on that sleigh ride, after the last big snow."

"I knew you were alive," Hart said. "I just never showed it."

Aggie slowly sipped her milk. "Where will we go—on this sleigh ride?"

"Anywhere, I don't care . . . listen Aggie, if you don't want to go with me, just say so."

"I'll go."

"What?"

"I said I'll go."

"That's more like it!" Hart relaxed some, and took a bite of his cookie.

Ottie looked at the two of them, from over the top of her knitting, and shook her head, but she kept her mouth shut.

* * *

Now, I've heard both Aggie and Hart tell about their first date, and the truth is, they are the only ones who know what really went on that night. But, I was young and romantic once myself, and I fell in love with the mother of this stubborn girl. I think I have a pretty good idea of how the evening went.

The moonlight filtered down between the tall pines, and its light reflected from the drifts of snow, creating a striking contrast of black shadows on white. The sleigh glided silently across the frozen countryside. Occasionally the sleigh bells would jangle. The horse's gate was slow, and Hart didn't encourage it along.

Desperately Hart searched his brain for some stimulating

conversation, and could think of nothing to say. He wanted to impress Aggie, but could only think of milking cows, breach-birth calves, sharpening tools, and shoveling manure. He quickly discarded each topic. Aggie, who usually had plenty to chatter about, sat quietly on the wooden seat beside him.

Hart realized that beneath a warm, fitted, wool jacket Aggie wore her prettiest dress. Unknown to him, beneath the dress she wore several skirts and petticoats to keep warm. He could smell the musky scent of lavender, which she only dabbed for very special occasions, and he could feel her closeness in the sleigh, which made him oblivious to the cold night air. Two deer walked slowly along the edge of the valley, and as the sleigh approached, they darted into the forest. They were does. Aggie smiled, and looked at Hart, and he blushed slightly.

"Would you like to stop and see George and Rachel?" he asked.

Aggie looked ahead to where the moonlit sky outlined the Hale's Hotel. "That would be nice," she said.

Oil lamps hanging from the ceiling in the hotel's dining room cast a welcome light onto the snow outside. The young couple saw George's sharp silhouette, where he sat at his table near the window, and lifted a glass up to his mouth to drink.

It is hard to stomp off all of the snow before entering a building, and their stomping and shuffling noises accompanied them all the way into the lobby. George's voice bellowed through the doors which swung into the dining area. "Look who's here! It's Hart, and by golly, if he doesn't have our Aggie with him!" Slowly the old man pushed himself out of his chair. "Welcome . . . welcome. Come in! We don't see enough of you Aggie." He helped them off with their coats, hats, scarves and gloves, which were all hung by the door.

The normal smells of wood burning in the fire, and oil form the lamps, blended with that of roasting meats, and baked bread, which filtered in on warm air from the open door to the kitchen.

Rachel helped take their coats, and then gave each a big hug.

"It sure looks like a fine night for a sleigh ride," George said.

"Oh, it is!" Aggie grinned. "And, it is such fun."

Hart stood a little taller, and his eyes twinkled with satisfaction. "I knew you'd enjoy it, Aggie."

George's bushy eyebrows twitched. Seeing Hart with a

woman—a nice woman like Aggie, surprised even George, who thought he had witnessed just about everything in his vast years of experience.

Rachel herded them all toward George's favorite table. "Come in . . . sit down . . . Let me get you something to drink. What would you like? Coffee . . . Apple cider . . . George is drinking whiskey."

"Apple cider sounds wonderful," Aggie said.

Rachel looked at Hart, who said, "Cider is fine for me too."

George shrugged at Hart's request, and Rachel went to the kitchen for the cider.

Holding a chair for Aggie, George said, "Sit yourself here by the window."

Hart frowned awkwardly, and George pulled a chair out beside Aggie. "You too," he said to Hart. "Sit here . . . There now. I was sitting here meself, keeping me eyes on a couple of deer. Maybe they will come back." Very carefully he lowered himself into a chair.

Hart noticed that George looked older with each visit. "How are you doing, George?" he asked.

"I tell ya, Hart, I'm cold. The old blood just don't flow like it used to." He winked at Aggie. "And it used to flow fever hot!" He poured some whiskey from a tall clear bottle, and returned it to its spot in front of him on the table. "The liquor helps some—warms me up a bit. Tell me now, how is Ottie?"

"Fatter than an old cow ready to drop her calf," Hart said. "It won't be long now."

"And the babe, Little Frank—what's that little rascal up to?"

"Mischief, as usual! He learns a new word every day. You really have to watch what you say around him."

Rachel brought in three cups filled with cider, and pulled up a chair between George and Hart. George leaned back in his own chair, and became unusually silent, as he listened to the others chatter about little Frank; the new wagon road which was closed because of the deep snow; the many sleighs that were out lately; the weather; and the fact that Henry might come back from Sacramento at the end of January, before the birth of the baby.

George sipped his whiskey, and watched the two visitors. It must have puzzled him to see Hart and Aggie together like this. Frank Campbell recently told George that he intended to court

Aggie. Now, here came Hart—hot on her trail. George surely remembered the day, a couple of years earlier, when Hart stood in that very room, and insisted that he would never let a woman run his life, the way he imagined Ottie was doing to Henry. Yet, there sat Hart, with twinkling eyes and rosy complexion betraying his inward feelings—that, and a sudden interest in small talk.

"George!" Hart almost shouted to pull George out of his daydream.

"Huh?"

"I asked if you heard the news about Elvira Colby."

George, usually current on all local gossip, asked, "What about her?"

"I don't think you were even listening to us," Hart said. "We were talking about our new neighbor, Alex Beaton. He just moved into the area, and is already marrying Hiram Colby's widow, Elvira."

"Sure, I heard about that," George said.

"It seems like all the available young women are getting married off," Rachel said.

Aggie blushed slightly. *She* was an available young woman, and so far had not experienced a single proposal!

"Well, it's a good thing," Hart said sincerely. He glanced out of the corner of his eye at Aggie. "It's not right for a woman to be alone."

George raised his glass. "Well now, listen to the man talk! 'It's not right for a woman to be alone.' Ha! And, what about a man, young Hart? Do you still think it is better for a man to live alone?"

"Men are different," Hart said defensively. "I'm not complaining about being a bachelor, mind you, but . . . Well, I just might surprise everyone, one of these days, and settle down myself."

"That will be a fine day," George said. "I'd like to see it—the day Hartwell Franklin Turner gets married!"

Hart's cheeks became uncomfortably warm, and he stared at his hands. "I'd have to find the right woman first," he said quietly.

Rachel smiled, and looked knowingly at Aggie. "Well, Hart, maybe you've found her."

Aggie's gaze dropped to where her hands were folded on her lap. Aware of her own flushed face, she scooted nervously in her chair, and wished someone would change the subject.

Hart reached out to the table, stood up, and with half a smile, said, "It is getting late, Aggie, we really ought to go."

Much relieved, Aggie rose and said, "Thanks so much for the delicious cider."

"Any time you have a yearning for cider, you come back, Lass," George said. He put one hand on the table and used it for leverage to lift himself to his feet. "And, if this young man gets out of line with you, come and see me! I'll set him straight for you, Love."

Once more, the bright shade of pink darkened on Aggie's cheeks.

* * *

Hart directed the sleigh around the hill and headed north. He was in no hurry to get back home.

They rode in silence for about a mile, and the only sound, in the crisp, clear night, came from the horse and sleigh swishing across the frosty snow; and the jangle of the sleigh bells. The moon darted in and out, between wispy clouds, and cast shadows of snow-draped trees on the white carpet below. Vapor rose from the horse's nostrils, as obediently it trudged along. Its head nodded in hypnotic style, as it pulled its burden down the well disguised road.

"Rachel is right, you know," Hart said, breaking the silence.

"Right about what?"

"About me already finding a bride."

"And who would that be?" Aggie asked. She stared straight ahead, watching the horse's hooves—avoiding Hart's eyes.

"You know . . ."

"I've never seen you with a woman, nor was I aware that you were courting anyone. I can't imagine who it could be."

"Are you saying I have to court you?" Hart's voice wavered, as he tried to hide his irritation.

"Me? Why would you want to court me?" Aggie asked. Her eyes were wide in mock surprise.

"If I want to get married . . . You're saying I have to court you first!"

Aggie didn't reply.

Hart worried now, in silence, wondering if maybe he had been too bold—too fast. His shoulders stooped, as he realized his pitiful attempt at proposing was a failure. A girl had a right to be courted that was a fact—it was the custom.

Aggie turned to him, and he felt the pressure of her knees against his. "Hartwell Turner, if you aren't the most exasperating man I have ever met! It is customary for a man to *ask* a lady—if he intends to marry her! You have never ASKED me!"

The pounding in Hart's chest left him speechless. Feeling clumsy and foolish, he cleared his throat, and tried to speak. His normally loud masculine voice became a mere whisper, "Well . . . will you?"

"*Will I what?*" Aggie was almost shouting.

"Will you marry me?" Hart asked sheepishly.

A tense silence followed the question. Even the horse stopped in the trail, and refused to go one step further without encouragement from the driver.

Aggie sighed deeply. "I will on one condition."

Hart's eyes searched her face for some expression—some indication of her intentions. "What condition?" he asked.

"If you will court me."

"Court you?" The corners of Hart's lips turned upward. "I'll court you, Aggie!" He flipped the reins and the sleight began to move once more.

They rode in silence, and Aggie kept looking at Hart, as if she expected him to say something. Finally she asked, "Why do you want to marry me?"

"Why? Well, because you are . . . ah . . . well, I mean . . . we are already like a family, Aggie."

"She looked sadly at her deer skin gloves, and Hart knew she didn't like his answer.

"What I mean is, little Frank calls me Uncle, and he calls you Aunt..." Hart searched her face for a smile that didn't come. "It's only proper we get married!" He grinned, and then straightened his smile when he realized that Aggie wasn't laughing.

Hart reached over, took her hand and squeezed it. He said, "I have always wanted to marry a good cook." He bent forward and peered into her face, looking for some sign of a smile. "You're a good cook, Aggie."

Aggie half-smiled, and shrugged.

Hart patted her hands, "We will make a great team, you and I."

The sleigh reached an area, near the center of the valley, where the headwaters of the Feather River gathered together—swelling in the winter months, and making passage dangerous, if not impossible. Hart turned the horse back toward the ranch.

"Why did you say yes?" he asked.

Aggie took her time answering. "You remember the day of Ottie and Henry's wedding?" she asked, after much thought.

"Yeah."

"Well, I saw you for the first time, standing next to your brother, and I think I have been in love with you since that very first day."

Hart put the reins down on the whip rack. The horse knew the way home. He turned to face the pretty young woman, who agreed to be his bride. Taking both of her hands in his, he pressed them against his chest.

"I remember that day so well. I remember you. You were so pretty—so alive! I couldn't look at anyone else. I did *not* want to get married then. I guess that's why I've ignored you the way I have. I guess I knew that if I paid you any mind, I would fall in love in a minute!"

Hart's confession of love surprised Aggie. She didn't know what to say, so she just squeezed his hands and smiled.

Encouraged, Hart continued, "When Frank Campbell took notice of you, and began flirting, it almost killed me! I realized then how I felt—how miserable I would be if you weren't around. I love you Aggie, and that's a fact."

Aggie bit on her lower lip, as a tear rolled down her face.

"Hey now, don't start crying. It's too cold! That tear will freeze to your cheek." He lifted her chin, kissed her lightly on the cheek . . . then on the lips, as his arms enfolded her in a tight embrace.

"I'm so happy," Aggie whispered into his ear, as she felt the shadow of whiskers brush against her face. "I really am happy!"

Hart pushed gently away from her, letting his hands slide up her arms to rest firmly on her shoulders. Smiling, he said, "I'll court you Aggie. Why you've never seen a beau as sweet as I will be! There will be winter bouquets, and sleigh rides. And, when Henry returns in the spring, we will marry."

CHAPTER SIXTEEN - 1871

The news of our daughter's engagement reached us by mail, which, in the winter, came so infrequently that several weeks passed before we received Aggie's letter. Rachel read the letter at least ten times, as she paced the kitchen floor.

"This is a terrible way to get the news that your only child is getting married!" she complained.

I laughed—unaware that for the next half-hour I would listen to my wife express every human feeling, from rage to joy. Rachel's only acquaintance with the Turners had been at Ottie's wedding, and she still considered them total strangers. On the other hand, our little girl was taking the first step necessary to provide us with grandchildren.

My own apprehension came in knowing that all I had feared, for the last two years, had come true. My daughter was making a permanent bond with a Republican.

*   *   *

The future groom also took up the quill, and composed a letter to someone special—his niece back in Maine. He had corresponded with Hattie Hale from the day he arrived in Sierra Valley. Every major event in his life had been marked with a letter back home. When Hattie received this letter from Hart, I'm sure her astonishment balanced with our own:

Dear Hattie,

I have the most surprising news for you. In fact, no one could be more bewildered than this old confirmed bachelor! I am getting married.

I wrote you once about Aggie Galloway, the girl who came from Downieville, over a year ago, to help Ottie. Well, Cupid had his way! We are going to get married on the last day of March. Henry should be home from the Senate by then.

There is good news for him also. His little daughter was born two days ago, on January 22nd. She is a tiny little bit of a thing, and reminds me a lot of you when you were born. Ottie has named her Mary Calista, after your ma. I think she did that for you Hattie, to let you know that we all love you out here.

Your pa is beginning to show his age. He does not get around like he used to. He has been sick a lot this winter, and drinks whiskey to keep warm. I wish you could find a way to join us here in California. It would be good for George to have you around, and of course, you know we all want you here.

     Your loving Uncle,
     Hartwell Franklin Turner

* * *

  During the winter of 1871, sleighs glided across the valley on a better snow pack than they had seen in years. Henry returned home as soon as he received the news of his daughter's birth. This left Hart and Aggie free to spend more time together.

  Hart courted Aggie, just as he promised. In the evenings he hitched a pair of horses up to the sleigh, and together they rode off across the snow covered fields. Other lively young people joined them on these excursions, and as the number of sleighs increased—each one packed with as many friends as it could hold—these outings quickly became wintertime adventures,

  Their laughter, and songs, and the jangle of sleigh bells echoed across the valley, as they lined up like elephants in a circus. Someone would yell above the boisterous group, "Where will we go tonight?"

  And another equally loud voice rang out, "The Buxton Hotel in Randolph" or "Robinson's Dance Hall". Once, when the river froze solid, they crossed the valley to the far north-eastern side, to visit the Summit House.

  No matter what the destination, the routine didn't vary. In the silent moonlit night, they slowed down the teams as they approached, letting a hush rule the energetic crowd. The trick was to delude the watchdogs, park their sleigh, and sneak to the door of their chosen victim, who unsuspecting, would answer their simple knock, and find a laughing crowd of merrymakers shouting, "Surprise!"

  One evening, late in February, Hart insisted that the jubilant party surprise George and Rachel Hale.

  Across the icy night they flew, approaching the back side of Hale's Hotel, because they knew George's habit of sitting and looking out of the front window.

  After the customary shouts of joy, the throng pushed its way into the quiet dining room. The Hales immediately brought out refreshments from their well stocked pantry. Above the laughing, talking, snacking and drinking, Hart raised his hand in the air, waved it back and forth, and said, "Listen everyone!"

Unable to get the crowd's attention, he stood on a chair, and banged a spoon against his half-empty cup.

Silence fell slowly, as conversations dwindled off. Hart jumped off the chair and said, "George, come over here. There is a special reason for our surprise party tonight. I have something for you."

He took an envelope out of his pocket, while George toddled over, with help from Rachel, who steadied him as they went. Hart handed the envelope to Aggie, and unfolded its contents, from which he read,

Dear Uncle Hart,
I am on my way! Nothing could stop me from attending your wedding, and meeting mama's namesake. Tell my father I will be there soon.
Love, Hattie

The glass George held in his hand slowly descended to a nearby table. His knees shook underneath him, as he lowered his entire body into a chair. Rachel reached out to help him, but ended up just patting his shoulder.

With a pretentious smile, Hart waved the letter and asked, "Well George, what do you say? She is coming home!"

George rubbed the gray stubble growing on his chin and, almost in a whisper, repeated the words, "She's coming home . . ."

"Come on everyone," Hart shouted, and raised his glass to the ceiling. "A toast to George's daughter: Miss Hattie Hale. May she have a safe and speedy journey!"

"Here, here!" many said in agreement, as they raised their glasses high.

Soon the boisterous crowd returned to their sleighs, and was off again into the chilly night.

George smiled as he watched them go. I believe that was the night he put a cork in his familiar bottle of whiskey. The young widows, who came out from their rooms to join the rollicking crowd, cleaned up the dining room, while George sat with his wife at their special table, and looked out into the dark night, which swallowed up the sleighs, and left only the question of change—a future suddenly altered by the prospect of once again seeing the child he left behind in Maine—a child who his new wife, Rachel, had never met: the offspring of a different life, and a forgotten time.

* * *

Senator H. K. Turner's early return to Sierra Valley brought with it the onslaught of political bickering, manipulating, and overall away-from-home preoccupation, which Hart became accustomed to, and considered just another part of his brother's life.

While little Frank learned to carefully hold his brand new baby sister on his lap, his father Henry spent a good deal if time across the valley, in Loyalton, helping organize a new Odd Fellows Lodge. His ears twitched constantly to the moans and groans of his constituents, who complained bitterly about the 15¢ tax they had to pay to complete the Yuba Pass Wagon Road.

I heard similar complaints in Downieville. "It's not right taxing only Butte and Sierra Townships," men complained. "The whole county should have to pay."

My democratic friends from Sierra Valley added additional grumbles, "Sierra Township already has to pay a special road tax of 25¢ --now they add another 15¢... That's not fair! We pay a total of $3.10 in taxes, while the rest of the county pays only $2.70. Isn't that unconstitutional, Judge?" they asked.

Oblivious to the turmoil brewing in the county, Ottie and Aggie made plans for the wedding. Rachel talked me into letting her take the stage to see our daughter. "There is no way I am going to let my only girl plan her wedding without me!" was Rachel's comment.

She purchased a lovely, smoky blue satin, and packed it away in her bag; and for the first time in our married life I watched *her* ride off.

I felt a terrible lump in the pit of my stomach as I helped Rachel into the drafty stage. "Are you sure you'll be warm enough?" I asked, as I looked at her lovely tailored coat, and matching bonnet tied beneath her chin.

She held out a hand covered by a soft leather glove, and whispered, "I'll be fine."

"You have the blanket?"

Rachel patted the seat next to her, "It's here," she said, as she smiled and shook her head gently. "You worry like an old mother hen!"

"The sleigh will be cold," I said in my defense.

No matter what the weather was like in Downieville, or Sierra Valley, she still had to cross over those snowcapped mountains. Somewhere above Sierra City, the stage would reach the snow line, and all the passengers would leave that normally dusty canvass shell, and transfer to an open sleigh which would take them over the steep snow covered Yuba Pass, and on down to the valley.

* * *

Silence . . .

Back at the cabin, it fell around me like a cage. The fire burned slower and put out less heat. The kitchen longed for the fragrance of freshly baked bread, and homemade soup. I missed her terribly! So, I sat and stared into the fire, and visualized her face, sparkling with joy, as she and the girls fashioned a bridal gown from the precious material Rachel so carefully picked out.

A few days before the big event, I rode to Church's Corners.

As a lawyer, I could stand before a crowd of people, and appear calm and in control—when in fact my knees shook and my fingers trembled. That was perfect training for the father of the bride. I suppose if you put my nervousness on a scale with the other men in our little group, who shared my apprehension, Hart's would weigh the most. I speak from experience when I say it is not easy for a man to give up his freedom.

Hart walked the floor—back and forth. He tried to smile, and hide his fears. "This may be a small wedding, Judge," he said, "but it sure will draw a lot of attention. I'll have a State Senator for my best man; the honorable Judge Galloway will give the bride away; and we have guests coming in all the way from Maine!"

Those words made George Hale shudder. He waited for his daughter with a strange reserve. I could not imagine how he felt. My wife and I experienced an unwelcome loneliness when Aggie left us as a young woman. I would have found it impossible to leave her when she was an infant. But, thank God, I never felt the pain of a widower, so I did not judge George for the choices he made.

Hattie Hale arrived in time for the wedding. She charmed us all with her loveliness and wit. I tried to see a resemblance to George, but somehow I felt I was searching for a common link between the beauty of a rose, and the thorny old vine on which it grew.

I dismissed all of Hattie's youthful charm as second rate; however, when on March 31, 1871, I faced my daughter in her exquisite smoky blue wedding gown. Listening to my heart pound, one would think I was the bridegroom. For the first time, these old eyes interpreted my child as a grown woman. She stood erect, and a high ruffled collar complemented her proud chin. There were hand sewn tucks down the front bodice of her dress, tailored to her slim attractive figure, and over her delicate shoulder draped a matching cape, with edges scalloped in gentle flowing curves.

She reached out and placed her hand on my arm, and together we slowly walked down the aisle. Suddenly nothing seemed fair. Step by step, as we walked toward the altar, where Hart waited with the Justice of the Peace J. E. Beard, it did not seem right that I should *give away* my beautiful daughter to someone as undeserving as Hartwell Turner.

Yes, I admit, I did like Hart, but in my nervous state, I gritted my teeth when the judge asked, "Who gives this woman in marriage?" and I answered, "I do."

The truth was I didn't! My plain little girl had just been transformed into a beautiful princess, right before my eyes, and she deserved no less than a handsome prince—not a danged Republican.

CHAPTER SEVENTEEN - 1871

The fidgeting noise of blackbirds and cowbirds rose loudly from the marsh where they built their nests; and chickadees, bluebirds, jays and robins flew to the tall trees with bits of straw and strands of hair from the horse's tail, which they picked from special places on the fence. It was spring—a season that stirs the spirit of a man with the same gentle shake it uses to rouse a hibernating old grizzly bear.

Now, I knew Aggie was a completely grown up woman, but I worried about her all the same. My mind buzzed with impossible sensitive questions that I didn't dare discuss with Rachel. For instance, was Aggie prepared for the demands Hart no doubt made on their wedding night? Does a girl get this information from her mother? Had Rachel given Aggie a mother-to-daughter talk? And, if she had, what did she say? I know, that many times during those weeks after the wedding, I peered over my reading glasses at Rachel, with these questions on my mind. For she asked, many times: "James, what is the matter with you?" and I shook my head and left my curious mind unsettled.

Of course, I would never know if Aggie was prepared for the passion of a virile young man, but I learned she was happy. She adored her new husband—and he was equally devoted to her.

Meanwhile, a headache developed in the eastern section of H. K. Turner's district, Sierra Valley. The proper ownership of much of the most fertile and productive farm land in our county was being questioned, and the government threatened to take back thousands of acres under, what they called, the Swamp Land Act.

The anxious and infuriated land owners assaulted Henry with questions:

"The government can't take away people's land, can they? It's got to be unconstitutional."

"I come here, back in the early '60's, Henry, same as you. I took up land, legal like—preempted, just like the law said. I built a house for my wife and young-uns. I got cows . . . and a barn now, and they tell me I've been living in a swamp. They're crazy!"

"They promised us that when the surveyors came, and they got this county properly surveyed, we could take this preempted land,

and purchase it at $1.25 an acre. They promised! Now they're going back on their word. It ain't right, Henry."

On and on, the complaints came. People were confused and scared. Most of the land, which the government threatened to take, lay along the gently flowing headwater of the Feather River's north fork, which originated in the middle of the Sierra Valley. The Turner's Ranch was quite a distance from the river, along the edge of the mountains, and remained unaffected by this quivering fate. But, the Turner brothers knew these ranchers well, and their hearts went out to them.

This entire hornet's nest began the previous fall while Henry's full concentration was on the Yuba Pass Wagon Road project. This innocent looking announcement appeared in the republican-slanted county newspaper, *The Mountain Messenger*:

NOTICE TO SETTLERS

"The state of California, having claimed as Swamp and Overflow Lands certain tracts in Townships 21, 22, and 23 . . . which tracts have not been represented as such on official plates, or in the returns of the United States Deputy Surveyors, I propose to hold an examination of witnesses for the purpose of determining the character of said lands as affected by the provisions of the Swamp Land Grant of the 28th of September, 1850, at the office of the United States Surveyor General in San Francisco on the first day of December next at 10 o'clock.

Sherman Day
United States Surveyor General for California"

Several Sierra Valley residents were called as witnesses, and it was definitely a hardship to expect these men to leave their families and homesteads, during the threat of winter, and travel more than 200 miles over the treacherous mountains to San Francisco,. The first step the farmers took was to have the meeting place changed. Their objections succeeded in having the inquiry moved to Loyalton, a small village on the south east corner of Sierra Valley, and the date was postponed until May 1871.

* * *

The time for the meeting had arrived. April storms ceased. Travel increased on the road through Turner Canyon.

In spring, the calves were born, and milking began in the dairy. By May the last snows had fallen, the ground thawed, and it was time to plant. Hart was hardly surprised when Henry strolled up to him, with that gosh-I'm-sorry expression on his face, and said, "You know I have to attend those meetings in Loyalton. I can't get out of it. Everyone is in an uproar over this swamp land matter. The government has claimed over 20,000 acres of our Sierra Valley farm land as 'swamp', and we know that is not true."

This time Hart agreed totally. "It's a pile of horse manure," he said.

"I hate to take off again, right in the beginning of our busy season. It seems I am always called away on one thing or another, leaving you with all the responsibilities of the ranch."

"It's just my luck to be the brother of our popular state senator!"

"Are you sure you don't mind?"

"I'd like to drop everything and go to those meetings myself, Henry. I'd tell those greedy mongrels what they can do with their Swamp Land Act. But, since you have a smoother tongue, and I know more about cleaning barns, I guess I better stay here and shovel, while you go to the meeting and shoot them down."

Henry smiled. "I don't know what I would do without you, Hart."

* * *

Every day Henry road across the valley to Loyalton for the hearings. Every night he returned frustrated and irritated.

The settlers who testified were angry, and to prove their point about having good, productive land, some of them stretched their stories way out of proportion. They were soon the butt of jokes all over Sierra and Plumas Counties. They should have just told the truth: Timothy, and other tame grasses grew successfully enough, in their location, to support small herds, and those herds produced some of the finest butter and cheese in the county. Some farmers actually dug ditches for irrigation in areas the government called "swamp land".

The confusion could be blamed on Mother Nature. Every spring, high in the surrounding mountains, the deep layer of winter packed snow would melt, and cause pregnant streams to swell, and give birth to the north fork of the mighty Feather River. Thereupon a flood of water would spill over her fertile banks. These overflow lands, fingered by the government, housed families and farms—some had been settled there for as long as twelve years. Houses, barns, outbuildings, and fences marked territory built with sweat and tears. These so-called "swamp lands" were homes.

If the settlers lost this battle, disaster would face our economy. Federal government takeover of 20,000 acres of Sierra County's most fertile farm land attacked not only the small farmer; it was a direct slash at the county's pocketbook. Empty farms create nothing—no cows, horses, sheep, hogs—all taxable produce. With the stroke of the Surveyor General's pen, this tax producing land would become summer pasture for monopolists from San Joaquin County, who wanted Sierra Valley for grazing. The farmers, fighting so desperately for their land, paid $3.00 an acre in taxes. If they lost the battle, the land would be assessed for one tenth of that, or 30¢.

Every local politician I knew had their ears turned toward the proceedings that took place in Loyalton. But the first week in June, the meetings ended. It looked like the decision fell *against* the swamp land proposal, and Henry once more took over his duties as a working partner on the Turner Ranch.

In August we were all shocked to find another notice in the paper. This one called for more meetings to investigate the problem of swamp land in Sierra Valley. This time the meetings were held in Randolph, and began on October third.

The only comment Henry made to his brother was, "Well, at least Randolph is closer to home."

October: The month when winds blow, and farmers work as hard as squirrels preparing for the isolation of winter. Young steers are sold for beef, or to be trained as oxen; hogs are butchered and cured; potatoes and other root vegetables are dug and put in cold storage; the dairy is cleaned; manure is taken from the barnyard and dug into next year's potato patch, and other garden areas, to set over the long winter months; snag trees are fallen for firewood, which is cut and stacked in long rows (at least five cords) for heat and fuel. It was October . . . and once more Henry had to be gone.

When the investigation ended, and we moved into November, it looked as if a few hundred acres of land would be declared "swamp lands", and the rest would go to the settlers—but nothing was definite.

Henry Turner may have been State Senator, but his hands were tied on this issue—it was a Federal Investigation. He wanted to help his neighbors, but all he could do was listen to their troubles, and give words of advice. The farmers petitioned the Sierra County Board of Supervisors for help, in what they called a "land war". Someone in San Joaquin County had power. They wanted the land for their own, and had appealed the Surveyor General's decision. This plea caused the matter to be sent to the Secretary of the Interior for deliberation. Our County Supervisors decided it was in their best interest to help Sierra Valley, and agreed to give them $300. Generous as it may sound . . . it was $200 less than was requested.

The November days became extremely cold, and it was time for Henry to return to Sacramento for the long Legislative Session. For the first time he would take his family with him, and while they packed, I'm sure his mind was on the unsettled question of the ownership of much of his district.

Aggie and Ottie knew they would miss each other's company during those long, cold, winter days, but the excitement of adventure and new beginnings softened their tears.

Their last shared joke was about Frank Campbell.

It began when Hattie Hale arrived for the wedding. Coldness that had settled around George's old heart, melted with the sunshine that Hattie brought with her. George began to take more interest in his 160 acre ranch, and he put renewed value in his community. That summer the Board of Supervisors appointed him the job of road viewer, a position that allowed him to help make the decision on which roads in the valley should be declared as public roads.

When the first frost swept through the poplar trees that September, dotting the evergreen forest with splashes as bright in color as the summer sunset, Hattie took a job teaching at Rocky Point—in the same school where Ottie had taught a few years earlier. This, of course, grabbed the attention of the two young Turner women, who watched with added fascination when Hart's friend, Frank Campbell, took a sudden interest in the little neighborhood school.

Aggie and Ottie giggled, and exchanged knowing glances, as they listened to Frank's explanation, "I just purchased a ranch in that district, and it's my civic duty to help out with the school!"

They weren't the least bit surprised when Frank began to openly court the new school teacher.

CHAPTER EIGHTEEN - 1872

On March 5, 1872, wedding bells rang once more for the Turner family, when Frank Herra Campbell married Harriet Calista Hale.

Rachel used any excuse she could to travel to Sierra Valley to see Aggie, and the wedding provided her with just the opportunity she needed.

"After all," she teased, "it is a family wedding."

She knew I would grumble. I despised any connection with the Turner family, and resented the fact that our daughter had married into it.

Henry and Ottie returned, from Sacramento, just in time for the wedding, and their two adorable little children upstaged even the bride, in her beautiful satin gown. Little Frank talked like a magpie, when a few months earlier he could hardly put a sentence together. And the baby, little Mary, was actually walking. She toddled around during the reception, touching everything she saw, and stealing everyone's heart.

George bought a brand new black woolen top coat, for this special occasion, and it had black satin inserts in the lapels. His chest bulged forward, showing a yellow striped satin vest, and a blue and yellow striped silk tie, and stiff white starched collar. He looked vaguely like an old penguin, as he strutted around pointing out to everyone that Hattie was *his* daughter, and that he was responsible for the lavish spread of food—which I admit was pretty good. If that didn't impress someone, he mentioned more than once that he was one of the first trustees of the little church in Sierraville, where Hattie was wed.

I stood with Hart in a neutral corner and watched our women, who huddled together and expressed every detail in their conversation with their hands, as they tried to catch up on an entire winter's events in just a couple of hours.

Henry drifted over, smiled at Hart, and offered me his hand in a firm handshake. "How are things in Downieville, Judge," he asked, just to be sociable.

I concocted a smile, and said, "Things don't change much in the winter."

He patted Hart on the shoulder, and said, "It's been a *long* winter."

Hart nodded. "Yep. But a good one. I will say, though, it sure was quiet around here without Ottie and the babies."

Henry smiled. "It was a frustrating session this year." He seemed to be directing his conversation at both of us. "I hate to return and fight the same battles. That bill, to form a new county, came up again—Donner County. Thank God it didn't pass! Can you imagine Sierra Valley being part of Donner County, with Truckee as our County Seat? The fellow who introduced the bill wasn't even in favor of it. The whole thing is a fiasco! The buildings, furniture, and books alone would cost the new county close to $50,000. They would have to take over our portion of the old county's debts—about $40,000. Then there would be salaries—another $20,000. That means the new county would have to raise bonds of $225,000. Just imagine the screaming we would hear from this valley then! They whined about the 15¢ tax increase put on them last year to build the road to Downieville."

I was reluctantly impressed. Senator Turner really knew the facts!

Hart smiled, and rubbed his chin. I could see his mind working.

Henry seemed to be able to read his brother's thoughts. "You know I am up for re-election."

"I guess you'll be gone a lot—campaigning," Hart said.

"I will try to keep it to a minimum."

I was encouraged by the fact that it was an election year once more. But, the democrat's chances of unseating the Senator were mighty slim. He was too good, and too popular.

CHAPTER NINETEEN - 1872-1874

The easy years go quickly. Ones when blessings fall like gentle rain on unsuspecting lives. They are jotted down on pages in family Bibles, and kept forever in corners of thankful hearts.

November 24, 1872: Harry Agustus Turner, born to Hartwell and Agnus Turner. That is what Rachel wrote in our family Bible. But in our hearts we recorded: Our first grandchild—a sweet, healthy baby boy, with ten fingers and ten tiny toes.

November 1872: H. K. Turner was re-elected Sierra County's Senator, for the State of California. That is what was recorded in the Turner family records. "It was a shoe-in!" is what I remember most about his re-election. Campaigning was practically unnecessary. His record in the Senate even won the respect of many leaders of the opposing Democratic Party, including myself. What Hart remembers is the fact that Henry was home long enough that summer to set down plans for producing bricks on the ranch, and they actually began production.

One good year followed another. Sierra Valley suddenly became alive with the sound of hammers and saws. The Swamp Land Matter was resolved, and farmers, who had not built, because they were afraid of losing their land to the "swamp thieves", were now confident in their ownership. Pent-up-dreams suddenly burst forth in the form of fences, barns, and houses-with-more-than-one-room.

Once the Turner Brother's Brick Yard became a reality, they were flooded with orders for bricks needed for chimneys for the valley's new dream houses.

Good crops of potatoes, hay and fine sweet butter, were not just rewards of hard work, during those years—they were a welcome blessing.

Hart built on to his small cabin, and Aggie beamed with pride. She was the housewife of a home comparable with the finest in the valley.

Henry returned from the Senate in the spring of 1874, a happy, strong man, sporting a satisfied smile. He loved the Senate. He loved his farm. He loved his family. Life was good!

CHAPTER TWENTY - 1874

"Fenstermaker sold the hot springs!" This was the kind of news that spread quickly around our county, stirring up great interest. Fenstermakers Hot Springs, was a popular resort located at the southern tip of Sierra Valley.

"Who is the new owner?"

"Jack Campbell."

The name Jack Campbell provoked even more interest than Fenstermakers Hot Springs. Campbell: Sierra County's popular sheriff. If the Hot Springs wasn't lively enough already, old Jack Campbell would make it famous.

Before the ink dried on his deed, Campbell stopped Henry one day on the street in Sierraville. With waving arms, and glowing eyes, Jack described his plans for remodeling. He overpowered Henry in size, and his bulk, combined with a booming voice, made him very intimidating. But his attitude that day suggested that Jack was impressed with Henry's title—Senator H. K. Turner.

"Now, I tell you what, Henry," he said. "We Irish men have to stick together—brothers, right?" He slapped Henry on the back. "And besides . . . you're a good Republican. I heard you've got a good brickyard. Bricks would be perfect for the new hotel I have planned for the Hot Springs. You've got the job, if you want it, man."

Henry knew that Hart would not understand if he turned down this job. So far, they only filled orders for chimneys. A job like this would boost their business. But, to work for Jack Campbell could be a regrettable experience. Jack was one of those men you either loved or hated, and his name was not found on Henry's list of favorite people.

To avoid a direct answer, Henry said, "Well, Jack, I will have to check with my brother. He handles the business end of the ranch."

"Ha, man, I thought for sure you would be the one to talk to! It will be a monstrous building—and modern—a fine hotel! I'll make it worth your time. Talk to your brother, man, and get back to me. I'd expect your labor too, and I'll pay a good price."

Henry could find no way to wiggle out of the deal. Hart considered it a stroke of good luck, and they hired B. F. Lemon, from Sierraville, to help Henry with the construction, while Hart continued to run the ranch.

Like an ill wind, changing directions before a storm, Campbell changed his mind. Instead of a brick building, he decided on a gigantic three story Inn, made of wood. Henry had shook Campbell's hand, and committed himself to the job, so even though Jack changed the building material, Henry felt obligated to stick with the project until it was completed.

The summer of 1874 went quickly. The farm and dairy once again fell into Hart's capable hands, as Henry rode off daily to the southern tip of Sierra Valley to work on Campbell's hotel.

That was the year Henry became a carpenter.

* * *

A wagon clattered past Hart and Aggie's house, ringing a bell of warning to anyone who might be headed up the hill. Hart turned his head away as a large cloud of dust drifted in his direction. Rays of sunlight sparkling through the dust were a sad reminder that it would not rain, or even snow, in the near future.

The wagon rolled on down the hill, taking its thundering clatter with it. Traffic on the road had slowed considerably since the farmers finished their harvest, and sent the last of their produce up to Downieville.

Every day, all summer long, clouds of dust billowed up from the teams of horses and huge wagon wheels, and seemed to swallow up the ranch. Aggie never left young Harry's side. The active two year old could easily dash out in front of the rushing horses, as they barreled past the house. So, the slow-down in traffic was very welcome when autumn finally arrived,

Aggie took deep breaths of fresh air as she listened to the wind which blew through the branches of the trees, while the small snow birds whispered sweet melodies from their lofty hiding places. Sounds once suffocated by summer's rattle, and the clatter of the horse teams, wagons, and mule skinners, suddenly reclaimed their natural balance on the Turner Ranch. Even the angry scolding of the cantankerous squirrel sounded like music to the deafened ear. The sound of nature had become a luxury that they looked forward to each autumn, when traffic dulled, and the song of the forest emerged.

All the preparations for winter were complete, and Church's

Corners enjoyed a peaceful pause, as the farm hands drifted off to their winter occupations. Spuds, and many of his friends, considered the ranch a temporary home—where they worked for their keep during the off season. Their loins ached for the feel of buckskin, and they looked forward to the softness of their fur coats, and their coonskin hats. These mountain men spent the unexpected long Indian summer exploring the hills, trailing the prize animals, and preparing their traps. The fur bearing animals would not reach their prime condition until the weather got cold.

I don't know a man who doesn't hunt. It's not only born into a man—natural, it is also good sense. No farmer with a mind for business would kill his own stock for meat. He hunts wild game. And Hart was no different. He could bring down a nice mule deer, or place a goose or duck on the table. But trapping? Trap lines were run for fur, not meat, and although the pelts were nice, and often brought a good price, Hart considered the time spent as wasteful. So he listened with neutral interest, when Spuds and his friends talked about their winter adventures.

It was during this pause in the weather, the first part of November, when one of Spud's friends, Sam Berry, turned his horse from the trail and rode into the Turner Ranch. He wore the typical buckskins, but that is as far as his likeness went to the average mountain man. Sam loved literature. He read continuously, and his appreciation of current affairs led him to seek out knowledgeable men, such as Henry, for stimulating conversation. He talked with a bit of a brogue, from the old country.

"Hello there Hart, is Henry about?"

"Nope . . . He's at the Hot Springs—Campbell's. He's finishing up the work on the new hotel, before he takes off for Sacramento again."

Sam looked disappointed.

"Come on up to the house, and have a cup of coffee with me," Hart suggested.

Sam dismounted, and walked alongside Hart up the hill, where Aggie kept the coffee pot always warm, on the back of the wood stove. She poured each man a cup as they discussed recent hunting adventures.

Sam took a sip of the dark brew, and then said, "I was up in Hamlin's Canyon, up above Randolph, hunting grouse, an' I came upon some bear tracks! Me thinks it had to be a might big bear—maybe even a Grizzly! I only had me shotgun, and I surely don't want to come upon a bear of such size with nothing to protect me, so I back tracked. I followed his tracks back to a rickety down cabin, and found where he had been feeding on a young heifer. I surely would like to trap a bear like that!"

"You better watch out if it is a Grizzly, Sam. Why, it would kill you before you'd have a chance to say hello."

"Sure, and it's true! But, I've figured out how to get him, Hart. I went to Abe Church, and I got me a steer head, and I took it up to that old cabin. I took me a rifle this time, and I lay to wait. I tell you, I waited for a whole week. And, sure enough, the old bear came back! It was a grizzly, all right. In all be born days, I never seen anything so fierce and so *big*. I couldn't get a shot in, because he was too far away. I kept meself hid out, and watched him eat the beef head. When he got his belly full, he left. I tell you, Hart, me knees are still a-knockin'!"

Hart smiled. "You better watch it Sam. Next time he will have you for dinner. I sure don't like the idea of a giant Grizzly hanging around these parts."

Sam nodded his head in agreement. "I'd like to get me a big bear like that." He took a long sip from his cup of coffee. "Trapping should be good this year. I hear folks say it's going to be a might cold winter. Last winter was fine—a good one for trapping. I got otter, mink, and pine martin—fine pelts. The fox and coyote were good, and lynx was prime."

Sam finished his coffee, went on his way, and Hart never thought much about their conversation until a couple of weeks later, when, on November 24th, Sanford Morrison rode up to the ranch. Sanford was the man who shared a cabin with Sam Berry throughout the winter

Hart watched the horse and rider approach. The stiff way Sanford sat in the saddle; the careless, unexpected, advance; the lined expression on his face—everything about him indicated something was wrong.

"What's up, Sanford?" Hart called out, before the man had a chance to dismount.

"I'm not sure, Hart, but I think Sam may be in trouble. I thought I'd better come to the Corners, and round up more men for a search party. There are men from Randolph and Sierraville already out looking, but they're not having any luck."

Hart glanced toward the lofty mountains. That long awaited snow storm had come, and it left behind a white robe, draped over the forest green mounds, and several feet of snow fell at the higher elevations.

"Sam left two day ago with his long board skis to check and re-bait his traps," Sanford said. He should have been back that afternoon, but he didn't show up. I went out searching the next morning. I searched all day, and couldn't find a trace of him. There is already four to five feet of snow up there, and it looks like another storm coming in. I'm afraid he's up there with a broken leg or something." Sanford shook his head, as he looked toward the gray sky. "I think those skis are too fast, and too dangerous."

Sanford Morrison rode off to round up more men for the search party, and Hart went to the house to get his things ready. "It's snowing in the mountains now," he said to Aggie. "Sam's tracks would be covered. We'll be lucky to find him."

Aggie packed her husband a lunch, while he put on his woolens, and checked out his skis. "At least they are already waxed," he said.

Hart rode off with fourteen other local men, in the direction of Randolph. Each man had a rifle, and some carried skis lashed to their saddles. Long after the sun set, Hart returned home—cold, hungry, and frustrated. The snowy wilderness, where they searched for Sam, left no trace—not a clue, of what happened to him.

The search resumed at dawn, and every able bodied man from the area trudged off toward the mountain—some on foot, and some with skis. They combed the canyon where the lost trapper had disappeared.

Over a hundred pairs of searching eyes came, and divided into groups of two and three hunters. They explored every hiding place. They looked behind boulders, searched through areas dense with tall brush, and looked anywhere a man might crawl to seek shelter. They agreed to fire a rifle three times, if they found Sam.

This was probably the biggest hunt ever witnessed by Hamlin's Canyon. All of nature perked to attention at the smell of Man. Deer, that innocently descend from their snow covered summer shelter, bounced off in every direction, unaware that they were not the object of this man-made madness.

Every cold ear listened attentively, and the quietness of the forest sent chills of fear through the anxious hearts of the searchers. They stopped to eat, beneath the shelter of trees, and listened silently—hoping to hear the three shots.

Hart and Isaac Church, on their skis, worked their way down a steep ravine, while below them, on the same mountain, Abe Church, Abe's brother-in-law Frank Rowland, and a local trapper named George Pettingill, explored with careful deliberation. Pettingill motioned to his companions. "Come down here. I think I found something interesting."

The two men slid down the small embankment that separated them. Pettingill squatted. His skis were still lashed to his boots. He carefully brushed new fallen snow from some deep depressions. "Look here. Bear tracks—big ones."

Abe put all of their fears into words. "Do you think Sam may have met up with this bear?" Abe had special interest in Sam. The trapper had worked for him every summer since 1867, and was a good farm hand—also a good friend.

The three men decided to follow the tracks back up the canyon. Their bones ached from tiredness and cold. The tracks were not easy to follow, because gusts of wind had blown clumps of snow from the trees, concealing them, and obscuring the trail. But, Pettingill was an experienced mountain man, and an expert at tracking, so they slowly worked their way up the mountain.

Above them, in the cold shadows of the tall pines, Hart and Isaac carefully moved down the gorge. The small groups could see one another, and soon they would meet—then they could go home. Try again tomorrow.

That was when Hart spotted something unusual, and motioned to Isaac. Together they waved at the group below. "Up here! We've found something!"

With renewed energy, the three searchers moved quickly up the hill, and rushed to where Hart and Isaac stood. There before them, in a burned out, gigantic pine tree, rested Sam's seven foot tall skis, and one pole.

Pettingill investigated the black wooden cavern. "It looks like a grizzly was making his winter home here."

He pointed his long barreled rifle skyward, and let go with three blasts—the welcome sound that kept every searcher's ear at perked attention—a signal that announced that the search was over.

Behind the tree, a few feet away, blood stained the snow, leaving a trail that told a story. Apparently an ill humored wind blew two trees down in front of the blackened out tree, where the enormous bear had begun its winter hibernation. It must have felt trapped and disagreeable. Unaware that the tree was occupied, Sam Berry placed his skis there, and when he discovered the angry bear, he ran off. Sam tried to jump over one of the fallen trees, but fell. Like a flash, the bear attacked him. It ripped off his coat, vest, shirt and even the flesh—all the way from his neck to his waist—exposing the ribs. The men saw broken, mangled, and torn hands, where Sam had tried to protect himself—most likely to protect his face.

It was a one sided fight. Sam's knife and axe remained sheathed on his belt. The bear overpowered its victim—clawed at the man, and left an unrecognizable mass of bones and flesh.

Silence once again fell upon the canyon, as each man weighed the cost of the tragedy in his own heart.

The chill of a setting sun drove the men to move quickly. They took off their skis, and set about the chore of removing the body from its bloody resting place. They lashed it to a couple of small fir saplings, and then strapped their long skis back on to their boots, knowing they could transport the frozen body much faster that way.

They went about their task like soldiers—two man teams. Working together, they slid across a new cover of soft snow, to take back home the remains of the unfortunate mountain man.

During the next few days, a posse tracked the bear. They followed the tracks several miles, through rugged canyons and over high jagged cliffs, going south of where Sam Berry's body was found. They searched as far as Webber Lake, but they lost him, like others who tracked this same blood shedding Grizzly nicknamed "Clubfoot" because of the shape of the footprints he left behind.

Hart returned home from the experience tired, disgusted, and chilled to the bone—barely in time to say good-by for another winter to Henry and Ottie, who were ready to leave for Sacramento.

CHAPTER TWENTY-ONE - 1875

The spring of 1875 brought Henry back to Sierra Valley, but it did not bring him back to help on the ranch. Jack Campbell's Hot Spring's Hotel was still not complete, and the senator-turned-carpenter needed to help with the finishing touches.

Our little grandson, Harry, was almost 2 ½, and I'll admit we considered him a pretty special little boy. We found all kinds of excuses to travel to Sierra Valley, but our visits were always short. So, when we found out that Aggie was expecting again, Rachel was delighted. Not only would she have another grandchild to brag on, she would also be asked to stay at Aggie's and prepare for the big event.

Old Doc Schubert no longer lived on the Turner Ranch. I thought it comforting to have a doctor so close, but Rachel shed no tears when she heard the old fellow moved on down the road to Sierraville, and was building a new cabin there. The only contact my lovely wife had with Doc was when Harry was born, and she disliked the fact that he smelled like the rotting end of a wine cork. "A doctor should have more respect for himself than that," she complained. "And look at his clothes. Why you'd think he slept in them—he probably does!"

The one thing Rachel didn't complain about, nor anyone else for that matter, was the fact that the man knew his medicine. He had what he called his "lee-tle pills", for just about everything, and the local folks swore that Doc's medicine worked.

With a new baby coming, I wished the doctor hadn't moved on; but Hart assured me that the road to Sierraville was open and clear, and he could be fetched quickly when the time came. That didn't keep Hart from pacing the ranch like a nervous bobcat, as the day got closer. Aggie had no trouble when she gave birth to Harry, and we were assured that she would probably do as well this time too. But, until the event actually took place, everyone became a little apprehensive.

I envisioned Rachel soaking up all that love from her only daughter, and only grandson, and never once did I imagine the chores required to prepare for the entrance of a new little Turner into the world.

I'm sure their mouths never stopped gabbing, while they cut Aggie's old sheets into squares. But their visiting slowed down some when they got out the big tub for the laundry. They boiled the squares in lye water for several hours, along with pillowcases and whole sheets. I wonder which chore was harder; avoiding the splash of the caustic lie, or keeping a frisky little two year old out of the way. Luckily, they had some warm days, and traffic on the road wasn't too bad yet, so they could hang everything out to dry. The object of all this cleaning was to make bed pads.

They brought the laundry inside, covered the table with one of the sheets, and dumped everything in the middle. Then, again keeping little Harry away from their project, they stacked newspapers, and covered them with sheet squares, pinning the neat stacks together with sheets and pillowcases. I'm sure Ottie provided the papers, and I couldn't think of a better use for Henry's subscription to that Republican blab-sheet, *The Mountain Messenger*.

Then, of course, they had to make diapers for the new baby. There were a few of Harry's old diapers left, but they were pretty worn. New ones were made from squares of Canton cotton. The women hand-hemmed them at the edges, because Aggie didn't have a sewing machine back then; however, that was the kind of love-work Rachel enjoyed—dreaming and praying all the while for a handsome, healthy infant. The diapers too, were boiled in lye water, dried, and placed in clean pillowcases. Aggie's nightgowns had to be sterilized also.

The day everyone waited for turned out to be June 4, 1875. I was working at Kentucky Mine, as supervisor, when one of the men brought me the news, "Hey Judge, you're a grandpa! That girl of yours went and had another boy!"

Another grandson! I did not waste time getting down the mountain. Turner Canyon had a proud new meaning to me. Never mind that it was named after those Republican men—I now had two grandsons with that same name, who, if I got my way, would grow up to be voting, fighting, Democrats!

A big surprise awaited me at the Turner Ranch. Rachel proudly picked up the baby from its cradle at the foot of Aggie's bed. She handed the small bundle over to me with a big smile, and Aggie said, "Papa, we've named him James."

I gave up hope long ago of passing down my name. There

would be no more Galloways, at least not from my branch of the family tree. But here in my arms, I held another James. I was actually struck dumb, an experience I have felt only a few times in my life! Rachel denies my interpretation of this story, because she says I kept her awake all night, with my jabber, about little James becoming the future democratic President of the United States.

Hart became a new man in my eyes that day. You can't help but admire someone who names his son after you. I saw in Hart a diplomat (a very nervous one) as the family poured through the house to see the baby. Under the same roof, he entertained the leader of the Sierra County Republicans: his brother, "Boss" Turner; and the leader of the Sierra County Democrats: his father-in-law, "Old Fire Eater", James Galloway.

Both Henry and I treated each other with mutual respect, and if there were any heated discussions during our visit, it began when Frank Campbell mentioned the Debating Society he recently joined, which met throughout the winter months at the Rocky Point School. The latest topic of discussion was: "Should Suffrage be Extended to Women?"

Someone asked Henry about Campbell's new hotel, and he smiled widely. "Thank God, we've finally finished. Jack has ordered new furniture from the city, and when it arrives Campbell Hot Springs will be officially opened." A sharp edge cut through Henry's voice when he talked about Campbell.

I turned to the Turner's brother-in-law, and asked, "You two aren't related, are you? . . . You and Jack."

Frank looked puzzled for a minute, then smiled and shook his head slowly.

"No way are they related," Henry said. "If they were, we wouldn't have let Frank in the family!"

All of the Turners, including Frank Campbell laughed. I grinned myself. Was there dissension among the ranks? I knew Jack Campbell to be a strong-hold in the Republican Party.

Hart smiled openly. It was a great day for him. A new son—and more good news: The construction was finally completed, and Henry would be able to help on the ranch for the rest of the season.

* * *

It had been such a mild winter, that many times the ranchers did not even have to feed their stock. The prosperity felt good. With the cash they saved, many bought new farm machinery—mowers, reapers, and rakes. The summer of 1875 was truly a fine summer.

The question that should have entered one's mind was, "Is this the calm before the storm?" Because, in fact, that is exactly what it was.

The winter to come began early. That November, Henry and his family left for the Legislative session in a snowstorm. No one thought it unusual. It often snowed in November. But, the temperature remained cold enough, and it snowed often enough, that winter never once paused to let the sun shine through.

A white New Year's Day, 1876, followed a white Christmas. Then the snowy-crystals that decorated the valley floor, turned to ice, and remained. Chimney ash drifted, and settled, changing the dazzling white landscape into ugly shades of gray.

After that, everyone welcomed the occasional snow storms. They enjoyed watching the clean fresh, blanket fall over the frozen soot-covered ice.

In March, when Hart and Aggie began to look for signs of warmth and spring, dark clouds answered with more bad weather. It stormed so heavily that roads were not just closed; they were lost under several feet of snow.

Hart shoveled to clear a path, only to turn around and shovel again—every day, for what seemed like all day. Henry was in Sacramento. The Turner's hired hand, Spuds, was fighting his own battle with the weather, somewhere up on the mountain. The only person around to help was Aggie; so her already rough red hands took up a shovel.

Small, gentle, white flakes suddenly became the enemy. In some parts of the valley, cattle began to die of starvation. Ranchers could not help one another (which was their custom in a crisis), because they all fought the same battle at home. They were *all* snowbound—each man totally on his own. Hart had enough hay put away to save his cattle, but he had to shovel all day long, making trails from the house to the outhouse, to the woodpile, to the barn, to the water ...

By the middle of March, the snow-pack reached four feet, and tall crystal-white walls bordered the trails, and each shovel full of snow made those walls taller.

They faced another problem when the snow got that deep. It could not slide from the roof of the house. There was no place for it to go! The weight of it on the rafters worried Hart, so he climbed up on the roof and tried to relieve some of the pressure by shoveling and tossing the snow somewhere—anywhere. So he added to the drifts that were already gigantic mountains surrounding his house—and then Henry's house also.

Harry's constant cry throughout the winter was, "Outside!" He loved the out-of-doors, even in bad weather. So when Aggie went out to help shovel, she bundled the child up, and took him with her. He played in the trails, dwarfed by towering walls, which Aggie feared would slide down and bury him.

Most of the time, Aggie stayed indoors with Harry and the baby. But from within their winter cage, they could not even watch Hart shovel. The snow was so deep that it covered any view from the windows. It also kept the daylight from shining in, and Aggie had to keep the oil lamp burning even during the daylight hours.

The wrath of winter went on, unceasing that year. In my mind, I always thought of Sierra Valley as "down the mountain", when actually it was "over the mountain", and rested at an elevation much higher than Downieville. We didn't get the jolt of bad weather, that Sierra Valley experienced, but because of the extreme storm, communication was totally cut off, and we didn't hear the extent of it until much later.

When the snow stopped falling from the sky, it lay as a silent blanket over the valley floor, at a depth of over four feet. And winter didn't end there. The sun hid itself, refusing to come along and melt it all the way.

When Hart was finally able to turn his attention away from the long, tunnel-like pathways, and check to see if his neighbors survived the great storm, he discovered that he had been lucky through it all. Snow hides its destructive wrath inside itself. The four foot depth people witnessed that year was actually deceptive, because snow settles to about half the depth of its fall, and it packs heavily wherever it lands. It damaged many barns in the valley, but worse than that was the cattle that suffered a horrible death of starvation.

George Hale came through the storm in pretty good shape; however he talked about selling out. The first week in April, Hart went over on skis to visit, and George told him that Abe Church's brother, Ezra, already bought the ranch and hotel.

CHAPTER TWENTY-TWO - 1876

Spring! Splotches of ice, tucked away in shadowy places, were the only reminders of the winter gone by. My boots caked with mud could cause frowns that were instantly washed away by the sight of Rachel's sunny daffodils nodding their golden head in the welcome sunshine. The trail was open to Sierra Valley. It looked more like a tunnel, dwarfed by walls of packed snow. But, when the pleasant word reached our home that traffic had resumed over the pass, Rachel nagged constantly about traveling over the mountain to see Aggie, and "her little darlings", as Rachel called them; and it wasn't long before we made the trip.

I had warmed to Hart some, that last fall, but with spring in full bloom, I discovered another side of the man I had not seen before.

While the women chatted about babies, diapers, cooking, and who knows what-all, I joined Hart as he headed down the trail to the barn. We leaned over the rough corral rail, where the warm sun left its mirror image on thousands of hoof print puddles around the yard. Hart scratched the ears of one of the calves. Mud clung to bits of hair on the animal's legs and tail.

"We've got thirty nine head here, not counting the milk cows," Hart said, beaming proudly.

"And if you count the milk cows?"

"Seventy-four. We more than doubled the herd! We ended last year with thirty four."

I raised my eyebrows, and scratched my chin. "That's wonderful Hart. Considering what happened to a lot of the farmers in this valley, I'd say you're mighty lucky."

Hart nodded his head slowly. "I'd say so too, Judge, but Aggie's convinced me that it isn't luck. She says we're blessed."

I smiled. "She's probably right."

"I never took much to church going until I married Aggie," Hart said, as the calf scampered across the corral. We watched as a concerned mother cow lifted her head and mooed loudly as her youngster darted between the other cows. "Aggie reads the Bible a lot, and whenever things get to looking pretty bad, she quotes scripture. The verse that got us through this horrible winter was, 'All things work together for good, for those who love God.' There's more, but I can't remember the rest." He shook his head.

"She's right you know. At least things worked out well for us, and I don't think anyone loves God more than Aggie."

I nodded in agreement. All those years I thought we wasted, insisting Aggie read from the Bible every day, to improve her reading and grammar, did not go unrewarded after all. In those days I was more concerned with her studies, than her faith.

"All of our neighbors lost cattle this winter—all but us." Hart looked squarely into my eyes. "Explain that, Judge. We prospered!"

I shook my head and shrugged.

Hart turned his eyes back to the pen. "We didn't lose a single calf this year."

* * *

When Henry returned from Sacramento, announcing that he would not run for re-election, and that he was stepping down from the Senate, a startling change was in store for everyone, especially Hart. Henry spent the entire summer working on the ranch! The additional herd made his presence welcome and necessary—unusual as it may have been.

Because the political fires never seemed to excite Hart, I considered him rather dull, and managed to forget how important he was to my daughter and her growing family. On a later visit, in the summer sometime, I realized how much Aggie really cared for her husband.

The hot, still air of summer robbed us of our appetites, and made it difficult to sleep. After supper, the children were tucked into their beds with just a sheet for a cover. To the tune of chirping crickets, Rachel and I went for an evening stroll, down the road to Church's Corners and back. We watched the moon change from a gigantic ball on the horizon, to a distant sphere, as it climbed high in the sky. Its blue glow spread mysteriously upon the peaceful meadow. Its reflection danced on the rippling water that trickled along in a ditch beside the road.

On the way back to Aggie's, we passed Henry's house. The lanterns were lit, and I could see Henry sitting and reading a newspaper, by the light of the lamp. The sight made me uneasy, as if he were doing his homework, while I was out playing. I suddenly felt it was time to end this short vacation and return to the new home we established in Sierra City—and get back to work.

That is what clouded my mind as my wife and I silently walked, arm in arm, up the hill. Suddenly Rachel tugged at my sleeve. We had been married long enough that she didn't need to verbalize her intention for me to stop, and quietly observe something she spotted on the trail. I heard the chirping of crickets and the croaking of frogs—but the trail was empty.

"There . . ." she whispered, pointing toward our daughter's house.

The moon outlined two people melted into a single form. They stood on the porch—Aggie, in her calico print dress, absent of color in the dim light; and Hart, in soiled and patched work clothes, with his shirt sleeves rolled up above his elbows. With muscular arms he gently pushed Aggie away, and stood for a moment gazing at her.

"Aggie, are you disappointed?" he asked.

Aggie tried to move closer to him, but he held her off. "Disappointed? . . . About what?"

"Are you disappointed that you married me."

For a moment, it seemed as if the crickets and frogs stopped their serenade. Aggie's hands went to her hips, in an aggravated gesture. "That is the silliest question I think I have ever heard!"

"Then answer it."

"Hart, we have two beautiful children, asleep in the house. Two wonderful little babies—and you ask me if I am sorry I married you?"

Hart's strong jaw didn't move, as he stared off into the night. His hair was tangled, as usual, from the hat he always wore around the ranch, and his beard, never quite trim enough, spoke of a rugged earthy man. But the mood, his depression, felt as thick as the humid night air.

Aggie reached out and touched his arm. "We have this house . . . and a good life. I couldn't ask for more."

"You could, Aggie. You could have had a lot more. Look at Ottie, and her fancy dresses. Look at her hands, Aggie. They haven't had to scrub filthy clothes in boiling tubs of lye soap! While in Sacramento, the Senator's wives send their clothes to the laundry. I don't see her patching up old pants and shirts."

Deep silence, known only to lovers, passed between the young couple on the porch, as their eyes searched for assurance and truth. Aggie's hand slid down her husband's arm, where she clasped his fingers in her own, and lifted them to her waist, and rubbed his rough knuckles. Hart was right about one thing. Aggie's fingers were red and chapped—a sad comparison to Ottie's smooth young-looking hands.

"Tell me, Aggie, I have to know. Are you sorry? Sorry you got stuck on this ranch, with nothing but a dowdy old farmer for a husband? Are you sorry that you didn't marry someone like Henry?"

Aggie began to pat his hand. "Let me tell you about Ottie. She is my best friend, and my sister-in-law. I love her dearly. But, she is a *lady*, Hart. She was born to live a life like that—I wasn't."

"Yes you were!" Hart's voice boomed outward, loud and clear. "You are as much a lady as anyone I know. You're a fine woman—the best. You deserve the best!"

"I have the best."

"You have nothing but a hard working man, that doesn't seem to get anything out of life, but more hard work. Look at Henry. Everything he touches turns to gold. He is always doing something good. All I ever do is work."

Aggie pinched the thick hair that grew on Hart's arm. "Hart, I love you. You are the kind of man that keeps the world turning. I wouldn't trade you for all the senators, governors, or presidents in the country! Remember, darling, behind every hero there is a hard working man."

Hart lifted her chin, and kissed her lips. "I love you, Aggie. I'm so glad you're my wife."

The tug on my sleeve invited me back down the trail. It seemed Rachel thought it best to extend our walk a little longer. When we got out of earshot, I asked her, "Are you sorry you married *me*?"

She laughed. "Well, if I am, it's too late to do anything about it now!"

CHAPTER TWENTY-THREE - 1876

In mid-summer, Rachel and I took an emergency trip to see Aggie. The emergency, according to my dear wife, was that our grandchildren were growing up without us, and little James hardly knew who we were.

"Henry is down the hill," Hart said. "Come on, I want to show you what we've done." Hart insisted I walk down to the meadow, behind the barn, where he proudly showed off the brickyard. What started off small was becoming a growing business.

The Turner's hired a few men to help during molding time, when they dug out the clay, tromped it into the right consistency, slapped it into the molds, and laid the bricks carefully out to dry in a flat area, covered with fine sand. When I arrived at the ranch, the bricks lay in long rows, drying in the sun. It was there, that I saw the grasshoppers.

Hart was not a man to swear, and I don't remember ever hearing him say he hated anything—except grasshoppers.

The greedy little critters invaded Sierra Valley, and it was a big joke in Downieville, because around the County Seat we had no idea of the extent of the grasshopper invasion.

They covered up the brick yard, making the bricks look like they were cluttered with fallen leaves, only *these* leaves crawled and jumped! The fields were alive with motion, and the clicking noise of a common grasshopper was multiplied by several hundred.

They arrived in swarms during the previous summer: Where they came from—no one knew—but they brought with them unbelievable power to destroy. They hid in the fields, as grasshoppers do, and ate their way through acre after acre of productive farm land. Much of the hay and barley crops in the valley were badly damaged by the insects.

Hart removed his hat, and swatted above the bricks. "Get out of here, you . . ." He came close to swearing.

Henry looked in my direction, and said, "It's a good thing we thought ahead, and got this brick yard going. As long as those filthy insects are around, we won't make any money selling hay."

Hart flipped his hat back on his head. "I'm worried about the dairy cows," he said. "They need hay, and lots of it. Those long-legged, tobacco spitting, monsters are chomping away on next winter's feed."

The two brothers bent down, and began to pick the bricks up off the ground, where they had dried for a little over a week; and they loaded them into a wheelbarrow. I suppose I should have helped, after all, Hart was my son-in-law, but I had on my "traveling clothes", as Rachel called them. She always insisted I pack my best duds when I traveled out of town.

Above the brickyard, along the Yuba Pass Road, the rumbling of the traffic blended with the scrapping sounds of bricks. As Hart and Henry worked, they ignored the racket of the wagons loaded with produce heading up the mountain; and the supply wagons that came down, jangling their bells of warning, as they came barreling around blind curves, hidden in clouds of dust. Maybe each had its own distinctive sound, because the men seemed to notice the daily stage that usually bolted through the ranch, in the direction of Sierraville. Instead of its normal non-stop rush, the stage slowed as it approached Henry's house. Immediately both brothers turned to look.

I also turned to see what had grabbed their attention, just in time to watch the stage roll to a stop at Henry's gate. Two men, dressed in dark suits, jumped down from the canvas topped coach, and began to dust off their clothes with their hands. The driver threw two small satchels to the departed passengers, and hurried the four horse team on down the road through Church's Corners, then off toward Sierraville.

Hart touched the rim of his hat. "I wonder who that could be."

We watched the two men take of their hats, use them to beat more dust from their trousers, then the plop their hats back on their heads, pick up their satchels, and walk up to the white picket fence that surrounded Henry's yard. Ottie came to the door, and pointed in our direction. The men handed their bags over the fence, turned, crossed the road, and walked down the hill to the brickyard.

I recognized the smooth step of Dan Cole, and the energetic bounce of his co-conspirator, Dr. Alemby Jump. Suddenly I felt like a rabbit falling into a den of wolves. If Henry were truly "boss" of the local republicans, then these two were definitely his closest collaborators.

The ex-senator actually looked embarrassed, as his friends approached. He removed his old work hat, and it left a clean ring on his forehead, outlined by a dirty hat band line.

"Dan . . . Alemby . . . It's good to see you. How was your trip?" Henry asked, as he removed his right work glove, and shook hands.

Hart stood with one hand on his hip. His eyes narrowed in a frown, where his hat shaded his face.

Henry continued, "You've met my brother, Hart . . . and, ah . . . of course, you know Judge Galloway."

"Yes."

"Yep . . . Howdy Hart."

Hart tipped his sweat stained hat, and mumbled, "Hello."

I just nodded, and mumbled the same.

Alemby ignored our suspicious stares, as he surveyed the long rows of bricks, and cheerfully said, "Well, you men sure look like you have a mighty big project in mind."

Henry wiped his brow with a handkerchief, which he pulled from his back pocket; then he plopped his floppy hat back onto his head. "It's for the new Masonic Temple they are going to build in Sierraville."

Dan rubbed his chin. "I thought you Turners preferred the Odd Fellows."

Henry smiled. "Sure we do. But, I take business where I find it. Actually, Mr. Nichols is building a store in Sierraville, with the Lodge Hall upstairs. It's a pretty big order."

Alemby nodded, and then said, "Well Henry, have you thought over what we talked about?"

Henry glanced quickly in Hart's direction, and then his eyes moved over toward me. "Actually . . . ah . . . Hart, why don't we quit for the day? Dan and Alemby have had a long trip, and I'm sure they would like something cold to drink."

Hart's lips tightened. He didn't answer. He just took off his work gloves, and stood there holding them, with his arms crossed in front of his chest.

The brother's eyes met in a threatening stare, and Henry's chin rose slightly. "Besides," he said, breaking eye contact, "It is getting late, and we've accomplished a lot today." Like a practiced politician, he turned a pleasant, forced smile towards his friends. "Come on Dan . . . Alemby . . . Let's head up to the house."

Hart stiffly slammed his hands back into his gloves, picked up the wheelbarrow by the handles, and pushed it over to the drying shed; where silently he unloaded the bricks, stacking them in diagonal rows, one inch apart, where they would continue to dry beneath the protection of the shed's wall-less roof.

It angered me to see my daughter's husband treated this way, and I wondered how often Henry had left jobs half finished, in favor of "more important" matters.

When the wheelbarrow was empty, we walked up the hill together. I let Hart talk, hoping he would solve the mystery of this republican reunion.

"I just can't believe it, Judge," he said. "Henry promised! When he returned this spring, he said he would *not* run for re-election. So, what are those leeches doing here?"

Leeches? I wondered whose side Hart was on—politically.

Hart ground his teeth together. "If they talk Henry into running, I'll . . ."

I raised my eyebrows, waiting for an explanation of just what Hart *would* do. But he glanced at me, smiled slightly, and said, "Well, I don't know what I'll do—but I can tell you now, I won't be happy. I need him here—especially with the brickyard. We hired an extra hand to help Spuds with the milking, and the dairy; and we have those who help at the brickyard, but there is just so much one man can do."

* * *

It was not long before I learned the purpose behind the Republican's mysterious visit to Church's Corners.

Early in February, the California Legislature passed a bill for the election of delegates to serve the state in writing a badly needed, new constitution. Who would be a better choice than Sierra County's favorite Republican, the man who proved himself to the people of our county: ex-Senator H. K. Turner?

Again, I guess I envied Henry his position. He was at the top of his career, and could easily snatch the election to fill the coveted seat.

California's old constitution was written in 1849, by men who, for the most part, had come West with the wave of gold seekers. They were all newcomers to the Territory—immigrants from every part of the world. I had no hand in constructing that first constitution, but I know the type of men who did. We were all the same then—self-seeking opportunists. Suddenly we were a state, and some form of organization needed to be constructed. The result was a constitution plagued with problems from its birth.

All over California, giant monopolies grabbed up the land. The Central Pacific Railroad controlled over eighty-five percent of all the railroads in the state. There were no rules to govern their fees, so they charged whatever they could get away with, and the price of a train ride varied from customer to customer. Citizens screamed at the policy, and demanded regulations.

Taxes: Everyone's nightmare! Yet, the first constitution reserved only one section on the subject of taxation—and that was found under the article on "Miscellaneous Provisions". If you can imagine a county allowing its Board of Supervisors to set the standard of taxation, and the county assessor deciding on property values—with no guidelines—that is exactly how our state was being run.

More problems came when gold wasn't so easy to find anymore, and those old gold miners gave up their claims. They still lived by the get-rich-quick philosophy, and it didn't take them long to discover the stock market. The used the market as a game of chance, buying and selling, with no regulations. As a result, our state's economy began to quiver.

Then along came the Chinese. The newspapers went wild with this one, painting hatred across the country at the speed of a never silenced printing press. Folks used to meet the ships in the old days, just to watch the Chinese men disembark, all looking the same in their pajama-like outfits, their long hair braided down their backs. Each one carried his belongings in two baskets, tied at each end of a pole that he carried over his shoulders. The novelty soon wore off, and resentment replaced curiosity. The Oriental's unwillingness to blend into our society bred a hatred which was fed by their foreign habits: They worshiped what we called "an unknown god", they dressed strangely, and had unusual eating habits. What really sparked anger was the fact these small bodied foreigners worked for practically nothing, and still sustained a way of life they found satisfying. Soon people shouted "Heathen!" and beat them unmercifully. Personally I feared that the Chinese who remained in California would take up all the available jobs, lower our pay scale, and throw the entire state into a depression.

Both the Democrats and Republicans wanted *their* people on the committee that would write the new constitution, but we both faced a greater problem than all of the Chinese, monopolies, or taxation woes.

It all began on the streets of San Francisco, with Dennis Kearney. He came straight from Ireland, with a tongue as sweet as any Irish tenor. With his fist in the air he screamed, "The Chinese must go!" and "The rich will have ruled us until they have ruined us! We will now take our affairs into our own hands!" And on his heels came scores of working men and in their wake arose a new political party: the Kearneyites, or Workingmen's Party.

The popularity of this new party spread across the state on the heels of bold promises. Their delegates rose up everywhere. Democrats and Republicans suddenly faced a strong and fearless third opponent. Overnight we discovered our chances were pretty slim of electing our own delegates to sit at the Second Constitutional Convention.

* * *

One day, not long after Henry's Republican friends met with him at Church's Corners, I saw Henry up at Downieville. He and Dan Cole walked onto the porch of Dr. Alemby Jump's house, and disappeared through his front door. I knew it was not illness that brought them to see the doctor. They were forming campaign tactics, just as we Democrats were doing on the other side of town. I, or course, sat in with the better of the two parties. But, I imagine the conversation was about the same.

"The biggest problem we have to face, in this election, is the Kearneyites. Kearney has too many followers now. And if you ask my opinion, they are all radical fools."

"I read about it in the paper. But to tell the truth, that is all I know—what I read in the paper."

"It is as big, or bigger, than anything you may have read. The Workingmen are a popular party now. It's not the Republicans we will be facing in this election, it is Kearney."

"We can be thankful that not all the Workingmen are behind their radical leader—but, they are a strong group. Their platform is narrow and self-serving. If they get a majority at the convention—which they just might do, only God knows what kind of constitution will develop!" "So, what do we do? How do we get the seats?"

The delicate moment arrived, when the political machine began to turn, and minds searched for answers.

The only answer to our predicament was to throw our votes with the Non-partisans. This solution stirred the conversation into a fever pitch. But the decision had already been made by the Central Committees of both the Democrat and Republican Parties: Let the fight be between the Non-partisans and the Workingmen.

"Let me get this straight. Are you saying the Republicans and the Democrats are joining forces against the Workingmen, and voting Non-partisan?"

"That's right. So we will have to run our candidate on an Independent or Non-partisan ticket."

Now, I found this news very upsetting. Never in my adult life had I voted any ticket other than Democrat. This was the most difficult fight in all my political experience.

* * *

The battle the Republicans faced was identical to ours. But the conflict Henry pondered was within his own conscience.

When he told Hart of his decision to run, Hart was ready for him. "You can't be serious! We need you here at the ranch. I thought your political days were over."

"My political days will never be over, Hart. I did think my days as a candidate were over, when they expanded the boundary of my senatorial district—there is no way I could spend the time campaigning all over the north part of the state. Sierra County was big enough."

Hart stood in his tall angry stance—both feet spread apart, and hands firmly on his hips, elbows outward.

Henry continued, "But, this is different. Can't you see, Hart? We will be writing a new constitution for the state of California—a constitution that will decide who can own land, and how our taxes should be paid, and to what amount. I don't see how I can turn down the opportunity to participate."

Hart sighed, and let one arm slip down to his side. He never won against the cunning tongue of his brother, who made politics sound so important. There was no arguing with the Senator, the man the Republicans could always count on—good old "Boss"

Turner.

Knowing he won another battle with Hart, Henry smiled. "That's not all. We've decided I should *not* run on the party ticket."

Hart blinked. "Is that ethical?"

"We are fighting the Workingman's Party, and what *they* have in mind is not ethical! I've been told that if I run as a Republican candidate, I am guaranteed to lose. There are members of my own party who would not vote for me."

Hart shook his head.

Henry shrugged. "Consider the alternative. If I lose, then another man, most likely a Workingman, will be sent in my place."

Hart shook his head again. What Henry was doing just didn't seem right to him. It sounded dishonest—patronizing.

* * *

The election was held on June 18, 1878.

While the Turner brothers rode to Sierraville to cast their ballots at Atwood's Store, I was over the mountain casting my own vote.

This was the first time I ever voted for a candidate not listed as a Democrat. I read down the list of names until I found H. K. Turner, listed on the Non-partisan ticket, and I marked my X. It wasn't as if I were voting for the adversary. The Central Committee had made the decision for me. I knew Henry to be a level headed politician . . . So, I marked my ticket, and dropped it into the ballot box.

When the votes were tallied, Henry pulled 400 votes—a good showing—enough votes to send him back to the state's capitol. The other man our county chose to represent them was a lawyer, named Ed Barry (also a Republican), who ran under the Workingman's ticket.

CHAPTER TWENTY-FOUR - 1878-1879

The Second Constitutional Convention: a politician's dream comes true! They started from scratch, and rewrote the entire constitution of the state. I read everything I could find on the subject, delving into conversations with old colleagues at every opportunity, expressing my point of view on what decisions should be made on each topic brought up before the convention.

Only one thing could have upstaged such an even on my calendar—and it happened. On September 28, 1878, the first day of the convention, my daughter gave birth to her third son, Thomas Kennedy Turner. No one needed to tell me who the baby was named for. I probably knew the first Tom Turner better than his own sons did.

As I looked down on the newest addition to our family, sleeping soundly in a pine wood cradle, I wondered about the puzzle of life, and how easily some otherwise mismatched pieces fit together. Some twenty years earlier, old Tom Turner gave me the courage I needed to approach Rachel, and now my grandson was also his grandson, and namesake. What a strange web our lives weave, touching memories from the past, and dragging them to the surface in unexpected ways.

I read the convention reports in the newspaper, with curious interest, and was fortified by the knowledge that I could get a firsthand account of the proceedings from Henry when he returned to Sierra Valley.

The group of men chosen for the prodigious task came from all corners of our society. Some possessed experience in the legislature, and knowledge of the law—business men, lawyers and even one corporation president. Others, mostly from the Workingmen's Party, had no talent whatsoever in making this kind of decision. Their insight came from trades such as rigger, sign painter, lithographer, tailor and cook.

It was a tremendous undertaking, especially considering the strong prejudicial feelings of many of the representatives. However, +-the delegates were separated into committees, to debate and outline their ideas. Henry was assigned to the Committee on Revenue and Taxation, which in his estimation, was the worst and most complicated of all the state's problems. A former state senator from Sacramento County, Henry Eagerton, was elected to head this committee. Back when he was Senator, Turner served with Eagerton, in fact, they quit the same year.

According to our Henry, Eagerton was an impressive man with a smooth tongue—able to stand up and take charge. He was a well known lawyer, who many years ago had been the prosecutor in a famous murder trial that led to the purification of San Francisco. Henry admired the man, and was glad to see him chair the committee

It must have been a strange Christmas for the Henry Turner family that year. Henry's committee began its report on Christmas Eve. That night, Henry tried to be both dignified Senator, and jolly old St. Nick. I wondered how well he made the transition. I would think that the pumpkin pie and Christmas cookie smells, and the laughter of nine year old Frank and seven year old Mary, could transform even the grumpiest politician into a merry old Santa Clause.

December 26th—Henry was back at the convention, and serious discussions began.

* * *

It took five long months to frame the new constitution, which was finally completed on March 3, 1879. It contained 22 Articles, of 233 Sections—as compared to the old constitution which had 13 Articles, of 156 Sections. The only thing left was the acceptance, or rejection, by the people of California—us, the voters.

I made my way to Sierra Valley as soon as Henry returned from the convention. Feeling much like a horse that had been kept too long in the barn, I longed for specific inside information from the brother of my son-in-law; and I was disappointed to find a tired, and frustrated, whipped politician.

"It was a joke: A mockery!" Dark circles underlined Henry's eyes as he looked into mine—as though he knew I would understand. "We have a new constitution for the people of California to vote on, all right; but if they decide to keep it, there will be nothing but a troubled future for our state."

We sat on Henry's porch, trying to enjoy one of those first warm spring days. Hart sat in a wooden chair, looking across the road toward the barn and field. The road was unusually quiet. No wagons rumbled down into the valley. Because of the snow high in the mountains, travel was still difficult. Only an occasional rider would slowly pass by, and wave. March 1879 was an easy time at the ranch. The calves weren't dropping yet, and the ground hadn't thawed enough for plowing, or making bricks.

Hart's eyebrows wrinkled above his deep set eyes, and he said, "But I thought you told me we *needed* a new constitution."

"We did Hart. There were major problems with the old one. The legislature had a pretty free hand with the tax payer's hard earned money. It could tax anything, anytime—and even set its own salary . . . as high as it wanted. Those things had to be changed."

"Isn't that what you did?" Hart asked.

Henry stood up from his chair by the door, walked to the edge of the porch, and sat on the porch rail. He reached into his coat pocked, and pulled out a pipe and a small pouch of tobacco—a new habit that developed during the course of the convention. I wondered if he were ignoring Hart, and my mind stirred with questions of my own.

From inside the house came laughter, and the chatter of women and children, which always seemed louder when Ottie was present, even before she had the children. I smiled, knowing Rachel was in her glory. It would be hard to calm her down that night, and I knew I would be listening to her "re-telling" for hours after we went to bed.

Henry lit his pipe, and the smoke rose between us, giving off the scent of apples... or cloves? Finally he spoke, "We went forward to make great changes . . ." He stopped mid-sentence.

Hart and I waited for him to continue.

He looked up. "Judge, did you know there are over 200,000 people in the city of San Francisco?"

200,000! I shook my head in negative surprise. "I knew there were a lot," I said, "but not that many!"

"That is one fourth of the population of our state," Henry said. "The next biggest city would probably be Oakland, or Sacramento. Sacramento has about 20,000."

I contemplated the unbalance, while Henry continued to talk. "That means that out of 152 delegates elected to the convention, over one fifth were from the big city of San Francisco."

He didn't have to explain the meaning behind this statement, but he did anyway. "We had a total of 50 misguided

Workingmen—ostrich headed Kearneyites! And, if that weren't bad enough, there were 35 foreign born delegates—mostly Irish."

While Henry took an angry puff at his pipe, Hart remarked, "What's wrong with that? We're Irish."

"Hart our mother was Irish, and our father was English, but *we* are American—born in the United States of America. We had men at the convention making decisions for us, who hadn't been in our country long enough to realize the *power* generated by freedom."

Hart shrugged.

"There were just too many self-interest people involved. And, the fact that there were so many foreign born delegates, caused a stir among the others. Everything caused a stir! If there was the slightest reason for provocation, someone jumped on it. If it had been possible, I think some of them would have written our entire constitution around one factor—get rid of the Chinese!"

Henry's evaluation of the Constitutional Convention amazed me. Rumors had circulated that things were not well at the Capitol, but I thought Henry would be a man to rise above it all.

"You sound pretty disgusted," I said.

"I am. This convention did something to me. How can we compare the interest of our small farming communities with those of a city with 200,000 people? And, what kind of a vote are we going to have? I just don't feel I can help anymore, Judge." The corner of Henry's lips moved upward as he caught my eye again. "I guess you'll be glad to hear that! I think ex-Senator H. K. Turner is going to hang up his hat."

Why wasn't I glad to hear that? H. K. Turner was, and had for many years been, the wheel that moved the local Republican Party. If ever I had a political enemy, it should have been him. But, my mind knew that Henry was an intelligent man—one who our county could be proud of. He just happened to belong to the wrong party.

I watched in silence as he re-lit his pipe. His eyes were slits, but I felt them peering at me through closed lashes. I smiled slightly, trying to cover my true feelings.

"Yep Judge, I think it's time to leave it for someone younger to figure out. I feel like I'm getting too old . . . I long for the good old days."

Hart grunted. "You mean the good old days when a man could

shoot anyone who disagreed with him?"

Henry smiled. "Yeah . . . those good old days!"

* * *

We voted on the newly written constitution on May 7, 1879. Kearney's city of San Francisco turned it down, Sierra Valley turned it down, but when all the votes in the state were counted, a majority of 10,000 votes accepted the new constitution, and for the most part, it went into effect on the Fourth of July, 1879.

CHAPTER TWENTY-FIVE - 1882

I'll admit, I doubted Henry's honesty, when he talked about dropping out of the political scene, and leaving it to the young. He talked about being "too old", and I, his senior, knew better than that! Blood just seems to run thicker as we get older.

I kept my eye on Henry, which meant visiting the valley more often. He surprised me—and Hart too. Henry turned his interest to improving the ranch. His hands and clothes were actually dirty, from hard work and sweat. And, on my occasional visits, he seldom asked about Downieville, or the activities of the court house. I looked forward to great elections without the interference of ex-Senator H. K. Turner.

Visits to Aggie's home, were always a treat for Rachel and me. But, now that Henry was no longer a burr under my saddle, these moments in Sierra Valley, watching the grandchildren sprout up like rampant weeds, were even more enjoyable.

I stepped out onto Aggie's porch, one spring morning, in 1882—three years after Henry's drop from politics. The ground had thawed enough to plow, and I breathed in the crisp, sweet, earthy smell. The first calf of spring had dropped the night before, but most of the cows were still bursting with expectancy. Clouds scattered across the sky, as if in a hurry to reach the deserts of Nevada, and I pulled the collar of my jacket closed.

The irregular "thump . . . thump . . ." sounds came from the direction of the wood pile. So, I jogged down the steps, and around the house where my grandsons were stacking wood. Harry was a wiry and active nine year old, and my little name sake, Jim, was a sandy headed, serious and adventuresome six.

As the boys threw chunks of wood into the wheelbarrow, their breath became vapors that rose in the air, like steam from a kettle on the stove. Hart stood by, letting his axe rest some, as he watched them. Henry leaned against the wall of the shed, chewing on a dried piece of hay. The men's attention was captivated by the two boys.

"Be careful Jim," Harry said.

"I am being careful!" Jim threw a piece of wood at the wheelbarrow, and missed.

"See there!" Harry frowned. "Don't throw the wood. You always miss."

"You throw the wood, so why can't I?"

"I'm bigger than you and . . ." Harry stopped mid-sentence, as he saw me approach. "Hi Grandpa!"

Everyone turned to look my way. I rubbed my hand through both boys' hair, and walked over to join the men.

"I see you're down from the mountain again," Henry said, with a warm smile.

"I've got to keep an eye on the Turner Ranch, Senator, and make sure you are hard at work, and staying away from the County Seat."

Henry raised one eyebrow. "Actually, I just got back from Downieville. Didn't Hart tell you, I've been gone for a few days?"

My heart fluttered. I looked at Hart, and he shrugged, and said, "We've got more important things to talk about than you, Henry."

Henry shook his head, and grinned. "I've got good news. In fact, I was just going to fill Hart in on our newest project."

Hart and I exchanged looks, with the same question on our eyes—*it better not have anything to do with politics!*

"We are going to build a vault!"

Sometime during the first two months of 1882, Henry heard that Sierra County planned to build a vault. He had his own personal branch on the local grapevine, and never missed a thing that was going on in the county. The vault had little or nothing, to do with politics, but the ex-Senator made his move. With all the training and experience of a seasoned politician, he rode to Downieville to the special Supervisor's Meeting that was held to discuss the matter.

"How did you get the bid so soon?" Hart asked, keeping one eye on the boys.

"Politics, brother: pure politics! I had my bid ready, just in case the project came up—and everything worked out to our advantage."

He was doing it again—manipulating the leaders of our county. I marveled at his persuasive talents, and believed he could probably talk a gnarly old mongrel dog into eating out of his hand.

"How much did you bid?" Hart asked.

"$1500, I think we can do it for that, and make a good profit."

Hart's face reddened. "You were supposed to sell them the bricks, not contract to do the work! What about the ranch, and the rest of our brick business?"

"This is a great opportunity Hart. We not only get the publicity, but the money too! We can hire someone to take my place here. Think of it: Our Bricks Built Vaults!"

"Pa, do you think this is enough wood?" Harry shouted. The wheelbarrow had overflowed, despite Jim's reckless help.

Hart glared at Henry one more time before he turned to the boys with a softer expression. "Now that looks good, boys. You've done a fine job."

"Jim and I can take it up to the house, Pa. You can keep talking to Grandpa and Uncle Henry, if you want."

"That's a pretty big load for you boys." Hart put his hands on his hips. He had cut the chunks of Lodge Pole Pine into the largest pieces that would fit in the stove, so that they would burn longer.

"We can do it, Pa," Jim insisted, as he ran between his brother and the wheelbarrow, taking the long handles in his small fists. His eyes were wide and pleading.

Harry pushed at his little brother, who wouldn't budge, and so together they tried to move the heavy load forward. The wheelbarrow inched along in short clumsy jolts, with Harry shouting orders, and Jim constantly getting in the way.

"What do you think of my boys?" Hart asked me. His voice was full of pride.

I could have come right out and said that I thought they were probably the cutest, smartest, and strongest little boys in all of Sierra County—even the state; but instead, I grinned, and said, "By the way they handle that wheelbarrow, I'd say they show a strong resemblance to the Turner side."

We followed the boys slowly around the house. The conversation about the vault was over. I sensed a feeling of relief on Henry's part. He had not volunteered much information about how he swung the deal, and I had a few questions about it myself, but I would have to find the answers later.

"Have you told Ottie about it yet?" Hart asked.

"Not exactly."

"What do you mean, 'not exactly'? Either you told her, or you didn't." There was a sharp edge to Hart's voice as he glared at his brother.

"She knows we got the bid, but I haven't told her that I rented a house for us while I was in Downieville."

I am sure my eyes widened in surprise. Henry in Downieville? I didn't like the idea of him close to his republican associates. Hart accepted the entire situation much more gracefully than I. "What do you think she will say?" Hart asked.

"I promised Ottie, a long time ago, that I would never leave her alone again. I think she expects to go to Downieville with me."

"She's pretty well settled in here, with the new baby," Hart said. "I don't think she will be too happy."

The new baby was a girl—born in October. They named her Lottie. Apparently Henry wanted to name her Ottie, but the wife objected, and said, "One Ottie Turner in this family is more than enough." The name Lottie was a compromise—one of the few compromises Henry Turner ever made.

I thought of Aggie. She was expecting her fourth baby. All she could talk about, since Lottie's birth, was having a girl. "Wouldn't it be wonderful," Aggie would say—her eyes shined with the wonder of it all.

Then Rachel would join her dreams and say, "It certainly would be. We are outnumbered in men around this house."

* * *

When I returned to Downieville, I did a little investigating of my own, and discovered some interesting facts. The Sierra County Board of Supervisors had ordered themselves to build a vault—that was appropriate. But, they also decided to accept bids for the project at the same meeting! This double-dealing hand they played, fed the mistrust I already harbored for the one hundred percent Republican board. It was obvious to me, who dealt the cards which seemed to be stacked in Turner's favor. My guess was that a close friend of Henry's, Dan Cole, who was also a member of the board, told Henry about the county needing a new vault. Good old Dan. Knowing the right people always paid off.

Years of serving as a judge, combined with old age, taught me an important lesson about justice. It is an obscure word, full of questionable shadows, out of focus reasons, and blurred realities.

Through my investigation, I learned that Henry had *not* offered the lowest bid. In fact, he was under bid by $200. The other bidder's name was Hardy, but it didn't matter what his name was, or how much he bid—he would have lost anyway. Is that justice? As a Democrat, speaking about the decisions of a Republican board, I would say: definitely *NO!* But, as a grandfather, who knew that grasshoppers were eating away the profits of *all* the ranches in Sierra Valley, including my daughter's; and knowing that if it weren't for the brick yard, the Turner Ranch would probably go under—and my handsome grandsons might go hungry . . . under these circumstances I would have to say it was justice—it was right. I was glad that Henry "won" the bid.

* * *

What a profound magnet God uses to pull us into his perspective. Henry once resolved not to involve himself in the local political arena, yet circumstance pulled him into building a vault next door to the Sierra County Courthouse. He must have felt like a retired gladiator placing stones around the walls of the coliseum, watching those less qualified than he, parade off and on to its bloody field.

But Henry applied his trowel like a professional, keeping his mind steadily on his work, stacking bricks on the level. The supervisors gave him a deadline of September first, five months away—an easy job.

I found more reasons than normal to visit the courthouse. Like other small town people, I was interested in the raising of a new structure in our town. And, I'll admit, I was curious to see if Henry would be able to keep his feet dry that close to the water. I tried not to be too obvious in my scrutiny. I had a friend whose office overlooked the red clay construction project, and one afternoon, while I happened to be visiting this friend, I found myself witness to a turning point in Henry's life.

The comfortable weather invited many of the windows in the courthouse to be open, and among the pleasant sounds of neighborhood birds and the scraping sound of cement against brick, came the booming voice of Dr. Alemby Jump. "Hey Turner, put down that trowel, and come over here a minute!"

My ears perked up like a hunting dog, fresh on a trail. From my lofty vantage point, I saw Henry, boxed inside what looked like a red brick fence. He picked a soiled rag out of his back pocket, and wiped his hands, as he walked over to the edge of the courthouse, where Dan Cole and Alemby Jump stood with another fellow I didn't recognize.

"Henry, I want you to meet a good friend of ours, from Forest City—the next sheriff of Sierra County, Francis H. Campbell." Dan smiled proudly throughout the introduction.

Henry held out a rough hand, tinted cement gray, and stared uncomfortably at the tall, handsome gentleman. Clearing his throat, he explained, "I'm sorry, Mr. Campbell, by my niece is married to a man with that same name. You wouldn't happen to be related, would you?"

The newcomer cocked his head to one side. ". . . Another Frances H. Campbell? I thought I was the only one! Where does he live?"

"Sierra Valley—on the west side—right over the Plumas County line. He's a good man and a friend of mine long before he married my niece. They call him Frank, his middle initial is H., just like yours. I can see confusion in our future all ready!"

Alemby nodded his head. "It gets worse. Guess who else is running for sheriff this year."

Henry shrugged. "I would imagine that Mr. Fish is going to run again."

"Nope . . . old Jack Campbell."

I knew of Henry's ill feelings toward this familiar name, and could imagine the hair rising on the back of his neck.

Jack Campbell. This man was once Sheriff of Sierra County for four years, back in the early 70's. When he bought the Hot Springs, near Randolph, from Fenstermaker, he changed the name to Campbell's Hot Springs—and hired Henry to build a hotel. Then, once Henry was committed, Jack changed the plan. Good old Jack Campbell—everybody's friend. You either loved the man or hated him, and I knew which direction Henry's feelings ran.

I watched Henry reach inside a pocket for his pipe. Carefully, he poured a small amount of tobacco from a pouch, and arranged it slowly, then lit it with the same deliberation. It was like watching a trout in clear water of the Yuba River, playing with the bait on a hook—with Alemby and Cole holding the line.

"Now, why would two good Republicans, like you, be going against an old county favorite son, like Jack Campbell?" Henry asked. He drew smoke through his pipe as he spoke.

Cole smiled. "Why Senator, you know there are those of us who are *true* Republicans, and there are those who aren't. Now our man here, Francis Campbell—he is a *true* Republican."

Henry's critical eye surveyed the bright blue eyes of the new contender. He was about Henry's age, with a little gray showing at his temples.

Finally Henry spoke, "I must be looking at a man who voted for Garfield."

"That you are!" Campbell nodded.

Garfield! Now that name was like music to my ears. Not because of his life, but because of the events following his death. A year before, in July, some filthy swine shot the President of the United States, James Garfield. It was a dastardly act that caused our President a long, lingering, two month death. The fact that the assassin was a Republican—killing one of his own, didn't hurt my feelings. The motive was apparently to see our Vice-President in office. The only good coming out of such a horrifying event was that it split the Republican Party.

There were now those Republicans, like Henry, who felt betrayed; and others who never liked Garfield to begin with. The later were men who Henry considered cowardly mongrels. Jack Campbell showed signs of being one of the later.

Holding his pipe in his left hand, Henry held out his right and shook hands with the tall stranger. "You have my support, Francis H. Campbell."

The gleam in the eyes of Dan Cole and Dr. Alemby Jump was the one you see on a fisherman when he sets the hook. It was as easy as that. They caught a mighty big fish.

With Henry back on their team, victory was assured—but this time, it seemed, they would be fighting other Republicans for their own party's nomination. Once the party's nominee was chosen, *then* they would take on the Democrats. A battle like this could get pretty hot; it all depends on how many enemies they made among themselves.

For Henry to back an unknown, against a popular candidate, like Jack Campbell, indicated just how badly the local Republican Party was split. That was good news! The bad news was, of course, that Henry was back in the game.

CHAPTER TWENTY-SIX - 1882

Distance—a problem our county has wrestled with from its beginning. The way a bird flies, nothing is very far away, but wagons and horses don't have wings. The treacherous Sierra Nevada Mountains, that mark most our territory, are outlined with deep canyons and rushing streams, making it impossible to go anywhere in a straight line. Every road and trail had the anatomy of a snake. So the traveler can never be in a hurry, and must pack for the shortest trip and plan to stay awhile—especially in adverse weather.

Because of this geographical problem, those who live outside of our County Seat sometimes find it difficult to attend public meetings—and so, this circumstance gave birth to excessive use of the proxy.

Henry devised his own mathematical equation from this fact: $P = P$, or proxy equals power—and he used it at every opportunity. He would say, "I think it would be a crime if a man couldn't vote at his own party's election, just because of distance, or illness. I'm doing him a favor."

When the Republican County Central Committee met in the Downieville Courthouse, on the first day of July 1882, the vault looked like something little more than a red brick wall.

Henry showed his face at the meeting dressed in a dark serge sack suit, with a matching vest beneath. He wore the jacket open, and next to his heart, within the inside pocket of his coat, he held the proxy for J. K. Walls. Henry had two-vote power—his own and the proxy; but he wouldn't leave it at that. He pressed the fact that Mr. Walls, before his unfortunate decline to attend, had procured the proxy of a Mr. Simon, and therefore Henry thought he was also entitled to this third vote of Mr. Simon's.

Now, the old, stanch, and sympathetic Republican Party might have let Henry get away with it, but not this new group. After loud complaints, disagreement, and shouting of uncomplimentary phrases, Henry was finally allowed only the legal Wall's proxy.

I enjoyed every delicious word I heard about the bickering that went on at the central committee meeting. These men struggled through every issue, and argued continually about the impending primary election. The voting members were Spalding, McNaughton, James, J. A. Vaughn, Dan Cole, our Henry, and the proxy for J. K. Walls.

Dan Cole and Henry stuck together and managed to get their way on almost every point. Then the project of choosing the delegates to the state convention came up before the committee. This was an important matter. These representatives would ultimately choose the final party candidates. Henry and Dan tried their best to nominate men from the old school, and fought all the way against the new reformers. The custom was for each candidate to submit to an oral examination.

McNaughton insisted on the same old question they always used: "Will you support the Republican ticket at the next general election in November?"

Henry stood. Raising his hand in the air, he said, "I object! I believe we should ask our perspective delegates: 'Did you vote for Garfield, or would you have so voted, if you voted?'"

This suggestion brought several men to their feet with shouts of "NO!" and "That will shut out some otherwise good Republicans."

Henry knew their definition of a "good Republican" differed greatly from his own, so he said, "Well gentlemen, I think the old test just might let in some 'good' Democrats."

Dan Cole stood, and demanded the floor. "Ex-Senator Turner is right! I think we should draft a new question this year."

The arguing continued with nothing decided. Finally the chairman of the committee, J. A. Vaughn, slammed the gavel down on the hard wood table, shouting, "Gentlemen . . . Gentlemen . . . Let's bring this question to a vote. Those in favor of the test 'Will you vote the Republican ticket at the November election?' will signify by saying: aye."

Spalding, McNaughton, and James said, "Aye!" in one accord.

"Now, those opposed, will signify by saying: no."

Vaughn, Cole and Turner, said, "No!" with Turner also voting Walls' proxy, bringing the majority over to his side.

Henry's suggestion for the "Garfield question" was carried.

Next, the problem of setting a date for the local primary came up to vote. Cole and Turner continued to stand firmly united.

With all the innocence of a hungry wolf, McNaughton suggested the primary be called on July 18th—a little over two weeks away. The candidates he supported were well known, and would not need the time it took to travel from one end of the county to the other on a political campaign. His candidate, Jack Campbell, could be elected solely on the popularity of his name.

Once more Turner stood in objection. Speaking for his proxy and himself, he demanded more time, and recommended August 20th—a month longer. Turner's candidate, Francis H. Campbell, was not well known outside of his own home town. He was a newcomer, and would be hurt by a short campaign.

I'm sure Henry felt betrayed when Dan Cole stood, and suggested a compromise of July 22nd, which was accepted by the committee.

After the meeting, Henry took Dan aside, and said, "July 22! What were you trying to do? That isn't going to give us enough time to run a decent campaign."

"I know," Dan said, resting his hand on Henry's shoulder. "But we have to compromise somewhere, Senator. As it is, the *Sierra County Tribune* is going to tear us apart. They'll scream that we were unfair. We only have three weeks left to campaign, so we will have to get to work."

"I'm afraid you cut our throat, Dan."

Dan shook his head. "I truly believe that if people in our county could get to know Francis, they will love him. They will elect him in a minute! He is an incredibly honest man. I've known him for many years now. Did I tell you he is a Sunday school teacher? Not only that—a Sunday School Superintendent, for the Methodist Church in Forest City. Alemby and I have been trying to get Frances active in the party for two or three years now. Sheriff would be perfect. He is a deputy now, for Sheriff Fish, and I am sure he could beat Jack Campbell, if given a fair chance."

Henry had a new black derby hat, which he held in his hands, and twirled it at the brim, absorbed in what his friend had to say. With a tone of forgiveness, he said, "Well Dan, if Frances H. Campbell is everything you say he is, we will just have to work extra hard getting the word around."

Dan smiled. "If we fail, we still have a chance at the convention. We only have to sell him to the Republicans for now."

Henry nodded. "Let's not worry about the general election in November, until we get him on the Republican county ticket."

Dan's hands moved to his hips, elbows outward, as he said, "And you usually get your way at the convention, right? . . . you and your proxy votes."

"I'm doing them a favor, taking their proxy votes," Henry said, as he placed his hat on his head, running his fingers along the brim. "If it weren't for me, they would have no voice at all!"

"Your proxy really saved us a lot of argument today," Dan said. "As soon as McNaughton found out you held the deciding vote, he didn't complain half as much."

"We're losing our magic, Dan. A few years ago, we could have swayed any committee, or convention, with our sweet talking words. We've always tried to be honest . . . and we've had good men. Now look at us. We have to depend on the proxy."

* * *

The north section of Sierra County is one of the most beautiful places I have ever seen; Laden with the type of dense forest and wild life that makes a wise man stick to the trail, for fear of getting lost. The mountains sweep upward to elevations of over 8,000 feet, topped with jagged rock formations which are hidden by snow throughout much of the year. Clear water streams cut passes through these mountains. Unless the miners upstream are stirring up the mud, the water ripples over the rocks reflecting a beautiful color of turquoise. In a short distance, the elevation drops to a low 2750 feet at a place called Goodyear's Bar.

To campaign in Sierra County, a politician has to take all of this into account. Downieville, our county seat, is the largest city in the county, but up in the surrounding hills are hundreds of voters hidden away in places like Shoo Fly, Shady Flat, Yellow Jacket Point, and Slap Jack Ranch. I think it would be impossible to reach everyone in the three weeks time the Republicans allotted their new candidates.

However, Francis Campbell did make a quick tour through the north section of the county, just a few days before the primary election. What impression he made on the Republican voters turned out to be of little importance, because the election was really decided at the local Downieville Republican Convention held August 17th.

My interest in local Republican Conventions has always been

limited to a defensive speculation—discovering what names would be found on the opponent's ballot. But, with Henry once again at the helm, I was curious to see just which way the wind would blow this rival vessel. And the wind indeed did blow. It turned out to be a hurricane, with poor Henry caught in the midst.

The convention began in the normal fashion, and as Henry's eyes surveyed the crowded meeting room, he must have sorted out his colleagues, and estimated a large enough number to give him a false sense of security.

Not long into the proceedings, a motion came from the floor to vote for all the candidates by secret ballot.

Henry jumped to his feet. "I object!" he yelled. "Each of us should be able to express our reasons for voting, for our candidates, in a loud and enthusiastic voice!"

Anger flushed Henry's face, and the pitch of his voice increased with each word. "Too many of our perspective delegates are not *true* Republicans."

The chairman's cold, hard eyes met his, and he said, "If there be no further objections, we will continue. There is a motion on the floor that the election of all candidates should be by secret ballot. Is there a second to this motion?"

"I second the motion," someone shouted from the back of the room.

Henry stood straight and tall. He spoke with a tone of desperation in his voice, "I object! Each delegate has the right to cast his vote with viva voice! I object strongly to the motion on the floor."

This kind of behavior was extremely out of order, for someone with Henry's knowledge of decorum. He was losing control.

The chairman continued, "Your objection has been noted, Mr. Turner. Now, if we may continue . . . A motion has been made and seconded, that the election of all candidates be by secret ballot. If there be no further objection, we will put the motion to a vote."

"I have further objection!" Turner shouted, "In fact, I have not yet begun to express the enormity of my objection."

The chairman slammed his gavel loudly on the podium. "Mr. Turner, you are out of order. We have already noted your objection."

"The hell you have! You haven't even had a taste of it. I am not the only one in this assembly of honorable Republicans that object to your conspiracy. I know exactly what you are trying to do! I believe there are a few in this room who are apparently ashamed of whom they are going to vote for. They have no more intention of following the will of their constituents, than they have of keeping the quartz and throwing away the gold. I tell you right now, that if those lily-livered cowards, who are afraid to cast their votes in the presence of the entire convention, get their way, and pass this motion—I will walk out! I will not sit in a convention where I am being denied the privilege of giving the reasons for my choice."

Throughout Henry's windy speech, the sound of the chairman's gavel echoed with authority, while he shouted, "You are out of order, Mr. Turner!"

Henry ignored him. "There are a few other *loyal* Republicans who feel the same. Am I right boys? Cone on, speak up . . . George? Dan? Alemby? Francis?"

The men stood as he called them by name. "That's right!" they shouted. "We'll walk out with the senator!"

Alemby Jump shook his fist. "We are not going to sit in a convention of cowards, who are afraid to back up their candidates with enthusiastic proclamations!"

The chairman quit slamming his gavel, and yelled above the confused murmur of the crowd. "If there be no further objections, we will continue. There is a motion on the floor that the election of all candidates should be by secret ballot. All those in favor signify by saying, aye."

"AYE!" was the chorus of voices from separate holdouts around the room.

"Those opposed?"

"NO!" came the equally loud shout that echoed across the convention floor.

"Since there are a majority of ayes, the motion is carried. The election of all candidates will be by secret ballot," the chairman said, without batting an eye. His gavel came down hard on the podium, with a final blow.

Loud moans, sharp gasps, and angry grumbles, started as a rumble, and grew into an emotional roar. Henry slowly surveyed the room until his eyes rested on, and glared at the podium, and the man of authority who stood there. Then he turned slowly, and walked from the Convention Hall. One by one, others followed him out of the door. A total of 23 votes left that day—some just paper proxies. But most were two-footed, red-blooded, Republican delegates.

CHAPTER TWENTY-SEVEN - 1882

Soon after the convention, I stumbled upon the three fallen patriarchs of the Republican Party: Dan Cole, Dr. Alemby Jump, and Henry. They stood in front of J. W. Brown's Hardware Store, on the wooden sidewalk, shaded by the veranda that Mr. Brown attached to this old brick building that had survived the big fire of '64. It's funny, but that is the same building where I first met Henry, when it was Charlie Gilbert's Tin Shop and Hardware Store. Good old Charlie sold it in 1872 to Dan Cole. Dan only kept it a couple of years, and then sold out to J. W. That old hardware store is an important part of Downieville's history. It is like an old friend—a favorite spot for men to gather and tell tales on one another.

The sizzling August sun blazed without pity. The three men held their jackets under their arms, and the sleeves of their white shirts were rolled up to their elbows. In one hand, old Doc Jump held a folded newspaper, which I recognized as the *Sierra Tribune*—the bias publication of the reform Republicans. I couldn't resist the temptation to stop and poke fun at those three quivering towers of strength.

"What's this?" I asked Alemby. "Are you reading the lies of the opposition now?"

Alemby shook his head like a gambler caught with an ace up his sleeve. "I just wanted to see what names they are calling us this week!" He turned to the inside page. "How do you like this one Judge: *traducer*?"

"Traducer? Let me see that . . ." Henry said; as he took the paper from Alemby, and read aloud, "Jack Campbell and his traducer . . ." Henry cursed. "I don't even know what that means. Where does the editor get these words anyway?"

"It means slanderer," I said. "It means you are libelous. I'm sure the editor means you, Henry. Good old Boss Turner is at it again, leading his flock astray."

The corner of Henry's lip followed his eyebrow in an upward swing, as he handed the newspaper back to the doctor, and asked, "What are you doing in town today, Judge?"

"I was just heading into the hardware store, and couldn't resist handing my condolences to the famous Republican losers—something I seldom get to do!"

"We lost, all right," Dan said. He shook his head, and looked quite discouraged.

Henry slapped him on the back. "Cheer up Dan! We would have lost anyway."

"Oh, you are really encouraging."

"We pulled 23 votes in our walkout," Henry said. He pulled a pipe out of his coat pocked, and began to stuff it with tobacco. "That means there were another 47 votes that were either against us, or undecided. We would have had to pull another 13 votes from that half-hearted crowd! I have turned this over in my mind a dozen times, and the most I could come up with, out of that bunch of turncoats, was six or seven that we may have persuaded. You could have pulled a few more, in your campaign for supervisor, Dan, but getting Francis Campbell in position as the candidate for sheriff was next to impossible. I don't think we had a chance."

Alemby rubbed his stubby chin. "I can't understand how so many good men became so mule-headed."

I was about to mention that *all* Republicans are mule-headed, when Henry said, "That rag in your hand, printed under the guise of a Republican newspaper is partly to blame." He stopped to blow puffs of smoke from his pipe, as he lit the tobacco. "What else did they say about us?"

"They called us a slanderous gang! Listen . . ." Alemby unfolded the newspaper again, and started to read, "'The *Tribune* is going to vindicate the selfish work of these slanderers, and hold them up as a mark for the scorn and contempt, for all honorable men.'"

"They cut to the bone," Dan said.

"They are a bunch of black sheep," Henry growled.

"Don't discredit them too much, Henry. I know some folks who believe every word they read." The doctor spoke as he folded the paper up once more, and stuffed it under his arm.

"Well, if they read this *Tribune* garbage, they deserve to be misled. *The Mountain Messenger* will tell them the truth, if they want to know what's what." Henry held his pipe clamped between his teeth, as he talked.

"We are just lucky that Vaughn is on our side. As long as he is editor of the *Messenger,* we have a voice," Dan said.

Henry and Alemby nodded in agreement. Then, as if my presence made me a confidant, Henry asked, "Well boys, what are we going to do now?"

As if reading my mind, Dan looked my direction, and said, "This is a strange battle we're getting into. It's not so much against Jack Campbell or the other candidates—it is against the Reform Republicans."

Henry took the pipe out of his mouth, and gazed at Dan. "Well . . . the only way I know of to fight them, is to aim at their top three candidates. The ones we didn't get to cast our vote against—because of their conspiracy."

My mind flashed to the write-up in the newspaper. He would aim against Wallis, candidate for state senator; Nelson, running for the assembly; and the third would either be the sheriff or supervisor seat.

"I think we should ignore the supervisor seat," Doc said. "People might think it is a grudge fight, and that could make it pretty bad for Dan in the future."

Henry nodded in agreement. "We are going to give it to Jack Campbell with all we've got!"

I'm sure I saw a gleam of a hungry hunter in Henry's eyes.

Dan took off his hat, and ran his fingers through the thick mop of dark hair, tinged with gray. "I don't know if I understand what you're saying, Henry." His eyes darted in my direction, and an uncomfortable blush crossed his cheeks. "Are you suggesting that we back the Democrats? I've never voted democratic in my life, and, pardon me Judge, but I don't think I want to start now!"

"It is not like the old days," Alemby said, with an impatient smile. "Republican and democratic platforms are now so similar, that it is hard to tell them apart. Isn't that right Judge?"

Totally embarrassed, with three pairs of Republican eyes waiting for an answer, I said, "That's why these third parties like the Workingmen's Party, keep surfacing." I thought I covered my bias very well.

The fire had apparently gone out in Henry's pipe. He chewed on the stem, and mumbled. "I'm to the point where I think I would rather vote democratic, than follow those cut-throat, lying, Garfield killing, reform Republicans."

Alemby nodded in agreement, and said, "I don't like this new

Republican movement either. I'm willing to throw my fists into the fight."

Dan shook his head. "I don't know. There must be some other way to do it."

Henry took the pipe out of his mouth, and sighed. "Look at it this way, Dan. The Democrats are running Mead for sheriff. He's run before, and lost. He doesn't have a prayer of a chance against Campbell. Jack will win! But . . . he is going to have to give it one hell of a fight. For the Assembly, we have the incumbent, Nelson—he has the election in his hand. Who is your candidate, Judge? Farley?"

I nodded.

"Well," Henry continued, "he doesn't have a prayer either. But, I would love to see Nelson shake in his boots! I want to see him dig in his pockets and spend a little money on this campaign!"

Alemby grinned so wide his teeth showed, but Dan squinted and gave no indication of giving in.

"And then there is Rawdon, the Democrat's choice for senator." Henry looked my way. "You democrats haven't won a senatorial seat in our county for well over ten years, and I doubt if your luck will change with this election. Our man Wallis will win. But, why not make it difficult? Let's show the Republican Party that we mean business. They are either going to act in a true Republican manner, or split the party."

Alemby nodded. "That's the spirit!" he exclaimed.

Dan's head moved in a slow affirmative nod. "I guess you're right, Henry. But, *you* don't have anything to lose. I guess I don't either . . ." His slow head shake began to move from side to side in a negative gesture, as a sad frown crossed his face. "I just lost my chance for re-election as supervisor of district two, when I stood up for what I believed, and joined your walkout."

Henry reached out and grabbed Dan's arm, just above his rolled up sleeve. "All right then, let's fight!"

Our little group broke up, and we went our separate ways. I found myself puttering around inside the hardware store, totally forgetting what errand had brought me there. My mind buzzed with the question of loyalty. Were these strong men joining forces with me, against their own Republican brothers, or had I just been smoothly swept up in one of Henry Turner's famous decoys.

CHAPTER TWENTY-EIGHT - 1882

It was late summer, but there was coolness in the air. A gentle breeze quietly picked up a single golden leaf from the branch of one of the trees near the bridge in Downieville, and softly sailed it to the ground.

I don't remember now why I was walking down the street in front of Henry Turner's rented house, but there I stood looking at the lovely form of Ottie Turner. She waved her hand and smiled, shouting out, "Hello Judge" as she walked down the path from her porch to the gate.

I returned here smile with all the warmth a man gives to a young lady he has known from girlhood.

"You just missed Henry," she said, guessing (wrongly) that was the reason for my unexpected appearance.

She pointed down the road toward the slim form of a man bounding off toward town, dwarfed by the steep mountain behind him.

I removed my hat, and for a moment we both stood there watching him disappear around a distant corner. Ottie said, "Do you know how many years I've spent watching Henry walk off, or ride away on one of his political endeavors?" I squinted at the thought of all the years that had flown by so quickly. "I couldn't guess," I confessed.

"Thirteen years! It sounds terribly unlucky, doesn't it," she laughed.

I shook my head, and smiled.

"Downieville hasn't changed much in all that time." She stood there, looking toward the steeple of the Catholic Church, where it rose up behind the St. Charles Hotel. The steeple stood like a sentinel on the barren hillside that only the old-timers could remember being covered with the dark foliage of the evergreen trees all along the deep canyon walls.

"What I miss most," I said, "is the silly laughter of two giggly little girls I used to know."

"We were silly, weren't we?"

"You were charming."

"It's funny, but I remember so clearly the day when Henry came into papa's store, looking for a school teacher. Aggie and I thought he was old! Now, I wonder why he never changes. He is 52, you know, and doesn't look much different than he did the day we met. Meanwhile, Aggie and I age with every year."

"If you and Aggie are getting old, then I must be antique!"

"I was just thinking out loud," Ottie said. She wiped her hands on the apron tied around her waist. "It's just that Henry has a new spirit in his life lately—a new bounce to his step. Whatever this new political battle is, it has put something back into his life that has been missing since he left the Senate."

"Politics has a way of getting into your blood."

"I guess so."

Ottie looked at her rough hands, which were beginning to show chapped redness around the knuckles. Her life in Downieville could not be compared to those affluent days in Sacramento. A slight frown shaded the old familiar twinkle in her eyes. Rachel once had that same sparkle when she was the young adventurer, and I saw it die as she bend down on her hands and knees, and scrubbed the hard wooden floor of our cabin; and when she leaned over a scrub board above a steaming tub of dirty laundry.

"Look at my hands, Judge!" Ottie held them up for me to see. "My life has been reduced to a world of buckets. There are buckets of vegetable peelings to feed to the chickens, buckets of left over scraps to feed to the pig, buckets of lard to be made into soap, buckets of ashes to take to the outhouse, and buckets of tea leaves to sprinkle on the carpet when I sweep."

"I guess you didn't have to bother with raising chickens and pigs in Sacramento," I said.

"We most certainly did not! And, I *bought* soap at the local mercantile store for a small amount of cash. Senator's wives do not save lard." Ottie's outspoken words surprised me. I was used to seeing her younger, gentler side.

"I thought I'd die back at the ranch, when Henry had to get up long before the rooster, and help with the milking. I don't know how Aggie can stand it!" She rubbed at her rough fingers. "Look at my hands! And, I used to send our dirty clothes to the Chinese Laundry. The worst part is, that I'll have to go back to the valley as soon as Henry finishes the vault—and then it will be chores from sunrise to sunset—every day!"

"There is no rest for the wicked," I said, raising my eyebrows and peering at her with a fatherly smile.

"I'm sorry, Judge," she laughed. "I do carry on so. Aggie and I are so close, that sometimes I think of you as my father. I didn't mean to complain. It is just that the children have been under my feet all summer, and those confounded buckets are lined up in the kitchen waiting to be taken to their destinations!"

A door slammed, and Frank tripped down the walk, with Mary skipping behind, arguing about whose turn it was to gather the eggs. "Don't slam the door! I just got the baby down." Aggie frowned. "The poor thing was up all night with a cough."

The children smiled when they saw me, and each one said hello.

Ottie said, "Frank, I want you to clean out the chicken coop—and be careful that the chickens don't go into the neighbor's flower garden again."

Frank's shoulders swooped down in a soulful slouch, and he politely said, "Okay, Ma," and turned toward the back yard.

"And make sure the chickens have fresh water..."

"I didn't slam the door, Ma. It was Frank," Mary said, as she looked upward with those big, bright, always innocent eyes.

I slipped my hat on my head, said goodbye, and wandered on down the street, as the two young Turner women walked back toward the house.

* * *

Henry's job in Downieville was easily defined: construct a brick vault as an annex to the Sierra County Courthouse. But, as usual, the ex-senator felt duty bound to much more important things: demolishing the Republican county ticket! This was like some fantasy come true for me, and I'm sure it must have been fulfilling a horrible nightmare—totally unreal—for Henry.

Dan Cole never did join the protest as strongly as Henry and Alemby Jump would have wished. Those two men began a smear campaign against Jack Campbell, like the county had never seen in all its years of dirty politics. They resurfaced an old suspicion we Democrats applied three years earlier, when we ran Mead for sheriff against their candidate. We claimed that when Mr. Fish was sheriff, he had not collected the proper liquor licenses. The smear worked well for us, and caused a full Grand Jury Investigation. Of course, Mr. Fish, an honest and upright republican from the state of Maine, was exonerated. The charges were fabricated, and I suppose it looked bad for Mead when it was all over.

I have to admit, I was not surprised to see Henry apply the same rotten tactics. Nothing works faster than repeating a suspicion already planted in the public's mind.

Henry and Alemby heaped coals on the cinders when they dug out the fact that, when Jack Campbell was sheriff, a few years back, Mr. Fish was his deputy—and collected the liquor licenses. That really set the tongues to wagging.

In all the local gossip spots, I heard comments like: "Do you think Jack Campbell was honest when he collected the liquor licenses? You know what a card he is—everyone's friend." and "You don't suppose he was getting kick-backs, do you? Special favors from the tax payers that he let slip by?"

Then, or course, we Democrats joined in the fun with our own ammunition, dropping comments like: "I sure wouldn't want to elect someone for sheriff if he's the kind of man who turns his head, and doesn't do his sworn duty!"

We should have given Henry an award for his choice remark, "Just check the records and you'll find out the truth."—a statement that dipped with intimidation. Of course, no one would bother to check out the facts, and such a statement from a prominent man, such as Henry, indicated that he could back up the claim with proof—which, of course, he couldn't, because the entire line of gossip was untrue.

As the insinuations got deeper, Henry and Alemby were labeled as "bolting mud slingers" by the *Sierra Tribune*. And, the more the derogatory names were flung at the two angry Republicans, the deeper the mud got. They didn't care. They were supporting Mead for sheriff—an honest and upright man, someone you could trust. I reveled in delight.

It was fun having Henry on our side for a change, and I enjoyed stopping by the construction site from time to time, just to chat.

"Well, Henry," I said one day, "I see that hanging around our county seat has given you a more *democratic* view of politics!"

Henry put down his trowel and pulled a rag out of his back pocket to wipe his hands. "How are you doing, you old buzzard," he said, with a smile. "You keep hanging around the courthouse. Are you waiting for the Republicans to drop?"

"Yep! And I understand they are dropping like flies!"

"Well, I figured it was time we experts showed you a thing or two. You old Democrats never did figure out how to beat the superior party."

"There is nothing I enjoy more, that watching Republicans fight with each other. It makes our job so much easier."

Henry shook his head and smiled. I decided that I won our little battle of wit that day—a rare delight, when challenged by someone of his expertise.

After a silent moment or two, I asked, "Have you and Ottie been down to the valley lately?"

Henry shook his head and stared back at the vault. "Haven't had a minute."

"I was just wondering how they are doing."

"I hope they are getting more sleep than we are. Our baby is almost a year old, and hasn't figured out the difference between night and day yet."

In the spring, Aggie's wishes came true, and she had her little girl—a pretty thing that Rachel talked about all the time.

"I kind of like the new little granddaughter," I told Henry. "She reminds me of Aggie, when she was a baby—actually the boys do too. One thing about you Turners, you've got a lot of boys!"

Henry sighed. "Uh-huh . . . don't tell Ottie, but I wish this one would have been a boy. I like the girls—love the girls—Mary and Lottie—but Frank is great. It's a blessing to have a son to help out on the ranch."

Henry had only half of my attention. My mind still pondered Aggie's newest little one. "I don't know where they got her name: Daisy. I thought 'Rachel' would be nice—after her grandma, you know. She would have been so tickled! But they decided to name it after a flower—and an ordinary one at that! They should have named her Rose."

A bead of sweat trickled down Henry's face, beneath his old floppy hat, and he caught it with the back of his hand, as it reached his cheek. "Last time I talked to Hart was when he brought up a load of bricks. He talked about building a sawmill. He is pretty serious about it, and wants us to be partners. Those danged grasshoppers have destroyed the dairy and cattle business in the valley—we've got to turn to something else, if this plague doesn't end."

I know my blue eyes betrayed the pride I had developed for my son-in-law, and I said, "Hart is a pretty ambitious young man. Aggie is a lucky girl."

"Ambitious?" Henry squinted. ". . . hard working, maybe."

"Last time I saw Hart he told me all about that sawmill dream of his. He sure is excited. When do you think you will have this vault finished?"

Henry shook his head. "The board has given me until September first, and I *would* like to stay in Downieville as long as I can, so I will probably string the job out until then."

"Too bad," I said. My mind reflected Hart's big plans. "That sawmill is pretty important to Hart, and he can't wait until you return to the ranch."

Henry sighed, "I suppose . . ."

The frown that crossed Henry's brow made me actually feel sorry for him. "You like being next to all the political fireworks, don't you Henry?"

He raised his eyebrows. "I should have been your son, Judge."

I laughed, and said, "I would *never* have a Republican for a son!"

CHAPTER TWENTY-NINE - 1882

Every season that touched Sierra Valley painted it with breathtaking splendor. Nippy autumn nights and breezy September days set the Quaking Aspen trees dancing in brilliant golden shades of yellow—like a sun, not sure it wanted to set. While the leaves still clung to the trees, Henry returned to his Valley home. Rachel and I were delighted when we were invited to join the Turner clan at Church's Corners for the big homecoming of Henry's family.

September 1882: reunion time.

Hart's chest ballooned with pride, as he welcomed the family into his home. His years of loving labor changed the small cottage into a fine large house—bigger than the Senator's place down the hill. It was a good thing too, because those little tykes of his never stood still a minute, and as they grew in size, it always seemed like more children raced around the place than actually belonged there. Aggie and Hart's family now numbered six; Henry and Ottie's totaled five; and at these get-togethers, Frank and Hattie Campbell always showed up, and they had three boys of their own. Then, of course, there were George and Rachel Hale; and the wife and me. It was quite a gathering.

The men always took to the front porch to talk, while the women gathered in the kitchen, and prepared a massive supper for the hungry crew. The children . . . well, they were all over the place.

Henry was the center of our attention that day, as he tried to explain his recent behavior to his Republican family clan: Hart, George Hale, and Frank Campbell. I tried to not grin too widely, as I listened and watched him squirm.

"You sure have created a stir here in the valley," Hart said, with worry pouring from his voice.

"Not just in the valley, Henry, but in the entire county!" George growled.

Henry said, "I hope we caused more than just a stir around here. I thought we caused a full-fledged rumble!"

Frank Campbell leaned forward in his chair, pulled a cigar out of his pocket, and bit off the tip. He offered one to me, and I gladly accepted. Frank was strangely silent that day. 1882 began as a beautiful year for the Sierra Valley Campbells, when Hattie gave birth to a pretty little girl, who they named for Hattie's mother,

Calista. But their joy lasted only a few short months, as the baby died in July—barely six months old. 1882 continued on for most of us, but it ended that tragic day in July, for Frank and Hattie. Frank became withdrawn and silent. I guess that was when he started smoking cigars, because I never saw him smoke before then.

When I lit my cigar, Hart asked, "But *why*, Henry? I know you don't like the new position some of the Republicans have taken, but by thunder, I sure never thought you'd ever be backing the Democrats!" He glanced in my direction, "No offence intended, Judge."

I held out my cigar. "None was taken, Hart."

George asked Frank if he had any more cigars. Frank found one, handed it to his father-in-law, and lit it for him; while Henry told his brother, with a few vulgarities thrown in, just what he thought of the new reform Republican movement.

Hart shook his head. "But Henry, in all the years you've campaigned before, you never resorted to mudslinging. Why now?"

"The mud was never so deep before!"

"Well, I guess I just don't understand," Hart said, with a big sigh.

The conversation switched then, and we talked about everything from the big building plans for the sawmill, to the rustic logging camps and robust lumberjacks of Maine and Canada, compared to the leathery hard-working boys that took over the woods in the West.

The day went by quickly, and soon the entire mob gathered around an extended table. The visiting stopped only momentarily when the blessing was given, and we began to feast on a wonderful meal of roast goose, with buttered carrots, and large baked potatoes grown in Turner's famous potato patch.

After clearing off half of his plate, Hart said, "If we are going to build this sawmill, Henry, your political days are over for awhile. I'll need all of your attention, and help. You can't go off on anymore campaigns."

"Don't worry. After this election, it will be all business for me—all lumber business. I've talked to Dan Cole quite a bit this summer. You know, he owns two mills up past Downieville. He gave me a lot of advice. We should have started this project years ago."

Hart searched his brother's hazel, blue-gray, always-changing-color eyes.

Henry smiled. "Really . . . I promise. I'll be around to help."

CHAPTER THIRTY - 1882

Hart didn't give Henry a minute to rest. The following morning the two men were up on the hill outlining every detail of a brand new sawmill.

Fall lingered on, and disguised itself brilliantly in the heat of Indian summer—warm and tranquil. However, the lull in the weather was as misleading as the sudden reduction of verbal assaults against Jack Campbell, which followed Henry's departure from the political front lines in Downieville.

When the wind came, it blew in from the north—cold and threatening. The kind of wind that makes a man pull the collar of his coat up around his neck, and glance knowingly at the darkened sky. It was the last days of September, sometime around the 22nd of the month.

Jack Campbell had sold the Hot Springs, and moved temporarily into a small house built on the Randolph side of Sierraville. He planned to move up to Downieville as soon as he won the position of sheriff in the upcoming election.

One year earlier, in August, the entire business section of Sierraville burned to the ground, and since then its sister city, Randolph, became the center of activity on the south end of the valley. Most of the merchants in Sierraville were insured, and they quickly rebuilt, but the clatter of hammers and saws chased a lot of the thirsty noon day trade down the road to either Cody's Saloon, or the Buxton Hotel, in the village of Randolph. On any given afternoon, you could likely find Jack Campbell in one of these two favorite watering holes, telling one of his famous stories, in that contagious Irish brogue of his.

Another Sierraville resident that could frequently be found in Randolph was George Wood. George was a lawyer with one of the finest collections of law books I had ever seen—they all went up in smoke during the fire, but with the insurance payment, he not only rebuilt his office, but I heard he started up a new library.

The events of that September day were told to us by the Turner's neighbor, Alex Beaton, who would not quickly forget the ride to Sierraville to visit his old friend, George Wood. It was the noon hour, when the two men left the law office and began to walk down the road toward Randolph. The usually easy going Alex woke up that morning in a fine disposition, but the day began with his horse refusing to co-operate, and then his wife requested he pick up a few things in town for her, and then George decided he didn't want to saddle up his horse, and would rather walk the mile to Cody's Saloon. By this time Alex's mood was as foul as the weather.

When a gust of icy cold wind blew down George's neck, he grabbed at his hat, and kept it from blowing off, then glanced over at his friend. Alex had his coat pulled up at the collar. His lips were pressed together as he pushed forward, leading his horse behind.

"You were right, Alex. I should have saddled my horse."

Alex just mumbled something that could have been mistaken for distant thunder—far off in the gloomy, dark sky. He pulled his arms closer to his body.

The two men were not alone on the road. Skipping down the street, with her pigtails bouncing behind her, and the wind whipping at her dress, was a little eight year old girl named Elsie Williams. The cheerful innocence of this child softened Alex's disposition. He was reminded of his own little girl, just about the same age.

As she came alongside the men, she smiled up at Alex, and slowed down to a walk, as she admired Alex's horse.

"Where are you going in such a hurry?" Alex asked.

"I'm going to fetch Uncle Jack. He's supposed to come home for supper now."

"You better hurry along, or you'll catch your death of cold!" Alex said.

As the girl passed them she skipped backwards with her back against the wind, her eyes still drawn to Alex's horse.

"That's Jack Campbell's niece," George said. "He never had any children of his own."

Alex recollected the story. Jack's wife, Maggie, had a sister with four kids, who were left orphans, so the Campbells took them in—they kept their parent's name—Williams.

"Aren't there four of them?" Alex asked.

"Um-hmmm . . ." George mumbled an affirmative sound. His eyes were riveted on a scene further up the road. There in the middle of the street, some distance off, stood the towering form of Jack Campbell. Traffic was at a standstill during this noon hour, and a couple of horses were tied in front of the saloon. A young man sauntered down the one step which led to the street from the porch of the Buxton Hotel. He approached the burly Irishman, just as the first roll of thunder clashed some distance away.

The two men talked briefly, and it looked as if Jack were spinning another of his yarns. Suddenly, the younger man pulled out something hidden beneath his coat, and ended their conversation with a shot through Jack Campbell's chest.

George grabbed Alex by the arm and gasped, "My God, Alex, he's been shot!" With those words George began to run down the road.

Alex, a man of slow deliberate action, couldn't get his feet to move. He realized that Elsie had turned in the road just in time to witness the bloody event. She stood rooted to the ground. Her eyes stared straight ahead, unblinking, like a night flying owl. She clasped her hands in front of her lips.

"Here, now, girl . . ." Alex went to her, and bent down on one knee. "You'd better not go down there. Let's go back home and get your Aunt Maggie."

Alex felt the little girl's body tremble in his hands as he lifted her to his horse, and climbed up behind her. Swiftly they turned toward Campbell's house, to relay the unwelcome news. A bolt of lightning flashed across the sky, not touching the ground, and when the thunder clashed, a few seconds later, Elsie began to cry.

Jack Campbell fell slowly to the ground, while the man with him glanced from side to side in fear. Cody raced out of the saloon. He waved his arms in the air, as he yelled at the assailant. The desperate man pointed the gun at Cody, daring him to come closer, and for a moment Cody stopped. The pause was long enough for the stranger to find a route of escape. He turned and ran off between the store and saloon.

George Wood reached Campbell's crumpled body at about the same time as Cody and some of the other men from the saloon and hotel. The brawny Irishman lay in a crumpled heap, and his face peered up at the blackened sky with a vacant humorless stare, while his life's blood oozed onto the dusty road, from a hole ripped savagely through his once white shirt.

"Is he dead?" a nameless voice asked.

Mr. Buxton, from the hotel, shouted, "Quick, let's get him inside! Someone fetch the doctor!"

"It's too late," George said.

"Grab his feet!" Buxton demanded, and George lifted one leg, while Cody reached for the other. With the help of Mr. Buxton, Mr. Dolley, and a few other men who had quickly gathered around, they were able to lift the lifeless body. Campbell was a powerful man, and in this awkward, unconscious state, his weight seemed to triple.

The excitement brought the street to life, and people raced about accomplishing nothing, as they gathered into small groups, and muttered to one another: "I think he's dead.", "Murdered!", "Who did it?", "Who shot him?", "I heard it was Dode Stubbs!", "Where did he go?", "Where did the murdering rat go?", "Where's the killer?"

At this point, someone mentioned they saw Stubbs race of between the saloon and the store. Some men with rifles, decided to chase after him as they shouted, "Someone killed Jack Campbell! Let's go after him!"

Alex arrived with Campbell's wife Maggie, and a couple of other women, just as this impromptu posse darted between the store and the saloon. Alex guided the women into the lobby of the hotel. Neighbors and friends moved back out of the doorway, to let them pass through. Jack's body lay on a long table. A small group of silent men stood a solemn watch, and several curious wide eyes peered through the dirty window glass, from the connecting porch.

When Alex went to fetch Maggie, he told her that Jack had been shot, but neither she, nor Alex, had any idea that Campbell had been killed. As the first wave of widowhood flooded Maggie's spirit, she lost consciousness, and collapsed in a dizzy fainting spell, while the other women held her, and whispered prayers that consisted only of the Savior and His precious name.

George Wood took Alex by the arm, and led him out onto the porch, past the onlookers, and into the dusty street. In a whisper, he said, "Alex, you better hurry back to Church's Corners, and tell Henry about this. Tell him he better arm himself. It doesn't look good. I expect someone will be coming after him."

"What!" Alex exclaimed. "Henry has nothing to do with this!"

George glanced back toward the hotel. "I know that—and you know that, but I also know he make quite a handful of political enemies lately. Politics can become a vicious game, and this time Henry may be caught right in the middle of it. Someone will have his neck for this, I'm sure of it."

Alex had come to trust George, during their many years of friendship. Besides his law practice, George had invested in several small business establishments. He seemed to have a lot of common sense, and a sharp mind. He knew the political battlefield well, and held the esteemed position of Representative to the State Assembly—Republican of course. Alex's interest in politics could only be described as passive, and he seldom questioned either George or Henry on their political judgments, so reluctance on his part was an exception. He shook his head in protest. "Henry would never even consider something as evil as this. Everyone knows that! He is one of the most honest men I know."

"Believe me Alex, there are some who would use this to see him destroyed, one way or another."

Alex was still not convinced, and shook his head from side to side.

"Do it Alex! Just do it!" Anger recoiled in George's voice. "Just pass the word to Henry. He will want to know."

"All right..." Alex said.

Still not convinced, he turned toward where his horse was tied.

* * *

Alex had lived in Sierra Valley for twelve years, and was no stranger to the inconsistency in the weather. He always kept his long, serviceable mackintosh tied to the back of his saddle. He put it on before he left Randolph, and as he rode along the fence line of Jared Strang's ranch, he watched the lightening flash feverishly across the sky, over his left shoulder. The rumble grew closer and closer. As he turned his horse onto the road which led to the Turner Ranch, the rain began to fall.

Ottie fidgeted nervously from chore to chore, while Mary sat by the window and watched for her father. She saw a rider approach from the direction of Church's Corners. The rain fell in torrents from the clouds, like a bursting dam, and it was hard to identify the approaching figure. When the horse turned toward the house, Mary raced to the door, saying, "Ma, there's a rider! He's coming this way. I think he is going to stop."

Ottie hurried to open the door. She rested her hand on the young girls shoulder, and peered through the onslaught. Vaguely she thought she recognized the stranger, who hovered on his horse—water pouring from his hat and down the sides of his mackintosh. Then she knew for sure it was Alex Beaton, when he spoke with that familiar, slight Scotch accent, "Is Henry around?"

Anxiety showed in Ottie's voice when she answered, "No Alex, he's not. He and Frank went up the canyon this morning with Hart. They are making plans for a water line to run to the mill. I'm sure they saw this storm coming, and headed back. Maybe they are up at Hart's."

Alex tipped his hat, and water dripped down in front of his face. He turned his gelding up the road toward Hart's house.

Light from the oil lamps outlined the windows as Alex tied his horse to the porch post. He tried to shake off as much dampness as he could before he knocked on the door. He took off his hat, and shook the water from the brim.

The door opened and the warm sound of laughing children drifted outward toward the storm.

"Alex! What a pleasant surprise," Aggie said, and then realized that no one would brave this weather unless there was an emergency. With sudden urgency she motioned him inside, "Is everything all right?"

Alex held his dripping wet hat in front of him, as he glanced around the room and found Henry seated at a table with his brother. There were papers scattered between them. They were drinking coffee and discussing business. Alex said, "I'm afraid I bring bad news."

All eyes stared in his direction, and all ears perked anxiously, as the wind whipped against the side of the house, and rain dripped noisily into puddles, from the roof.

Alex cleared his throat. "I just rode in from Randolph. Jack Campbell has been shot."

Denial is a strange and unpredictable thing. Henry heard Alex's words, but his usually sharp mind refused to accept the depth of the information that Alex was trying to relate. Jack was shot . . . in the arm? In the leg?

About the worst thing that could happen to Henry at this point in his campaign against his fellow Republicans, was for the object of his mudslinging to be violently killed. So, it couldn't be that tragic. Henry thought it *had* to be an accident—probably a minor wound.

The thought of Jack being laid up in bed for the rest of the campaign brought a smile to Henry's face. He shook his head at Alex, and said, "I suppose he wants sympathy! Wonderful—it will probably get him elected. Of course, he didn't have to go that far. He would have been elected anyway."

The color began to drain from Alex's face as he listened—astonished at Henry's response.

"Don't look so sad, Alex," Henry said, still smiling. "This will outshine any hunting story that Jack has ever told."

"Henry . . ." Alex held tightly to his hat with one hand, and reached forward with the other, as he said, "Jack is dead."

Slowly Henry began to realize the truth, and his face became as pale as his friend's. The senator never liked Jack, but he never wished him dead.

Now it was over—the vicious campaign was over. Jack won. Oh, he might be dead, but he cheated Henry out of the joy of the race. Not only had he cheated Henry by getting shot, but the implication of the act was a prize threat. Anger flared in Henry's nostrils. "He can't be dead!"

"I was there, Henry," Alex said softly. "I saw it happen."

Hart's eyes jumped nervously from Henry to Alex. "How did it happen?" he asked. When Alex revealed the details Henry slammed his fist down on the table. He muttered a few curse words. Then looked at Aggie, but couldn't find the words to apologize. He stood and walked to the window, where he stared out at the rain. "What kind of people are they, to let someone shoot a man down on the street, and then just walk away?"

"Do you think this had anything to do with the election?" Hart asked.

Henry turned toward his brother, and said, "I'm sure everyone will think so." A frown rippled his forehead, and his eyebrows cast unfamiliar shadows on his gray eyes, as the flickering light from the oil lamp deepened the lines on his face.

Alex bowed his head toward his feet, and shifted his weight. "I was with George Wood, when it happened. He said I should come and tell you, Henry. He said that maybe . . . Well, maybe you should arm yourself."

Henry nodded in silent agreement.

"I don't think so, but George insisted," Alex continued.

"George is right." Henry's voice was low—slightly above a whisper. "There are three things that make a man mad enough to kill: race, religion, and politics. I sincerely hope I have not been the ignorant instigator of Jack's death."

He turned toward his son, who sat quietly on the floor stacking blocks with his young cousins. "Get your coat, Frank. We better go home."

Alex left with Henry and Frank. "I'm sorry to have brought you such bad news," he said. Then he turned and hurried off toward his own house.

As Henry rode up to the barn, he could see the flashes of lightening up over the hill—probably somewhere near the County Seat. The clash of thunder upset his horse, and he had trouble keeping the animal in control.

Another time, another year, Henry would have welcomed a storm that brought rain to these thirsty mountains. On this day, it only added to the feeling of doom.

Somewhere Henry had been tricked. From some high majestic place in heaven, he knew God was judging this most recent campaign. It was obvious: the angry voice of the thunder roll, the raindrops which only lacked the salt of sweat and tears . . . and the mud. It stuck to the horses' hooves, as he led the poor drenched creatures into the barn. It stuck to his boots, as he walked up to the house. It stuck to his dreams that night. Henry wondered if he could ever stop the storm—if he could ever erase the memory of the mud.

CHAPTER THIRTY-ONE - 1882

The posse—over a hundred strong—searched the roads, alleys, villages, yards, barns and forest; yet they couldn't find a trace of the killer. Loggers, storekeepers, farmers, milkers, even the Indians who camped on the outskirts of Randolph—everyone hunted. It seemed Dode Stubbs vanished in the tall brush behind Dolley's Store.

Dode was not a well known man, before the murder, but within a few days, everyone could describe him, and probably spot him on sight. He was young—only 22 years old. He worked at Rawden's Planing Mill in Randolph, and lived in the Buxton Hotel. Where he got the name Dode, no one knew for sure, because the name signed on the hotel register was J. J. Stubbs. Surprising enough, he did not drink or gamble. However, those who knew him best said he was a hot tempered and foolish young man.

The day before his encounter with Jack Campbell, Dode started a fight with Cody, the saloon keeper. Using a fireplace poker as a weapon, Dode threatened to smash in Cody's skull. Cody is always prepared for his hot tempered clients, and he instantly produced a pistol to defend himself. Stubbs backed down. But, the next day, his friends said that Dode was carrying a gun, and he bragged that folks had seen the last time he would ever back out of a fight. Jack Campbell became the unfortunate next-in-line for an argument with Dode Stubbs.

Soon after that, I heard a vicious rumor which caused Henry to watch his back. It had begun: suspicion and innuendos began circulating, that H. K. Turner might be involved.

"The day prior to the murder," the gossips said, "Someone saw Stubbs exchanging money with a man named Ferguson. What was the money for? Who was this Ferguson fellow? You don't suppose it had anything to do with the election?"

The fact that Henry didn't know any more about it than anyone else, was of no concern to Henry's enemies. Their suggestions and implications made Henry's mudslinging look like a school yard prank.

* * *

The local constable, Henry Slipner, sat at his kitchen table, deep in thought. Stubbs was a reckless man who drew his gun faster than he could think—the kind of man who seldom considered the consequences of his actions. Slipner knew the type well. It was not premeditated murder, he was sure of that. So, Stubbs would have no plan in his mind for a safe retreat. Yet, he disappeared so dramatically, during the noon hour, when the sun was straight up in the sky. It was stormy—yes, but still light, with very little shadows to hide in.

The first impromptu posse had searched the thick brush that grew along both sides of a small creek, behind Dolley's Store and Cody's Saloon, and found no one. In fact, they did such a thorough job, in their hunt, that they destroyed the trail Stubbs might have left. But, Slipner's gut feeling was, there was no trail to follow. Several witnesses saw the desperate murderer slip between the two stores. So, where did he go?

While the posse prowled for answers, Slipner searched, interview, and listened with careful and deliberate attention. Jack Campbell may have had a lot of friends, but Dode Stubbs had a few friends too. Slipner added this information to the fact that the owner of the local store had a reputation for kindness (someone who takes in stray dogs); and the local constable had an idea which probably saved Randolph from seeing more bloodshed that week.

He waited until the sun set, and the moon's glow cast only indistinguishable shadows across the sleepy village. With a search warrant clasped firmly in his hand, Slipner tapped lightly on the door of the little house behind Dolley's Store, where Lynus Dolley lived with his pretty young wife, Amelia.

Amelia let him in. Her swollen belly pushed against the loose fitting, white flannel gown, suggesting that the newest Dolley baby would soon be born. As she led the constable through the house, she leaned backward, with one hand on her waist, and walked with her feet pointed outward.

"Sorry to bother you so late at night," Slipner said.

Mrs. Dolley answered in a soft, quiet voice, "That's all right, Mr. Slipner. I'm glad you came after dark. I hear the folks around town talk of a hanging, and it scares me plum crazy."

Amelia led the constable to a room where a frightened young man quivered in fear. Dode surrendered without a fight.

In the secrecy of the night, Slipner saddled two horses, and led his prisoner a short ways down the road to the south of town. Like two night prowling raccoons, they disappeared into the woods, and wound their way through obscure, lonely trails that led over the mountain to Downieville. Slipner avoided the road that led through Church's Corners, and over Yuba Gap, because he did not want to risk meeting anyone along the route to the county jail. That is how certain he was of a mob lynching.

The two men rode all night, and reached Downieville at eight o'clock the next morning. With a sigh of relief, constable Slipner turned his prisoner over to Sheriff Fish, not just for confinement, but for Stubbs's own protection.

I watched the town of Downieville come alive that day. The turmoil caused by the capture of Jack Campbell's murderer, was magnified, when an hour later a buckboard wagon rolled into town, along the Downieville-Sierra Valley Road, and pulled to a stop in front of the County Hospital. The cargo transferred in this humble wagon, was the body of the slain man—Jack Campbell. A crowd gathered around to watch. The remains were unloaded and handed over to the hands of the County Coroner, Henry Turner's friend and mudslinging partner, Dr. Alemby Jump.

* * *

Alemby held the scalpel above Jack Campbell's chest, and Dr. Sawyer assisted him. Neither man said a word. Outside, the crowd grew larger. They were mostly friends of Campbell's—waiting for the release of the body.

With great skill, and without a single tremble to his hand, Doc Jump did his work. He never wanted it to end this way—autopsy before Election Day. He later told Henry the unspoken words that nagged his mind through the entire procedure: "You son-of-a-gun, always looking for a fight! Well, you got yourself a good one this time!"

After setting the tools aside, and washing the blood from his hands, Alemby wrote the following verdict: *The ball, about 38 caliber, passed directly through the heart, and struck the backbone, where it lodged in the thoracic cavity, and where it was discovered.*

The doctor then surrendered the corpse to a host of the dead man's friends, who delivered the body to the local Masonic Hall, where a few hours later the town folk gathered to pay their respects. Campbell's was one of the largest funerals I ever attended.

Everyone was there. Everyone, that is, except a certain faction of the Republican Party, who, for their own welfare and safety, stayed off the street that day, and out of sight.

* * *

Before the murder, Constable Henry Slipner, and the rest of the leading citizens of Randolph, beamed with pride when they spoke of their little community. The main topic of conversation at the local mercantile store, and among men on the street, was the building of the new water system. With the method of subscription, these men managed to accumulate the $500 they needed to begin the project. They ordered pipe and hydrants; and construction of the reservoir was proceeding on schedule. They watched their neighbor town, Sierraville, engulfed in flames one year earlier, and that instigated this progressive activity.

Then Campbell was shot.

Suddenly, like an unexpected change in the weather, a bad temperament exploded within the town. Young men began carrying side arms, threatening anyone who disagreed with them. Black eyes and bruised swollen faces, shined like badges won in battle. The nods and smiles of the elder citizens, was wiped from the streets, hidden in fear behind closed doors and drawn curtains.

It seemed as if, when the bullet passed through Jack's body, there on the main street of town, his incredible spirit for controversy flowed out, and remained behind to haunt them.

Jack Campbell's eulogy, of course, emphasized his generous side. He always was one to give handouts to the less fortunate. His reputation for generosity mixed with his Irish wit, were the qualities his friends would remember, while his less favorable characteristics were memorialized by his enemies.

Stubbs, the villain with the gun, had drifted into Randolph one year before, got a job at the planing mill, and moved into the Buxton Hotel. Despite his fiery nature, he made friends fast, with equally excitable young men, who were willing to defend his reputation with brute strength.

A story went around, that in the shadowy corner of Cody's Saloon, one of these companions shouted in anger, "Stubbs is a friend of mine, Mister. You better watch what you say about him, unless you want to answer to my fists!"

"You don't look so tough."

"Let's take a walk outside, and I'll show you just how tough I am!"

These young men, who worked with Stubbs in the mill, stacked green lumber all day, and were without question the strongest men in town. A wise man would avoid a competition of physical strength with them, if it were possible to do so without looking like a coward.

So, he would offer a compromise, by asking something like, "How do you know so much about Stubbs, anyhow?"

"I work beside him, mister. You don't work beside a man every day without getting' to know him pretty good."

"He's a killer."

"Campbell asked for it!"

"Nobody asks to be killed."

"Listen. The day before he was shot, Campbell was sitting on the porch of Cody's Saloon, and got in a fight with Ferguson."

"That's not how I heard it."

"Well, you heard wrong."

"I heard Ferguson started the argument. He called Campbell a lot of filthy names—then threw a knife at him."

"Jack Campbell was a trouble maker. He always gave us mill hands a bad time. Then he ran for sheriff. Bull shit! Can you imagine him as sheriff? He'd have us all in jail."

"The word is that Ferguson paid Stubbs to do the killing."

"That's a lie. Fergy don't have to pay no one to do his fighting for him. But, you're right about one thin. If Stubbs hadn't killed him, Fergy probably would have."

"You don't kill a man because he disagrees with you! Campbell liked a good joke, and he got a little pushy sometimes. That's no reason to kill him."

"I guess you could say he finally pushed the wrong man."

"Stubbs killed an unarmed man. Campbell never carried a gun, and everyone knew it. All the years I've known Campbell, he never carried a gun."

"Then he was stupid. I've got my pistol strapped right here on my belt. There ain't no man gonna mess with me—and live to tell about it!"

Just like any other topic of conversation, people get tired and all talked out. It took about two weeks. Black eyes began to heal, and parents no longer jumped at the sound of gunfire, shot in anger by temperamental young men. Amazingly enough, no more blood was shed, and the town returned to its project of building the new water system.

CHAPTER THIRTY-TWO - 1883

The county lost interest in the big election. I guess we were all in shock. A new candidate, named Nicholson, replaced Jack Campbell's name on the ballot, and he lost to Mead. We Democrats finally had our man in office—Sierra County's new sheriff. However, the circumstances around the election threw the damper on our jubilation. We felt we won by default.

It was a long cold winter.

Folks waited for Dode Stubbs's trial, which would be held in the Downieville, at the County Courthouse. But, it was postponed. All the witnesses lived in either Randolph or Sierraville, and once the first storm hit the mountains, no one knew for sure when the big one would follow. Witnesses could not be relied upon to make the long trip in bad weather.

It was a long cold winter.

The progress of Turner's Mill also stopped. Henry never left the ranch much anymore, and spent a lot of time with his family. He got to know his son, Frank.

Together they cleaned out the barn; and before the ground froze over, they took the manure and dug it into next spring's potato patch. They planted onions and garlic. Then when the snow began to fly, they shoveled paths together—a trail to the outhouse, the well, and the barn. They hunted deer, duck and geese; and brought home fresh wild game for the table. They pitched hay to expectant cows, which were kept close to the barn in winter. And, on brisk mornings, when the night air dipped below the freezing mark, they broke ice from the water trough, so the cows could drink.

It was a long cold winter.

Sometime in the early part of 1883, I had an opportunity to travel to Sierra Valley. Our new sheriff, Mead, had business in Sierraville, and knowing I had family down that way, he asked me to accompany him.

He could have traveled by stage, which stationed sleighs at the snow line to take passengers over the mountain, but Mead didn't want to risk the chance of being stranded in Sierraville if the stage decided to cancel its trip back. So he decided to go it on horseback, and preferred not to travel alone. With special snow shoes attached to the horses' hooves, we took the tedious journey over the snow capped mountains, without much trouble.

I despised the boredom of winter, when the mines are closed down, and life is slow. I jumped at the chance to go, and Rachel complained that I would get to see the grandchildren, and she would not.

When we got to the valley, Mead went on to Sierraville, and left me at

Aggie's were I had a wonderful visit, while I waited for Mead's return two days later.

I saw a different man in Henry. Physically, I'd say he had gained years in a few short months since I saw him last. But, the most remarkable change was his attitude. Instead of Downieville being the center of his life, he seemed to have changed his focus onto his family—especially Frank.

Hart, the three grandsons, and I walked single file down the neatly shoveled path to the barn, where we found Henry and Frank inside, resting on a stack of hay.

"I see you two are hard at work again," Hart said, as our boys jumped into the hay to join their older cousin.

"We fed the cows, Uncle Hart," Frank said, "and Pa was just telling me about when you two were boys, back in Maine."

"Burrr . . . You think it's cold here," Hart said. "There's no place colder than Maine."

Henry put his hand on his son's shoulder. "And Frank was telling me about his dreams for the future."

"Yeah, I want to be just like Pa. I want to *do* something for the people. I want to be someone important."

"You will have to go to school Frank, and get an education."

"I go to school, Pa."

"I mean later—high school and college."

"Did you go to college?"

"Sure I did! I went to Bowdoin College in Brunswick, Maine."

The boys all looked at Henry with a new curiosity, but Frank's eyes especially sparkled with admiration. "What's college like, Pa?"

"Bowdoin College was not easy to get in to, son. It is an old established school—I guess it's the oldest college in Maine. Its history goes back as far as 1794. Just to get admitted, I had to prove I could write in Latin, and read the Gospel from the Greek New Testament!"

"You speak Greek?" Harry asked.

Henry shook his head, and looked up in my direction. "I doubt if I could now. That was a long time ago. We had to pass an entrance examination which covered not only Latin and Greek, but also algebra, geography—everything you would expect in a college entrance exam. I remember I was pretty proud to be accepted."

"Did you go to college with him, Pa?" asked young Jim as he looked up at Hart.

"No son, you Uncle Henry is a lot older than I, and Brunswick was several miles to the south. We lived in Whitfield. Your Uncle Henry had to move away from home to go to college."

Henry nodded. "Our father, your grandpa Turner, came west, and I wanted to go with him, but he insisted I go to college. Our ma died when I was just a little boy. Do you even remember her, Hart?"

Hart shook his head sadly. "No. Aunt Mary was the only mother I knew." The children looked puzzled, so Hart explained, "She raised us kids."

Henry nodded. "I never saw Pa again," he said.

My mind returned to that little old man, panning for gold on the Yuba River. I remembered his toothless grin. He was so proud of his sons then, and I knew he would be even prouder of them now.

"Your Grandpa Turner was killed in the mines, near Snake Bar," Hart said to the captivated children.

"And you went on to college and got educated?" Frank asked, obviously prompting his father to tell him more.

"I was 21 years old when your grandfather left for California. That fall I enrolled in college, and really gave it a try, but I was just not college material. I quit after two years."

"Me too, Pa. I'm not college material either. I guess I won't even try!" Frank said, and we all laughed.

Henry grabbed his son's head, and rubbed his hair with a knotted fist. "Oh yes you will. I'm warning you now, so you can study hard, and learn your lessons. Your mother was a school teacher; and she's a smart woman. And two years of college is pretty good for a man of my age, if I do say so myself."

They stood, and tried to brush off some of the hay from their clothes. "I wish I had stayed in school longer, and had more to show under my hat," Henry continued. "It sure would have helped out in the Senate." He looked at me and smiled.

I had been watching Hart. Through Henry's talk of college, Hart stood leaning against a post, with his arms folded tightly across his chest. He never once smiled, and sometimes looked down at his own feet. He never got the opportunity to further his education, and apparently it bothered him. I saw him flinch, when Frank grinned up at his father and said, "I think you're real smart, Pa."

We all walked out of the barn. The sun was shining. Henry took a long deep breath, and let it out slowly. "I feel spring in the air," he said. "And it sure feels good!"

CHAPTER THIRTY-THREE - 1883

The spring runoff has always posed a special threat to the homes along the Upper Yuba River. Downieville clings to the side of the steep mountain like a scared child clings to its mother with it is afraid. The mighty river flows through the center of town, and brings life to every creature in its path. High up on the snow capped peaks, the warm afternoon sun shines, and sends little trickles of water to feed the streams. They gather strength, and grow into a raging angry flood, which destroys the life it normally feeds. More than once I have witnessed a home slide into the river, and become smashed into splinters, as the rapids tossed it against the rocks.

It is nature's way, I guess. The promise of life and the threat of death, often reside together. Our more personal promise of life came over the winter, when Aggie announced that she was pregnant again. Rachel could hardly wait to join her during this special time. Although Aggie already had four children, and knew exactly what to expect, my wife pretended that she was needed by her daughter's side.

I helped Rachel onto the stage, that spring, with a touch of regret. I don't know why, but I felt perfectly at east leaving Rachel alone for a few days, but I hated it when she left me. She patted my hand, as I closed the flimsy door of the stage that would take her up the mountain to the snowline. She wore a black wool suit, and I don't know how many petticoats, and her coat had a fur collar, and a nice warm fur muff for her hands. She had on her best riding hat, with a veil, which she had thrown up onto the brim, it was black too, and long black gloves. She was attractive in black, but looked like she was going to a funeral, rather than preparing for the birth of her fifth grandchild! I knew she was perfectly safe, but the haunting feeling of anxiety crept upon me, and I shook it off as loneliness.

I tried to imagine Rachel arriving at the Turner Ranch. Hidden in her luggage were small presents for the little boys—mittens and scarves, and a pretty lacy new dress for Daisy. She enjoyed the grandchildren so much—maybe because she always wanted a large family, and we only had the one child. I knew "grandma" would hug and kiss those babies, while Aggie chatted on, like she hadn't seen a woman to talk to in years.

Strange as it may sound, Aggie told her mother that Jack Campbell's murder brought unexpected blessing to the Turner family. "It brought Henry home," she said. "Ottie is much happier now, and there is a new closeness between Frank and his father, that was not there before. And, thanks be to God, it has certainly lifted a burden from Hart's shoulders—having his brother around every day to help with the chores."

Rachel held Daisy on her lap, while Aggie talked. "Hart doesn't like to make decisions that pertain to their partnership without Henry's input. The sawmill is a real gamble. It is going to cost so much, and they have to get the money somewhere. So, they have decided to sell the dairy herd."

The picture of Aggie that day is indelibly printed on Rachel's mind, and she often speaks of it. The sparkle in our daughter's eyes, as she talked in her soft quiet voice, about Hart and the sawmill. She sat in an old rocking chair, close enough to a window that the sun filtered through and illuminated the youthful blond highlights in her brown hair, casting the illusion of a halo around her head. Her hand gently moved to the little table, alongside the rocker, and her long fingers drifted gently on the edge of the old black book we gave her so many years ago, when she was a little girl.

"Remember this Bible?" she asked.

When Rachel smiled, and nodded, Aggie continued, "It has been a God-send. It has helped me through so many hard times—and those scripture verses you forced me to learn as a child . . . I still remember them."

Rachel laughed. "See now, I wasn't as cruel to you as you thought!"

Aggie laughed too, and said, "It's a hard life here, but I guess you know that, don't you. I was so afraid for Henry this year. You know he started wearing a gun! Ottie was beside herself with fear, but she couldn't stop him—and maybe it was a good think, after all the trouble—'course I don't blame Henry."

Rachel looked at the little girl on her lap. Daisy had fallen asleep, with her head pressed against her grandmother's chest.

"It's like God promised . . ." Aggies softly patted her Bible. "'All things work together for good, to them that love God, to them who are called according to His purpose.' Last fall we faced the worst event in Henry's political career, and now, a few months later, it turns out to be a blessing for the entire family."

* * *

During that first week in April, shortly after Rachel arrived, Aggie took sick. Rachel tried every home remedy she could think of, and called in the neighbor, Mrs. Fletcher, but nothing seemed to help.

Soon, Henry's young boy, Frank, was sent on his father's horse, down the road to Sierraville to fetch Dr. Schubert.

Hart came in from the field, and waited on the porch until the old doctor rode up in his buggy.

"This way Doc, hurry," Hart said, and lead the way into the house, through the kitchen and into a large comfortable high ceiling bedroom, where Aggie lay doubled up in pain, on the four poster bed that Hart made for them during their early years of marriage. Rachel and Ottie leaned over her, placing cold wet towels on her forehead.

Rachel straightened up and stared at this homely old man that Hart called "Doc". He wore a dark overcoat, which was dusty from the road. In one hand he held his shabby black doctor's bag, and in the other an equally dusty, and battered old hat, which he must have just taken off, because his thin gray hair was mussed and tangled. He hadn't shaved recently, and Rachel's eyes jumped from his bristly chin to the red and porous nose. He walked slowly, and with the gait of a bowlegged old cowboy.

Hart seemed totally oblivious to the man's appearance, as he pleaded with him, "Doc, she's been sick for about a week—sick to her stomach. We didn't know if it was the baby. Now she's worse! She's got the chills, and she's hot . . ."

"Well, let's have a look at her," the doctor said, in a strong German accent.

Ottie moved toward the door, but Rachel didn't budge. She placed herself squarely between her daughter and this strange little man.

"Ottie, why don't you take Hart, and this woman here, into the kitchen, and make a good, strong, hot cup of coffee, while I try to find out what is wrong."

Ottie and Hart stared at Rachel who still did not budge.

"It's all right, Mother," Hart said. "This is Doc Schubert. He's going to take care of Aggie for us."

"We've met—when Harry was born," Rachel said.

Doc Schubert raised one bushy eyebrow.

"Doc, this is Aggie's mother."

Obviously the old doctor was not going to challenge Rachel's position, as he stood staring back at her. A slight smile of admiration lifted one corner of his mouth.

"I'm not leaving," Rachel said. But, she did stand aside, and give the doctor room to examine our daughter.

Hart didn't know what to do, and before he could make a stand one way or another, Ottie took his arm, and led him into the kitchen, shutting the door behind.

The doctor ignored Rachel, as he took his black bag, and placed it on a table near the bed. He took off his coat, and dropped it over a chair. Rachel was relieved that he now looked more like a doctor, in his dark vest and white long sleeve shirt with its stiff starched collar. He rolled up his sleeves, and began to fumble around the bag. Then he pulled out a stethoscope, and hung it around his neck.

"Well now, young lady, what seems to be the matter?" he asked, as he placed his hand on her forehead. Her flushed cheeks indicated a fever. She had a handmade, goose down, quilt drawn up around her, yet her teeth almost chattered, as she shivered.

"Are you cold?" he asked.

"Um hmm . . ." she answered, meaning yes.

The old doctor peered down at her, through his small wire glasses, as he carefully lifted Aggie's eyelids, and looked into her bloodshot eyes.

He gently took her face in his rough hands, and turned it toward the light that filtered in through the closed window. "Open your mouth."

Her throat looked fine, but her tongue was dry and red around the edges.

"Have you been thirsty, Aggie?"

"Um hmm . . ." she answered, again meaning yes.

Doc frowned as he took her wrist between his large fingers and felt for her pulse. He pulled a pocket watch from his vest, which was attached by a long chain, as he stared silently at its face. Her pulse was strong, but much too frequent.

He took the stethoscope from around his neck, and put it in his ears, holding the other end on her chest. He raised his chin, and closed his eyes. "Breathe for me Aggie. In and out . . ."

She breathed in quick, short breaths.

He moved the stethoscope father down on her abdomen, and listened for the heart beats of the baby, which was fully developed in her womb. It was there—a faint little rhythm.

Doc Schubert stood straight, and stretched, as if his back ached. He let the ear piece of the instrument, fall back around his neck. Then he bent over, once more, and began to prod gently around her stomach.

He didn't have to ask if it hurt. She screamed in pain.

Rachel moved closer, and Hart's pale face appeared at the bedroom door. "Is everything all right?" he asked.

Doc Schubert looked up at Rachel—somber, daring her to interfere. "I'm almost through, Hart. I'll be out in a minute."

Hart gently shut the door.

"Aggie, I don't want to make you any more uncomfortable than you already are. Have you been vomiting?"

"No, but I feel like I could."

"And, you seem to have a lot of pain in your stomach?"

"Yes."

"Well, I think if we bend your knees . . . That a girl . . . you'll be more comfortable." Doc said, as he helped her change positions. "There, isn't that better?"

"I think so . . . a little."

The doctor walked slowly back to the table, fumbled around in his bag some more, and replaced the stethoscope.

"What is wrong with me?" Aggie asked. "Is the baby all right?"

"Your stomach is inflamed, and that can be pretty bad. The baby is fine . . . I'm trying to remember when we decided it was due."

"The end of April."

"Well, it's hard to tell. But, this far along, the baby could survive. The main thing for you to do, young lady, is to try and relax. You just rest. I'll leave some medicine for you to take, and I'll be back to check on you." He patted her arm. "You just try to get better."

The doctor looked at Rachel, and motioned with a slight nod of the head, that he wanted her to follow him out of the room. He picked up his bag and coat, and went into the kitchen where Hart and Ottie waited anxiously for his report.

He carelessly plunked his coat over a kitchen chair, and sat down, placing his bag on the floor beside him. He breathed in deeply, and let out a big sigh, clearing his throat at the same time.

"It's not good Hart," he said, as he scowled and shook his head.

Ottie placed a steaming cup of coffee in front of the doctor, and Rachel fell weakly into a chair across the table, staring silently ahead of her.

"Well, what is wrong with her?" Hart asked.

"I believe her abdomen is inflamed. Let's wait a week, before we really decide."

"Wait a week! Isn't there anything you can do *now*?"

"I'll leave some medicine. Aconite is the only thing that has been any good at all, in cases like this. We will know in a week or so, if it is going to work."

Hart stood, and pushed his chair out of the way. He glared at the doctor, and then glanced at the closed bedroom door. He tried to keep his voice down. "What do you mean, in a week or so? Aggie can't be sick that long! My God, Doc, she's got four kids to take care of, and the baby is due in four weeks. What are you saying? Isn't there something you can do *now*?"

"The baby is fine, so far. It is just best to wait and see how the disease progresses, before we . . ."

"What do you mean, 'how the disease progresses'?" Hart's eyes were wide, and his teeth were clamped shut, as he tried desperately not to shout.

Rachel sat silently, trying to fight off a swirling dizziness. The doctor implied an awful lot in the tone of his voice—the finality of his attitude. Fear—sick fear, kept her from passing out.

Doc Schubert avoided Hart's angry stare, and he took a sip of hot coffee, looked sadly at the women, and said, "Hart, we can't be sure of anything just now."

Hart clenched his hands into hard fists, placed them firmly on the table in front of the doctor, and asked, "Are you saying that she might lose the baby?"

"That is definitely a possibility," Schubert answered, without much feeling in his voice.

Hart leaned closer, almost in the doctor's face. "A

POSSIBILITY!" he whispered loudly.

Ottie grabbed Hart's arm. "Doc is here to help us—to help Aggie," she said.

Hart sat down. He couldn't get mad at Doc Schubert, it wasn't his fault. Hart's still-clenched fists rested on the table, as he rocked, ever so slightly, back and forth.

The sudden quietness hung over the kitchen table like a cold, gloomy storm cloud.

Hart finally spoke again, with more composure. "How long will this disease last? How long will she be sick?"

Doc set his cup of coffee down on the table. He looked from Rachel to Ottie, and then to the man who minutes before had been angry enough to fight. His eyes were reduced to narrow slits, as he peered over his spectacles. "Do you want it straight, Hart?"

Hart stood again. His body trembled. His breathing was loud. He opened his mouth to say something, but no words came forth—just fast loud breathing.

Still squinting, Doc said, "Well then, let's just wait and see."

The old doctor stood slowly. He lifted his bag to the table, and searched its contents. As he took some vials of medicine from the satchel, he didn't look as opposing to Rachel as he had when she first saw him.

He set out a dark bottle with the words ACONITE hand printed on the label, then looked from Rachel to Ottie, not sure which pale, badly shaken woman would be in charge. "Give this to Aggie every hour and a half, ten drops to ten tablespoons. When she is not complaining of pain, you can give it to her every four to six hours."

His words rattled around in Rachel's head. Nothing made any sense. The doctor looked at her, raising his eyes over his glasses, he asked, "Maybe you should write this down."

"Yes . . ." Rachel looked at Hart, who sat hunched over at the table. "I need paper and ink."

Hart's eyes were glazed, but he said softly, "In the drawer, in the table by Aggie's rocker . . . there's a journal."

Rachel moved swiftly, and returned with a blank journal, pen, and bottle of dark ink. She sat at the table and wrote, as the doctor repeated the instructions again.

"Give her a sponge bath daily, with soda and water," he

continued. "The friction of scrubbing sometimes helps. Watch her diet carefully: rice water, corn starch, toast water, or weak gruel."

Doc Schubert's hand slipped over the handle of his black bag. "Well, I guess that is all for now."

"Thank you Doctor," Ottie said, and Rachel smiled weakly. Hart stood and walked with him out to the porch, where he watched until the doctor's buggy was out of sight.

During the week that followed, after continuous doses of Aconite (which I would have considered poisonous), and countless painful rubdowns (which brought tears, although the end result did relieve the pain some), Aggie did not improve. There were moments when she felt well enough to sit for awhile, but most of the time pain was her constant companion.

The message of her condition reached me at the mine near Sierra City, and I came down the mountain to see for myself how she was doing.

When old Doc Schubert returned to check on Aggie, he found me, the dragon of the local Democratic Party, standing in the parlor surrounded by Turner men. His eyebrows rose, and his eyes widened some, but he wasn't the first person I knew that seemed to forget that I was Aggie Turner's father.

The scrubby old doctor removed his hat, smiled as he looked me squarely in the eye, and said, "Hello Judge." Then he turned to Henry and said "Hello Senator."

His smile faded some when he confronted Hart, and asked, "How's our girl doing today?"

"Not good," Hart said sadly.

"Isn't there anything more you can do, Doc?" Henry asked. "Don't you have some of your special 'little pills' that you can give her?"

"Not for this one, Senator. No lee-tle pills this time." He slowly walked away toward Aggie's room.

A few minutes later, he returned with his hat in his hand. Dark circles, which I hadn't noticed before, underlined his eyes. He set his satchel down, pulled a handkerchief from his coat pocket, and loudly blew his nose. We all watched his every move for a clue of his diagnosis. When he returned the handkerchief to his pocket he said, "You might start giving her the Aconite mixed with brandy. Heat it up—serve it steaming hot." He sighed loudly. "Hot rags on her tummy will help ease the pain some. Soak them in the aconite-brandy concoction first."

Everyone welcomed Doc Schubert's medical advice, and his confident manner, but it angered us all that he could do no more. I expected chatter from the women, but they kept their thoughts to themselves, afraid to share their fears. Instead, they attacked the potatoes as they peeled them, and slammed the cutlery into the drawer when they washed the dishes.

We men, of course, could vent our frustrations in hard work and farm chores. In the evenings, when all the chores were done, Hart retreated to the woodpile, where he sometimes chopped for hours, throwing the wood angrily into a heap. If the boys went out to help, he would yell at them to stack it carefully.

Henry, who normally had something to say about everything, became unusually quiet.

And I walked. I stayed clear of the road, because of the traffic, the teamsters, and wagons. I just walked around the property—down to the barn, across the field, along the stream. Or I just paced, back and forth, like a confused angry animal in a cage, from which there was no escape.

All of us wanted to take Aggie into our arms, and rock her, and tell her how sorry we were—but we could barely touch her, she was in such intense pain. Even in her un-restful sleep she would moan. Rachel and Ottie took turns nursing her. They did not dare leave her alone, even at night. And, when night did come, in its quiet sleepless shadows, we cried—pleading to Heaven with our tears.

Rachel Hale and Hattie Campbell came over often to help with the children, and neighbors pitched in. They brought food, and beautiful bouquets of new spring flowers, which brightened up both Aggie's room and her spirit.

While we all suffered in our own little hell of grief, Aggie seemed to rise above it. Her constant faith and hope, during those pain filled days, kept her from falling apart. I'm sure that she guessed she would not live through this experience, yet, during the moments when the pain was less, she seemed almost cheerful.

She tried to pass on her courage, as she talked to us of the Lord and Heaven. "It won't be so bad, Mama," she said, as she took her mother's hand. "I am only going to exchange this world for a better one. Eternal life means eternal bliss with my Lord and Savior."

As I stood and watched, from the foot of her bed, I wiped at my own tears. Aggie smiled up at me. "Really, it's all right Papa. I do pray to live—for Hart and the children. . . . my dear family."

Pray to live for me, my heart cried out.

* * *

April 29, 1883—a day of surprise—the baby was born!

We had almost forgotten this precious little angel, as we fought our way through the daily jungle of fear. Yet, with a quiet little voice, she announced her arrival.

Doc Schubert stood at Aggie's side, and shook his head, as he listened to the faint breathing of this weak little infant. "It's a girl, Aggie, but don't hope for much. She won't live long," he announced.

True to his prediction, the baby lived only one day.

Aggie cried as I had never seen her cry before. Then the tears stopped, and she seemed to get better. Our hopes were renewed. She lay in her bed, propped up by pillows, pushed behind her back and beneath her raised knees, with hot towels placed on her stomach. Doc Schubert increased the strength of her medicine by mixing it with opium.

We were gathered around the kitchen table, eating our mid-day meal, when Aggie asked to see Hart—alone. They had not been alone together since she took sick.

Birds chirped happy songs from the trees, and seemed to mock us as we waited in the kitchen, just outside the bedroom door.

Years passed before Hart could talk about what happened that day inside their room, as Aggie's cold, thin fingers ran alongside his face, and into his dark wavy hair. With a look of pity in her eyes, she smiled and said, "I'm so sorry darling, to put you through all of this. And . . ." her voice trembled, "I'm sorry about the baby."

Hart's back stiffened, as he took her hand in his. "It's all right. Just get well, sweetheart—I want you well again." He kissed her fingers. "I don't want to lose you. I can't go on living without you, Aggie."

"Don't say that Hart! I don't ever want to hear you say that again." She put her hand under his chin, and lifted his face to hers. His eyes glistened with unspoken tears. "You *can* get along very well without me, Hartwell Franklin Turner, and that is just what you are going to do!"

He shook his head, and a tear rolled down his cheek.

Aggie rubbed the back of his neck with her fingers. "We have four very sweet, wonderful children, which God gave us to raise. I won't be around much longer, Hart…"

He glared at her.

She continued, "… you'll have to do it alone."

Hart took her fingers in his hand again, and brought them to his lips, "Hush," he whispered.

"Be strong for me, darling," she said. "Trust God . . . You must!" Again she lifted his chin, and made him look into her eyes. "I want to see you again. When your time comes to follow me, we will meet in Heaven."

Hart tightened his grip on her hand. Uncontrollably the tears began to fall. He realized he could not stop Aggie from leaving. Together they cried tears of parting—tears of eternal commitment. And when the tears were all spent, they knew they could face the inevitable, together.

On Sunday, May 6, 1883, at three o'clock in the morning, my beautiful young daughter went off to meet her Maker. She was barely thirty years old.

CHAPTER THIRTY-FOUR - 1883

What good was it to keep on living? What purpose is there in life, when a child you love so much dies? For thirty years not a day went by without Aggie on my mind. Oh, I know she was a grown woman, that she had lived a full and rich life, but Blessed Lord . . . she was my only child—barely 30 years old! Those were the exact words I prayed, over and over, through the muck of deep depression.

The spring flood of tearful nights kept me awake throughout that month, and into the next. I suppose Rachel and I would have drowned in our own sorrow, if Hart's pain had not seemed to outweigh our own.

When children are left motherless, it is common for the little fledglings to be farmed out to relatives or friends—families ripped apart during the very midst of their confusion and despair. We couldn't do that to Hart. Aggie would have rolled over in her grave, if she thought the family she invested her life and love in, were destroyed while her death bed was still warm. So, Rachel and I stayed on at the ranch to help with the children.

Hart mourned in a way that is probably not unusual for a man—but I was never so close to it before. While the sun turned its face toward the earth, and spread its warmth on every growing thing, Hart remained cold, and spoke only when it was necessary, and then in short, incomplete sentences. Like a stiff, dead, angry thing, he plodded through each day, doing the necessary chores to survive, demanding obedience from the children, like a strict unloving school master. Those little ones clung to Rachel for the warmth, love and understanding they once got from their mother. Their need became the healing balm for their grandmother. A balm that Hart badly needed, and that I had to find from another source.

Nights were the worst. I hated them. Rachel and I took over Aggie and Hart's large bedroom. Hart wanted nothing to do with that room anymore—as if he blamed it for his wife's illness and death.

Some other day, some other time, I would have floated to a heavenly sleep in Aggie's soft goose down feather bed, but those long nights were haunted by ghosts. Not the death bearing goblins of old tales, but the kind that floats around in your mind, conjuring up memories from the past: Words of love that were never spoken; Visits that were never made; Visions—past and future—of what life would be like if only . . . And then we listened to the deafening night sounds: frogs, owls, coyotes. Noises I easily slept through before, now thundered through the silence, and in my wakefulness, I could hear Hart stir the fire, add wood, pace the floor—and then later, when the entire world stopped to rest, and my eyes ached for sleep—I could hear him cry. He sat in Aggie's rocker, held her Bible against his broken heart, and sobbed like a forgotten child. Night after night, he performed the same ritual, and I began to fear not only for his sanity, but for his life.

We let a month or two go by, where it went I have no idea. I began to pass the word around that my lawyer shingle was now up in Sierra Valley, and these old bones longed to get rattling on a good testy case—one that would demand my knowledge of the law, my time and my energy.

I spoke with Henry about his brother, and wrinkles crossed the Senator's brow, as he peered at me with a downcast head. "I knew Hart was having trouble accepting Aggie's death," he said, "but, I hoped time would help—that it would pass."

"So did I."

"Has he talked with you about it?"

I shook my head sadly.

"Me either . . . I can't get him to talk about anything. He just plods along—lifeless. Is it always this bad, Judge?"

I frowned and shook my head again. "You know what's wrong with Hart. He lacks the pioneer spirit. In the old days, a fellow could handle just about anything—he had to. Survival was always on his mind. It was a way of life. I know, I sound just like the old man that I am, but it's true. I'm disappointed in Hart. Those little kids of his are depending on him, and he's left the entire load on Rachel's shoulders. She's a strong woman, always has been, but she's no spring chicken! The old gal is 64 years old. She loves those little grandchildren, but they are full of spice and vinegar, and by dinner time she's exhausted!"

"I think I've got an idea, Judge. This is a problem for old George. We need to take Hart for a little ride out to the Hale's—better yet, let's get George and Rachel to move on to the ranch. They are just renting were they are now, and George's health is pretty bad. His wife, Rachel, could help with the kids. Hart has that old cabin they could stay in . . . What do you think?"

I remembered those days before Aggie and Hart were married, when George was the shoulder Hart would cry on. Henry's idea seemed inspired. I smiled the smile of hope—something that had been missing for a long time.

The Hales moved onto the ranch the following week, and according to Henry's plan, all the women folk and children would have an overnight party down the hill at Henry's house, while us men folk talked business, and made plans for the Hale's "new" little cabin.

It was a masterful plan! "Talking business", not only gave us the excuse we needed to leave the families behind, but it also demanded Hart's presence. Having our meeting at Hale's relieved Hart of the haunting memories that his own home and Henry's invoked. Also, having our meeting at Hales, with the absence of wives, made possible one more important ingredient—George's bottle. Now, I think I've mentioned before, that I am not what you would call a drinking man, and neither is Henry or Hart, unless the occasion calls for celebration. So, under the guise of toasting George's new home, we talked him into breaking out the bottle.

"We're going to celebrate!" Henry said.

`He took George's brandy, and poured everyone a drink in the cups that I rummaged from Rachel Hale's cupboard. Hart looked upon the potent liquid as David must have looked at Goliath, and he picked up his cup with the reluctance that the young shepherd didn't even show, as he searched for soft round stones.

"Drink up brother!" Henry prompted him with an upturned hand.

We were seated at the small kitchen table, and Henry reached in his vest pocket, and pulled out a deck of cards. Without saying a word, he shuffled them and began to deal out five cards each. George grinned and wiped both of his hands on his chest. "What are we playing," he asked.

"Poker," Henry replied, concentrating on the deal.

Hart stood, jerking his chair away from the table. I reached out and grabbed it as it began to fall. Hart glared at his brother, then at me with a hate I had never seen before, darkening his eyes. "I thought we came here to talk business!" he shouted. "I'm glad

George has moved on to the ranch . . ." He looked at George, and his red, tired eyes softened a bit, so did his voice, "I *am* glad you're here, George . . . but, I'm not playing cards with you or anyone else! And I'm not drinking your rotten brandy! Have you forgotten my wife just died?" His eyes centered on me now. "How can you drink, and play cards, and party, Judge? Don't you care? Aggie's dead! She's dead!"

A cold chill ran down my spine. I wasn't as ready for this as I thought.

George took a few sips from his cup during the onslaught, and reached for Hart's stiff arm. "Whoa Lad," he said. "Sit yourself down here for a minute, and talk to us about it. We don't have to play cards, you know. And you don't have to drink my brandy, which you referred to in such irreverent terms. I hope you won't forbid the rest of us a drink of two. It's good for the rheumatism."

Hart slowly sank back into his chair.

"Now, what's this about accusing the fine Judge, here, about not caring that his lovely daughter has passed on to the hands of the Father?"

Hart glared at me, and I had no idea why unless he was mad at the entire world. Henry quietly began to pick up the cards.

George took another sip of the strong drink. "You're wrong Lad," he said softly, patting his arm. "Oh, you think no one knows how you're feeling. You're angry that the world keeps right on turning, while your love grows cold in the grave." Hart stared sadly at the table in front of him while George's head nodded in secret understanding. "That's how I felt when my darling Calista died. Sure, I've been through this pain too."

Hart looked at George with a new spark of interest. Had he forgotten about his own sister's death, so many years before?

George nodded with his lips pressed tight together for a minute, then continued, "I loved that woman like the earth loves the sun. And when she died I thought for sure that I would die too. But it wasn't part of the plan. Sure, I believe there is a plan—and you know that Aggie believed that too. She was a wonderful woman, like my Calista."

George held up his cup for Henry to refill. "I ran away, you know. I ran from the grand Atlantic Ocean, all the way to the Pacific Coast. And what did it get me?" George mocked a laugh.

"It didn't bring Calista back. And I almost lost my beautiful child because of it. You gave me my daughter back, you know, Hart. If you had kept your nose out of it, I would have lost her for good." He held his glass up. "Here's to you Hart. A fine brother-in-law, and never a better friend could a man find."

Hart wiped a tear from the corner of his eye. "I miss her, George."

"Ah Lad . . . You'd be a fine one now, if you didn't miss her, wouldn't you? We all miss her! But, life must go on. The heart is a mighty big package, and when a piece of it is taken away, we are sure the whole thing will break. But the good Lord made us stronger than that. And, maybe a part of your heart will always feel lacking, but you've got a big heart, and there are other small pieces that are crying out for your love. They have names too: Harry, Jim, Thomas, and Daisy—now there is a pretty little lass!"

The corner of Hart's mouth turned slightly upward, and he nodded his head in agreement.

"That's the spirit, Lad!" George beamed.

"What will I do?" Hart's voice was barely audible, and the desperation was real. "I can't die, like you said—the kids need me." His hand went to the handle of the cup. "I'm afraid if I take a drink, I'll never stop. I'll just drink myself to death!"

George smiled. "You can try to drink yourself to death, Lad, but it seldom works. It just makes you old, and sick, and racks your body and soul. I'll tell you what to do. You have that sawmill you wanted to build—build it! It will keep your mind busy. Hard work is good for a man. And have a drink, Lad. Your brother and I will slap you around if you become an incurable drunk, and the Judge will have you thrown in jail! It will ease your mind some tonight, and relax you enough so you can get a good night's sleep. Then in the morning, go to work on the sawmill. You'll be so tired by bedtime that you will fall asleep with your clothes on, I guarantee it."

CHAPTER THIRTY-FIVE - 1883

It is a well know fact that Maine and logging go together like potatoes and gravy. The lumber industry took root there, long before the Revolutionary War. As native sons, the Turner brothers knew—from a child's eye view—the rough-tough loggers who moved logs down the river toward seaport mills.

Logging in the Sierra Nevada Mountains would be somewhat different, with no waterways to transport the logs. Timber cut on steep volcanic mountainsides, had to be moved through dense forest land to the mill. Other industrious mountain men answered the challenge with the strength of mules. After loading the magnificent logs onto huge solid wheel wagons, they pulled the heavy load, slowly, along narrow winding roads. Sometimes outfits used ox teams to pull the burden along dry wooden chutes, which they built down the sides of the steep mountains. The task of sawmill building was only half of the problem the Turners had to solve. The bigger question was how to transport the timber once it was cut.

George was right about the sawmill, and how it would keep Hart's mind and body busy—and Hart devoured the occupation of his time, like a starving man at a banquet.

Henry's satisfaction came from using his mind, to think up new ideas. They had friends with sawmill experience, and Henry spent hours gathering information and knowledge. One of their close neighbors, and a good friend, Tom Fletcher, became a valuable resource. He once owned a mill near Church's Corners, and ran it for several years. Then there was Henry's old confidant Dan Cole, the builder of two prosperous sawmills north of Downieville. Advice was free, and often came without asking. Money, thought (important to any building project) was not as easily obtained.

They had already sold their large and productive dairy herd. So it became *essential* that they get the sawmill established. The Turner Brother's Dairy was no longer there to support them. Despite careful planning, and pinching pennies, they still discovered that they lacked the capital one needed to get a mill in working order.

Henry and his miracle mouth came to the rescue. He presented their case to Mr. Blachley, the owner of Church's Corners only blacksmith shop and town hall. The Senator spoke as if he were introducing a new bill to congress. He used his unique power of argument and persuasion, until he convinced Blachley that the Turner Brother's Mill was indeed a worthy project for investment. The blacksmith loaned them $2500, and took a mortgage on all of the Turner's property, including their homes, barns, and fences—everything.

* * *

It was good to see Hart smiling once more, as he reached up and pulled the water nozzle over, so that it pointed directly at the shot wheel. The force of water on the wheel moved a turbine that sent the circular saw spinning with a loud *twang*!

"It works! That's great Hart," I said. My many years mining taught me the satisfaction that comes from seeing a new project become a reality.

"Of course it works!" Henry said. "And she will saw through any log we put to her! Henry was the brains of this outfit, and devised the mathematics that brought such power to their mill. The men strung an eight inch pipe up the mountain for a quarter mile. The fall of the water produced a good force, which they accentuated by reducing it by a two inch muzzle. The shot wheel was small, only about 8 to 10 inches. The combinations produced power—sawmill power!

We stood beneath the rustic shed-like overhang that sheltered the saw from the weather, and watched the hypnotic spinning, as the blade sang its empty song. It seemed to plead for the touch of a good, strong, newly cut Ponderosa Pine.

Hart reached up and pushed the nozzle aside. It sent a flow of water onto the ground, were it ran into a ditch and on down the hill. The saw continued to spin with less and less force, until finally it came to a stop.

Henry slapped his brother on the back. "We're in business, partner, are you ready?"

"I've been ready ever since you brought that ox team over from the LeBroke Mill," Hart said proudly.

Cautiously, the Turners tiptoed into their new business venture, being careful where they spent money. Their home and their entire life's savings depended on them being successful. The new ox team, from LeBroke Sawmill in Randolph, was borrowed from the kind and sympathetic owner, Thomas LeBroke. The plan was to cut the timber themselves—close to home, and use the team to pull the logs to the mill, where, thanks to Henry's powerful water-driver saw, the logs would be cut into lumber.

The oxen were amazing creatures. Castrated as young calves, these cattle were meticulously trained to pull the heaviest burden, turning left or right at the shout of the bullwhacker's voice. An average ox weighed an easy 1500 pounds. Using a team of these beasts, Hart and Henry figured they could handle a small operation on their own. There was a constant demand for lumber in the area, and they were sure it would be easy to sell. Then with the proceeds they could continue to improve the mill, and build the appropriate buildings to support a full time operation.

All the excitement of a new adventure filled the Turner Ranch on the day Hart and Henry walked up the hill, carrying the long, narrow, crosscut saw. It was ten foot long, with a handle on each end, and a man at each handle. Each man carried a bright new, never used, double bladed axe, that weighed 3 ½ pounds. Everything about them was so brand spanking new, clear down to their flannel shirts, leather suspenders, and shiny corks—those logging boots with the sharp spikes that stick out of the soles. They looked like greenhorns and it was difficult to have the faith in them that I knew they expected from their family.

Rachel and I stood on the porch with the children, to watch the men cut the first official Turner Mill pine tree.

"Don't you boys get any ideas about going up there to watch. It's too dangerous," Rachel said to the three wide eyed Turner grandsons, who hung over the porch rail, when they were not hopping up and down the steps.

"I could help," Thomas said, in his innocent, youthful, high pitched voice.

"Your pa has enough to worry about, without having to watch out for you!"

Henry and Hart picked out their first tree: a huge Ponderosa Pine on the hill several yards from the house. It measured about 3 ½ feet in diameter and probably had been standing for over a hundred years. We couldn't see their smiles as they stood next to its thick trunk, facing each other. Hart took the first swing at the tree's base, and the children cheered. Then it was Henry's turn. Hart, the stronger of the two brothers swung left handed, allowing Henry to wield his ax with all the strength of his favorite right arm.

Soon the rhythmic thud, thud, thud, echoed through the woods and on down the hill. George Hale came outside, pulling his suspender up over his shoulder, and I could see his wife Rachel, watching through the kitchen window, with her night cap still snuggly tied under her chin. The pink haze of early dawn made the sky alive with color. George stretched and said, "Well, I see they're getting' an early start."

I smiled, nodded, and grunted. I never was much for conversation early in the morning.

Up the road came Henry's family—Ottie and the children. "Isn't it a lovely day?" Ottie said, smiling sweetly. "The children insisted on watching the big event, and I must say, I'm rather excited as well."

Up on the hill, the men stood back and admired their undercut. The children were bored by this time, and were playing along the side of the house. The women retreated to the kitchen. George was back in his cabin, eating a breakfast that sent delicious smells out of the Hale's kitchen window. I sat alone on the porch, on an old wooden chair, and watched the progress up on the hill. I guess I had indeed passed into the realm of old men—for they, more than anyone else, can get great satisfaction in just sitting and watching things happen.

The men picked up the crosscut saw, and began to make the back cut. They took the same stance as before, facing the tree from opposite sides, and took turns pulling the long saw. Back and forth the new blade flew, gnawing its way into the heart of the tree, until the massive weight from above was robbed of its support, and began to lean toward the undercut. With a loud cracking sound, it broke loose, and the men quickly jumped back and shouted "TIMBER!" And we watched, as the giant came thundering to the ground.

The children raced around to the front of the house, and the women dashed out from the kitchen. George and Rachel Hale stepped outside.

The magnificent tree tore its way through the virgin forest, bringing down limbs and smaller trees in its path. All of nature shuddered at its thundering roar, and the earth trembled in its wake. Dust clouds rose, where the trunk violently united with its roots.

And, as the substance from which all mankind is made, drifted upward through the branches that separate the heavens from the earth, it could be seen far and wide by those who traveled by the wayside, and they knew that a dream had become a reality—the Turner Brother's Mill was born.

CHAPTER THIRTY-SIX - 1884

I missed the challenges found at our County Seat, especially during the long, slow, colder-than-Downieville winter. While men like George Hale enjoyed playing cribbage, I would prefer to exercise my competitive skills by talking politics—a nice argumentative debate. I discovered that a walk down the shoveled path to Henry's house fulfilled this desire. Henry's gift of intelligently presenting his side of a controversy was almost as good as my own! I think Hart rejoiced that Henry and I found each other. It kept us both occupied, and he didn't have to listen.

Hale's health went steadily downhill that winter, and Hart kept him company. The men spent hours at a time sitting with a cribbage board between them. Sometimes Harry and Jim would join the men, and sit quietly in a chair, leaning against their father, soaking in his nearness. Little Tom and Daisy were too full of vinegar to sit still very long, and they stayed away. We discovered that Rachel Hale had a short temper around children, and it was best for all, if they stayed out from under her feet.

Because they didn't have the dairy herd to care for, chores were done quickly, compared to other years. Work still had to be done in the barn, because of the horses, a couple of cows and the chickens, but that was about all.

In the month of March—the year was 1884—the snow remained in cold dirty patches prolonging our wish for spring. And, amidst our quest for warmth and life, an unwelcome visitor once more knocked on our door—the death angel. This time it took our good friend, the Turner's brother-in-law, George Hale. His life in Sierra Valley spanned 25 years. He arrived in the valley with the announcement of the accidental death, of the oldest Turner brother—Merrick Turner; and departed with his own demise at the age of 69.

Of course, we were not surprised. His normally bad health became worse through the winter, and left him bent and crippled in pain. We greeted his destiny with sadness and relief.

His normally quiet wife, Rachel, told us they had been married 17 ½ years. On September 3, 1866, they took the long trip up to Downieville by mule train, and were married by Rev. I. B. Fish. In those days George's mind churned with dreams and plans, and he had the strength and enthusiasm to carry them out. They built the hotel on the southeast edge of Church's Corners, and were partners in its management. The time they spent as husband wife may have been short, compared to others of their advanced age, but to Rachel Hale, it was a lifetime—her lifetime. Before George, she did not exist. And after him . . . she feared emptiness.

Rachel Hale's spirit reached the depths of despair, then like the fresh breath of spring, Hattie came to the rescue. George's grandsons became Rachel's, and with tiny loving arms, they reached out to her and with wet little-boy kisses, they told her they loved her: James, George, and Charles Campbell.

They stood together on the hill above town, and the wind caught the black veil that hung from Rachel Hale's modest hat. With black gloved hands she grasped the arm of her son-in-law, Frank Campbell. "Please," she begged, "don't let us forget George. I hate leaving him here."

I wondered if her fears were justified. Who would ever forget George Hale? The delightful, kind man, with humor built into his soul. Does time erase all things?

The name Church's Corners joined old George in the cemetery that year, when the town's first post office was established. Ezra Church, the man that bought George's hotel, back in '76, became our first postmaster, and bore the privilege of officially naming the community. For some unknown reason, he disliked the familiar, and submitted to the Post Office Department , his mother's maiden name—Sattley.

I hated the name, and knew it would always be Church's Corners to me.

* * *

Love: Defined a million ways by poets, and held in high esteem by all. It comes in many forms, shapes and sizes, and for every relationship on earth there seems to be a unique expression of the word. We all loved George. Henry came West with him, to get rich in the gold fields. When Hart arrived a few years later—young and inexperienced, George took him under his wing, and taught him the facts of western life. He had been Hart's shepherd and mentor ever since.

I feared a return of the depression Hart struggled with the year before, but thankfully it never came. Hart made peace with God, and so with death.

Spring entered, draped in melancholy . . . the slow reflective kind. And so, March was ushered out, and April drug its feet. The men puttered at their work, and became experts at procrastination. April's daffodils began to droop. The one-year anniversary of our daughter's death approached, as May nagged like an impatient old woman.

Winter's snow had melted from the mountains above the ranch. The thawed ground and warm sunshine sent out the alarm that it was time to get down to business.

Down the road, about two miles from the newly named Sattley, lived the champion of cattlemen, Ed Freeman. He raised beef cattle, and ran herds up the mountain to Downieville in the early days, before logging became a local interest. The sight of his steers winding their way into those old mining towns sent the salivary glands of the old miners into quivering ecstasy. Fresh beef—a rare and welcome event! These days, old Ed found more profitable ways of selling his castrated male cattle. He let them mature, domesticated them, and trained them to pull the heavy wagons. *And*, he got a prime price for each head: Oxen—the muscle behind the logging industry.

Henry approached Ed Freeman, and bought four yoke, already broke, and ready to use in the woods. He pastured them in the field beyond the barn, where the dairy herd once grazed. Henry picked up a few other bulls and steer, but Freeman's were prime, beautiful creatures that weighted close to 1800 pounds each.

The next chore to be taken care of immediately: hire a driver. The Turners limited experience with ox teams became evident the year before, with LeBroke's team.

The men struggled their way through each step of the log-to-lumber process, and stumbled along like toddlers just learning to walk. On their list of necessary employees was a professional bullwhacker. A good man could transform "awkward struggle" into "smooth operation"—and that was their goal. Hire good men, and constantly improve production.

Henry's first stop, on the search for an ox-team driver, was Randolph; to talk to Tom LeBroke. Tom shook his head slowly, "It's a shame, Henry, but I think you waited too long. Everyone I know is already hired on somewhere."

From there he went by saloons, talked to loggers, and left word everywhere that he needed a driver. And he got the same response: negative shaking heads.

On the days that followed, Henry talked to Tom Fletcher, a man who kept in touch with the industry. He rode out to McNair's Sawmill, over toward Mohawk Valley—tried to tie in with someone there. No luck. He even went up to Downieville, to look for a driver. He talked to his old friend Dan Cole, but Dan shrugged his shoulders and said, "You might try Truckee."

Truckee: The hub of the wheel which spread out to the gold mines of Downieville, the silver mines of Virginia City, and all the places in between. The railroad at Truckee connected the Sierra Nevada Mountains with the fertile Sacramento Valley, and seaports of the San Francisco Bay. Truckee became our local import-export depot. Because of this, the roads in that direction were greatly improved, with stages running on a regular schedule.

Desperation showed its nervous head. Not a minute more could be wasted. All the other mills had snatched up the good loggers and bullwhackers before Henry could offer a bid. Pre-dawn hours found Henry down at the barn saddling his horse for the long ride to Truckee.

That afternoon he spoke to every logging outfit, saloon keeper, and mule skinner in that town, and found no help for his predicament, until someone suggested an old man who lived at Tool's Station, half way to Auburn.

"If that old Billy goat is still kicking, he used to be a pretty good driver," the informant said. "He's about the only one I can think of that ain't been hired."

All the way to Tool's Station, Henry's imagination taunted him with questions, "What if the man says no? What if he's dead?"

The Turner brothers spent a lot of money—really gambled, to get his sawmill into full operation that year. They borrowed money . . . the mortgage . . . *What if* . . . Henry shuddered to think of the consequence that not finding a driver could cause. He, or Hart, could run the team like they did last year: Slowly . . . carelessly. It would be just as well to put young Frank or Harry on the whip.

When he arrived at Tool's Station, the last of the setting sun cast a lively glow on the otherwise dull specimen introduced to Henry as Colonel Woods. Every speck of clothing the man wore was black—the garment of the Pennsylvania Dutch, and he had a beard as white as snow, straight down the front of his shirt, short but untrimmed.

Henry didn't care how he looked, how old he was, where he came from, or even if he spoke English. He wanted only to know if he could drive an ox team in a logging operation, and if her were willing to work for them in Sierra Valley. Henry was ready to offer the old man anything, if only he would stay with them one season.

Colonel Woods stroked his milky beard, and said, "Well now, you certainly sound like a desperate man."

"We've looked everywhere! I know we got a late start, but I just never realized it would be so hard to find a driver."

The old man smiled, but did not reply.

"It's a new operation. We built the mill last year, and did everything ourselves. But now we need to expand. It's a fine mill, with a circular saw, run by water power."

The old man nodded, but still said nothing.

"Mr. Woods . . ." Henry said in exasperation. "I am asking you to consider working for us. We have a brand new sawmill, and very few employees. We built a cabin for the crew, but you would probably have it to yourself this year...and my wife will cook for you. She's a good cook! We will pay you well."

"Who will swamp for me?" the Colonel asked.

"Swamp for you?"

"That's right, who will swamp for me? You know—clear the roadway in front of the team, and help me out when I need it?"

"I'm sure I could get one of the Church boys. There are a lot of young men in the area."

"I always choose my own swamper."

"It could be your decision. These are good, hard workers. I would trust them."

"Hmmm . . ." His eyes narrowed. "I suppose you want me right away."

"Well, yes sir, as soon as you could come."

He turned and started to leave the room, saying, "I'll go get my things."

"You mean you'll come now?" Henry asked, speaking to the man's back.

He faced Henry and frowned. "You did say you wanted me

right away, didn't you?"

"Yes! . . . Thank you Mr. Woods!"

The man held up his hand, waved it forward a couple of times, and said, "My name is Colonel. Just call me Colonel."

On the long ride back to Sierra Valley, the Colonel had very little to say, but Henry gained courage to ask him just how old he was.

"Seventy-five, sonny," he answered. "I'm weathered and old, but you won't find a better man with an ox team."

* * *

The Colonel was true to his word. He handled the ox teams as if he raised them from calves, and they responded to his voice like they shared some secret language.

The Turners hired Isaac Church's son, Charlie, to swamp for the Colonel. Charlie was a young man, a 24 year old farmer who took to the logging business with the enthusiasm of a cat at milking time. The Colonel did not have to yell at him to remove branches and rocks from the road in front of the ox team—and when they got in a tight corner, where the Colonel had to steer the huge, overloaded, solid wheel wagon, with the wheel cattle, Charlie would hang on to the brake like a professional. It took timing, and strength to keep the wagon from colliding with a tree.

With a good bull-whacking team, a couple of fallers, and a swamp-man, the Turner Brother's Sawmill put up 40,000 feet of lumber that season.

CHAPTER THIRTY-SEVEN - 1885-1886

During the next two years, I established a small lucrative law practice in Sierra Valley. People always got into trouble, and my democratic friends knew where I could be found.

At the ranch, I watched the sawmill explode around me. The Turners developed a full scale operation, borrowing another $1500 from their neighbor Abe Church. Hart's home sat right on the edge of all the activity, and at times I thought I was living in the headquarters of the lumber mill. Rachel complained about the dirt and dust. "The road was bad enough, but now with this mill here, it's impossible!" She was right. We seemed to *breathe* dust, and it settled on everything.

But the mill prospered. They sold all kinds of clear and common cut lumber, and folks grabbed it up as fast as they could get it: rustic wood and pickets for fences; lumber and molding for floors and ceilings; and their specialty, fruit and butter boxes. They kept the brick yard running, so Turner's Mill was also still the local source for bricks. They advertised in the newspapers and promised they could fill orders at short notice and at low prices.

All summer long they pulled the logs along dusty, dry chutes, which looked like flumes-without-water. A mile or two out in the woods, a crew fell the trees, and bucked them into logs, decked them and pushed or pulled them onto those chutes—sometimes using a tool called a cant hook, and sometimes using cables and oxen. Then with the help of gravity, and more ox-power, the logs scrapped and screeched their way to the mill.

Chute logging worked fine for downhill grades, but to move the rest of the timber to the mill they used strong wagons they called trucks. Deep in the forest, over hills, and down canyons, the logs were cut. Three yoke of cattle were often used to load the heavy logs up onto the solid wheel trucks. The Turners hired-on experienced drivers, who sometimes had their own six and eight horse teams. These magnificent creatures could easily pull a 10,000 pound load along a road, so narrow I often wondered how the wagons could slip through.

As I watched the logging operation, from the standing tree to the ready-to-cut lumber, I began to admire the way these tough loggers handled the animals. Every day they worked side to side with God's most splendid creatures, whether it was a mighty beast, or a towering tree. A man, barely over 5 ½ feet tall looks hardly capable of the task—and injuries did occur, even death—yet this breed of man, as unique as the trapper, does his work with an enthusiasm and enjoyment that I have only found , for myself, in a courtroom.

Each summer the loggers cut an extra 700,000 feet of timber, which they left in landings out in the woods. When the snow turned the ground cold and hard, the Turners took the sled out there to recover them. At that time, Henry and Hart had their own team of six horses, and during the winter they hired on two more teams. This way the sawmill never shut down, and the saw, with its squeaky twang, kept our teeth on edge all year round.

CHAPTER THIRTY-EIGHT - 1887

When the first snowflakes fell in the winter of 1887, Henry approached his 58th birthday.

"There are a thousand things I planned to do, Judge, and I never got them done," he growled, as he stood at the front window of his home and looked at the falling snow.

Knowing that those thousand things were probably Republican in nature, I reluctantly said, "You've still got lots of time, Henry." I said that just to cheer him up. I knew the panic *I* felt when I could see ahead *my* milestone sixty.

"I feel old," Henry said. "I've done a lot. I've seen a lot. I'll bet there isn't a race, culture, religion, or political background that I don't know about. I've seen fights—even murders—up on the Yuba, panning for gold. Those were the days, weren't they, Judge?"

I nodded in silent agreement.

"I've been Senator of one of the largest states in the Union. I built a road—and a mighty important road, too. I've built houses, barns, lodges, a dairy, a brickyard, a vault, and even a sawmill. I am married to the finest woman God put on this earth, and I have three wonderful, loving children. But..." He slammed his fist against the sill of the window. Then in a sad, quiet voice he said, "But there is still a lot I would like to do."

"You haven't joined the Democratic Party yet," I said, trying to avert his melancholy mood.

Henry turned and started to laugh. "You're right there, Judge! And that is not in my immediate plans."

* * *

The middle of December I sat reading the *Mountain Messenger*, not because I enjoyed the Republican nonsense sheet, but because it told all of the local Downieville news, and I still considered Downieville my home town.

The children taunted Hart about Christmas being only seven days away. Wonderful smells drifted in from the kitchen, where Rachel mashed boiled potatoes against the side of a pan. Daisy lifted plates carefully from the dish cupboard, and she helped set the table. We had a home here, and it was comfortable, warm and alive

I skimmed news about Sierra City. It mentioned the dreaded disease, Smallpox, but it seemed so unimportant at the time . . . "The citizens have taken steps to isolate the sick, and there is no danger of the disease spreading."

Daisy bounced around the room, announcing that dinner was ready, and I put the paper aside, and never thought about it again, until a couple of days later, when right in the middle of all the holiday festivities, three of our Sattley citizens came down with the pox: Mr. Coats, Ed Freeman, and one of Abe Church's children.

Now, if this new invader had been a killer bear, or a mountain lion, or even a man gone crazy in the head, we could have handled it easy enough by sending out a well armed posse. But, how do you stop an invisible enemy that sneaks into your house, and hides in the very air we all breathe? The answer is: with nervous panic and a lot of prayer!

The spread of this horrible disease is stopped by isolating the sick—but isn't that what they did in Sierra City?

A couple of days after Christmas, I borrowed the next issue of the *Mountain Messenger* from Henry, tromped back up the hill, and sat down at the kitchen table where Hart was sipping a cup of hot coffee. The date on the paper was Dec. 24th –Christmas Eve. Hastily I shuffled through the large printed pages until I found the news I hungered for—some kind of explanation of how the smallpox could have reached Sattley.

The article stated that a Mr. Lewis was arrested in Sierra City. His crime: he lived at the Mitchell Hotel, where the first case of smallpox was discovered. Immediately the authorities put the building under quarantine, yet Lewis left the hotel, and went all over town exposing people to the disease.

"Listen to this, Hart," I said, and I read the article aloud.

"That's stupid!" Hart interrupted me as I read. "No wonder it's spreading like a wild fire."

I continued to read, "'. . . he was found guilty, and sentenced to jail for 20 days, and to pay a fine of $20, if in default, to serve 20 more days.'"

"Twenty days! They ought to hang a man for that!" Hart said, ripping a bite from a hard role he was eating with his coffee.

"Um hmm . . ." My eyes had skipped down to another article. "That's ridiculous!" I said aloud.

"What's ridiculous?"

". . . The Sierra County Board of Supervisors. They were going to call a special meeting to appoint Health Officers, but they couldn't, because of a rule that insists on five days notice to make a meeting legal. Have you ever heard of anything so absurd? This would be an emergency measure. Any idiot knows how far smallpox can spread in five days!"

I looked at the blank, please-Judge-let's-not-get-into-a-tirade-about-this expression on Hart's face.

"I think I'll walk on down and talk to Henry," I said, as I peered over my glasses at Hart. "We need to establish a Board of Health here. Our local cases are being kept under quarantine, thanks to our good doctor, and intelligent neighbors, but measures should be taken to keep anyone, or anything, from coming in from Sierra City."

"Let our elected county officials handle it, Judge," Hart said. ". . . in fact, I'm sure they are. You don't need to get Henry involved. You know how he is when you mention the Board of Supervisors, or the County Seat."

Hart was right. Mention this to Henry, and he'd be off on another campaign—only this time it would be to purge the county of smallpox!

Hart was right about another thing. The Sierra County officials did have everything under control. Henry's good friend, Dr. Alemby Jump, the County Health Officer, made sure there were Boards of Health set up in all the districts in Sierra County, and he made sure he chose good men to do the job.

In fact, as Hart and I sat there talking, several men around the south end of Sierra Valley received word that they were picked to immediately establish a Board of Health, I was not surprised that our Republican Health Officer chose primarily men of his own party to fill the seats. When I learned their names, I reluctantly agreed that they were all good men.

From Loyalton, he chose Dave Keyes and Thornton Battelle, both long time residents of that community. From Sierraville came George Wood, the lawyer friend of Henry's that witnessed the Campbell murder, and Mr. Case, an outspoken religious man—the local school teacher. From a ranch between Sierraville and Sattley, there was Jared Strang, a cattleman and early pioneer in the area.

And from Sattley itself, our neighbor Abe Church was chosen, along with (I'm sure you've guessed by now), Dr. Alemby Jump's favorite man—H. K. Turner.

Apparently word had not reached Dr. Jump that Abe Church was under quarantine with his sick child, and could not comply with the doctor's request. But the rest of the group all showed up in Sierraville to make immediate resolutions to stop the spread of this frightful disease. The most important decision they made that day was to halt the run of stages and riders that came in from Sierra City.

Henry returned home flushed with excitement. He was back at the wheel. He smiled broader and seemed an inch or two taller. He walked up the hill to check on the mill, and found Hart and myself at the house. Hart had an almost empty cup of coffee in his hand, and we were watching an ox team unload a good sized load from one of the trucks.

"You'll never guess what happened to old C. C.," Henry said, with a twinkle in his eye.

C. C. Darling was Sierra County's Supervisor from Sierra Valley: a big Dutchman who threw his chest out when he talked and always chewed on an unlit cigar. The man was such a character that there was no telling what he was up to now.

Henry couldn't wait to tell. "Well, it seems when he rode up the mountain, on his way to the Supervisor's meeting in Downieville, he passed through Sierra City. Downieville's Health Board had men posted at the road into town, and they stopped him, and put him under quarantine!"

Hart and I laughed at the joke. No one deserved such treatment more than old C.C.

"Yep, they have him under quarantine—stashed away in Dave Atkins' cabin."

"How's he going to get by without his whiskey or cigars?"

"Oh, the Board of Supervisors sent him all the necessary supplies: bedding, whiskey, cigars and newspapers. They said someone else felt sorry for him and sent him a bunch of Dutch Almanacs. He is well supplied."

* * *

Does small pox ever pass through a village and not leave death in its wake?

While Sattley fared much better than Sierra City, it did experience a loss of the Morrison Brothers, Joe and Sanford. They were simple men, who did not demand much out of life. They hired on as farm laborers around Sattley area during the summer, and began their trap lines with the first frost. They were good friends of Sam Berry, before he was killed by the Grizzly bear.

Four restless weeks elapsed between the deaths of the brothers—from the end of December to the end of January.

We all hoped the ugly thing would have passed on its way by February, but it didn't. News reached the Sierra Valley Health Board, of which Henry was now president that five members of the Kelly family, in Loyalton, were down with the smallpox.

Kelly. I knew the name from reading the *Mountain Messenger*. Mr. Kelly was on trial at Downieville, but I didn't know the charge. Henry came home with the facts. On the way home from the trial, a member of the family spent the night in Sierra City, and contracted the disease there. Would this never end?

Henry was livid with anger—angry at people's stupidity. The disease could have been stopped so easily, had Sierra City taken the proper steps to protect its citizens. It made him sick. It gave him a headache. In fact, his whole body ached. He decided to lie down and rest awhile.

Henry never got to read the good news in the next issue of the *Mountain Messenger*, February 11, 1888. It said that Downieville received its first mail express from Sierra Valley and Sierra City—thoroughly fumigated.

The yellow flag, posted in front of Henry's house, waved its message to anyone passing by, "Quarantine!" The president of Sierra Valley's Board of Health had smallpox.

CHAPTER THIRTY-NINE - 1887

Alex Beaton is either the bravest, or the craziest man I know. I always thought of him as a kind hearted fellow, ever since I heard that he rode to the Turner Ranch to warn Henry that Jack Campbell had been killed.

What he did on a cold February day, in 1888, astounded everyone. He walked past the yellow flag that poked out of the soot covered snow in Henry's front yard.

"Alex!" Ottie screamed. "You can't come in here! Didn't you see the yellow flag?"

"Yes, I saw it," Alex said, as he stood in the Turner kitchen, with his hands planted firmly on his hips. "Where is he?"

"He's in there, Alex, but . . ."

Alex charged past her before she could say anymore, and entered the room where Henry lay.

Henry smiled, whispered, "Hi Alex . . ." then he dropped back off into a fitful sleep.

Alex bent down, wrapped blankets around his friend, picked him up, and began to carry him out of the door.

"Alex, you can't do this," Ottie insisted. "We're under quarantine!"

"I know, Ottie," Alex said, and headed for the front door, with Henry tucked firmly in his arms.

"But Alex . . ."

"Never you mind! I've seen this thing go through families too many times. It is not going to wipe out yours. You just keep the kids in the house—yourself too, until the quarantine is lifted. And, pray to God that you don't get it too."

"But . . . what about you?"

Alex smiled. "Well, it's too late now. I'm exposed—same as you. Guess I'll just have to stay with Henry 'till he's over it."

He lifted Henry up on the back of his horse, and led the animal up the hill to an unoccupied cabin near the mill. Henry drifted in and out of consciousness while Alex carried him inside, and laid him on a cot in the corner of the room. Then Alex went out, unsaddled his horse, and swatted him on the rump. The horse jumped, and raced off down the hill toward home. Alex then went back into the cabin and shut the door behind him.

When the doctor came by, he placed a yellow flag in front of the cottage, and left some medicine—digitalis mixed with zinc and sugar. It seemed to work as well as anything that had been found to fight off smallpox.

Alex was a devout member of the Odd Fellows Lodge, and through his participation in this fraternal order, he became an experienced nurse. He took to heart the responsibility of caring for his brethren, and was often called on to help out when one was sick.

Day after day, Alex watched Henry drift in and out of consciousness with the fever. Then the ugly, painful sores appeared and made Henry's skin hot and irritable. Alex gave him doses of the digitalis mixture, and wiped his brow with a cool wet towel during the fever, and sponged him off with warm water when the pox set in.

The sores burst, and Alex applied corn starch. By then Henry was well enough to sit up and eat a little, so his friend gave him tea, dark toast, and raw eggs beat up in milk.

Rachel had begun cooking for a crowd, and we left food at the gate for Alex, and at Ottie's gate for her and the children. We warned the grandchildren to *absolutely* stay away, in fact they seldom were allowed to leave the house during those "smallpox months". The school shut down, the mill shut down, and everything stood still while we waited for the disease to pass on through.

When Alex yelled from the door that Henry was sitting up, and taking tea and toast, we raced down the hill to tell Ottie the good news.

The trees around the house were draped in smoke from a bonfire she built in the yard. It didn't rise, the way smoke should, but stayed low to the ground—haunting. When she heard about Henry, her hands flew to her bosom, where she clasped her fingers tightly together, and started to cry. "Thank God, Judge!" she shouted through here tears. "Thank God!"

Ottie had to disinfect here entire house. The bed coverings and down mattress, that she had spent hours assembling during the first year of marriage, were all placed in a pile on the frozen ground, and burned, along with Henry's clothing—anything that he may have touched.

Inside the house she filled pie tins with sand. On the sand she poured small ant-hill-piles of yellow sulfur. She made sure all the windows were shut, and then lit fire to the sulfur. She took the children outside with her, and closed the door, letting the deadly smoke do its work, as it filtered into every corner of the house, killing every living thing.

There was no place she and the children could go, but to stand in the yard, bundled in their winter garb—and wait.

"I hate that yellow flag!" Lottie said, as she glared at it where it waved slightly in the ice cold breeze.

"It's not the yellow flag we hate, darling, it's the smallpox."

Ottie took a deep breath of cool air, and she hoped that she had killed whatever secret attachment the disease might have to her home.

Later, she held her breath, ran inside, and quickly opened all the windows to let the poisoned air out. She stripped the wallpaper from the walls, and scrubbed the floors and ceilings with lime water.

Those were the things that Ottie and her children did while Henry fought his battle with smallpox. When the quarantine was lifted, neither Ottie nor the children showed any symptoms of the disease. And, the house was spotlessly clean. Not even the pox could live through the treatment it received from Henry Turner's family.

The yellow flag was lifted from in front of the little cottage where Alex took Henry. We watched with searching hearts as Alex helped his patient into the daylight. Henry was thin, but surprisingly strong, and his scars were few, compared to others who survived this battle before.

Alex also miraculously escaped the pox, and became a hero in the Turner family's eyes.

It was the end of February. The disease had done its damage, and passed on to another place.

CHAPTER FORTY - 1888

During the first week of March, Henry was barely back on his feet, yet he caught the stage for the long ride to Downieville. It was a business trip. He had to file a foreclosure on a mechanic's lien against George Morrison, a brother of the two men who died in Sattley of the pox.

"The body may not look healthy, but inside I'm as strong as an ox, and ready to live," he said.

As Hart looks back on that day now, he realizes that he should have insisted on going himself. Every time Henry got near the County Seat, he got the political itch.

The warmth of the sun fooled all of us. Day after day it slipped across the blue sky, with only a wisp of a cloud for a partner. Although the bushes and trees held back their swelling buds, we thought we were witnessing an early spring. Yuba Pass was open for travel, and it seemed safe enough for Henry to make the overnight trip. Then a storm set in, and it kept the ex-senator at what Hart called "that den of temptation", for an entire week.

A special look; A grin; Sparkling eyes; One of the tell-tale things you can tell about someone if you know them very well. That is what Hart saw on his brother's face. Henry may as well have carried a sign that read, "I have been to the County Seat talking politics with my best friends."

When he showed up at the mill, Hart greeted him with skepticism. "Well, how was Downieville?" he asked. His voice dripped with suspicion.

Henry cleared his throat, and rubbed his hands nervously together. "You know—the same old thing."

Hart squinted and searched Henry's face for a shred of honesty. "You were up there talking to Dr. Jump and Dan Cole weren't you."

Henry refused eye contact. "Of course . . . What did you expect, Hart? I was there for a week, because of the storm, and those men are my closest friends."

"What did they talk you into doing?"

An uncomfortable crimson color rose to Henry's cheeks. He gritted his teeth together, and asked, "What do you mean? Can't I even visit my friends without you getting on edge?"

I was in the kitchen when I saw Henry walking up the hill from his house. I quickly finished my cup of coffee, and put the cup in the dishpan, and went out to greet him. I approached right at this point in their conversation, and was anxious to get all the latest Downieville news. I guess I interrupted. "Well, Henry, you're looking pretty good! Nothing like a trip to that old County Seat to get a man's blood flowing like it should."

In the awkward silence that followed, I noticed the secret daggers that flowed from one brother's eyes to the other.

"Explain that to Hart, will you Judge?"

Anyone who enters the world from a used cocoon knows the love-hate feelings that brothers face since birth. I sympathized with Hart, and didn't want him to think I was taking sides. I smiled and said, "There needs to be a man around with his feet solid on the ground, and Hart is our man."

The conversation abruptly changed to the swing of the weather, and the storm that passed through and kept Henry delayed. I stood impatiently listening, and felt like I'd been watching a baseball game that was called off in the fifth inning, because of darkness. Finally I could not stay silent any longer, and asked, "Well Henry, did they talk you into running?"

Henry's eyes flashed—first at me, then quickly toward Hart.

"Running?" Hart snapped. "Running for what?"

"Senator . . . Assembly . . . anything!" I said. It was election year, and despite the bad water Henry passed through a few years back, he was still one of the Republican's favorite sons.

Expressionless, Henry inquired, "Now what makes you think they would ask me to run?"

"It's election year! I don't have to explain things to you. I've heard people talking in town. Folks are wondering if you are going to run again."

Henry looked at the drifting clouds. He crossed his arms in front of his chest, and bit the lower corner of his lip. Hart watched him like an old barn cat ready to pounce. I could see I had opened a pickle barrel way too soon.

The nervous ex-senator took off his hat, and smoothed his hair into place. "I'm sorry Hart; I wanted to break this to you more gently. But, yes . . . I can be the Republican nominee for State Assembly, if I want it."

Forgetting for a minute on which side of the fence I belonged, I sprang forward, grabbed Henry's shoulder, and said, "Wonderful! That's great news! That is just what I wanted to hear!"

Henry's smile was curious, marked with upturned eyebrows. "I can't believe you said that, Judge. Do you think your team has a man that can beat the pants off of me?"

I stretched to the extent of my entire five foot six inches, and said, "To heck with the party, Henry! I am 70 years old and too old for this game anymore. The only fun I will have this election is to watch you reclaim your pride. You are the man, Henry! You can do it!"

Hart's complexion was changing like a chameleon—first an angry red blush, then a pale sickly blue, now a panicky yellow. I shook my head. "Come on boy," I said. "Be happy for your brother. The good Lord has granted him another chance to be what we all know he should be."

With lips sealed tightly shut, Hart shook his head slightly from side to side, and walked reluctantly forward. He reached to shake Henry's hand, and Henry met him more than half way—grabbing the rough, large knuckled, hard working fingers tightly until the edges of Hart's mustache turned upward.

CHAPTER FORTY-ONE – 1888

It was the last week in July, when the stage barreled past the sawmill and continued down the hill to Sattley, quickly coming to a halt in front of Henry Turner's house.

The minute I set eyes on the two passengers that climbed out of the rocky coach, I was reminded of the day the same two visitors came down the mountain to encourage Henry to run for delegate to the Second Constitutional Convention. Years had passed since then, and the two distinguished looking gentlemen had put on a few pounds, and were a little grayer around the edges, but they still demanded the same respect—Dr. Alemby Jump and Dan Cole.

Their starched white shirts and expensive coats were a startling memory of how my life used to be. Living in the middle of the dust-trap sawmill, my mind now believed all the world was covered with a small brown layer, and I expected every man to have at least a few smudges of dirt on his face, and his hand should be spotted with black stains from a combination of pitch and dark earth.

I rubbed my hands together in excitement. The campaign had begun. Behind closed doors they planned their tactics.

"There will be *NO* mud-slinging," Henry said.

"You realize mud is going to be thrown at you, over that Jack Campbell mess," Alemby said. "You may have to throw some back in self defense."

"This has got to be a clean campaign on my part, or I won't run."

Alemby shrugged.

Dan sat back and said nothing.

The Republican County Convention, in Downieville, was just a couple of days away. The party's candidates would be nominated for the county offices, and Henry's name, as a *state* candidate would not come up. But I'm sure Alemby and Dan would have loved to spring the good news to their colleagues at the convention. All they needed was for Henry to commit himself.

"Either the people want me, or they don't." The ex-senator stood his ground.

"All right, Henry, if that's how you want it, then that is how it will be." Alemby slapped his hands on his thighs. "I think I have a plan that might avoid any trouble."

Intently Dan and Henry leaned forward.

"Henry, your name causes some strange reactions in this county. There are those who would beg you to run again, like Dan and myself. Then again, there are those who still remember Jack Campbell, and would like to make a folk hero out of him. I think getting elected in Sierra County would be a toss-up as things stand now. But if your name comes up linked with Campbell's murder, it could jog enough memories to sway the campaign against you."

Dan nodded in agreement.

Alemby continued. "But, we now have to share our Assembly seat with Plumas County, where no one has ever heard of Jack Campbell, and couldn't care less. If you were able to pull the Plumas vote, you might win the election."

Understanding flashed in Dan's eyes, and he looked at Henry. "Do you mean I should not campaign in Sierra County at all?" Henry asked.

Alemby nodded. "That's what I think."

Henry stood, and paced the floor for a minute, and then he smiled, and said, "Alemby, you're a genius! But how do we explain this to the voter?"

"That shouldn't be so difficult," the doctor said. "We will hold your name back, and not file until the very last minute. Jerome Vaughn is still our friend. We will explain the situation to him, and ask if he would keep your name out of the *Mountain Messenger*. As editor, he should be able to arrange that. When the Sierra County voter receives his ballot, on Election Day, it will have your name printed on it. Hopefully he will remember your experience, and years of service, and simply mark his X.

Henry laughed. "You make it sound so simple."

* * *

All of the men now working at Turner's sawmill made the village of Sattley explode in population, and therefore earned for the town its own delegation to the Republican Convention. Henry, of course, was right there, and Isaac Church, who held the proxy for a third man.

The delegates from Sierraville now numbered five, but three of them couldn't attend, and they gave their proxies to Henry's good friend, George Wood. Something came up unexpectedly in

George's life, and he gave his proxy to LeBroke, Henry's sawmill friend. The only other delegate from Sierraville was old C. C. Darling, our local Supervisor.

The convention hall rumbled with a large majority of Henry's old friends, and the entire day slid by without argument or hard feelings. Among the candidates nominated to the party's local ballot, was Frances H. Campbell, the man who was cheated out of candidacy for sheriff during that unforgettable campaign, a few years back. Frances was now chosen by acclamation, as the Republican's choice for Alleghany District's Supervisor.

The public's mind eased some when Jack Campbell's murderer was sent to prison. And the memory of the dirty campaign, that hung over Henry's conscience all those years in between, had the permanency of the fog that hung around the cattails on a cold autumn morning.

The absence of ex-Senator H. K. Turner from the front lines of Sierra County's 1888 political battle proved to be no problem at all. Most folks were simply glad to hear from one less candidate. When a rare voice asked: "Why isn't old Turner around making all those promises that politicians seldom keep?" The answer was simple: He was called to serve on the Grand Jury.

In the middle of October, Vaughn stormed into Dr. Jump's office at the County Hospital. Alemby's insistence in holding the newspaperman quiet during the entire campaign was remarkable. "We don't want to even *mention* Henry's name in the paper until the very last minute," Alemby said.

"The last minute is now!" Vaughn's hazel eyes pleaded with the Republican stronghold. "We have to say something."

Alemby scratched his stubble chin. "Well . . . all right, but make sure it is short, and put it under 'Local Items' or something like that."

On October 20th, from the powerful pages of the *Mountain Messenger*, under "Local Items", we read: "Hon. H. K. Turner, Republican candidate for assemblyman, was up from the valley this week. He will not be able to canvass this county for want of time, but will make a through canvass of Plumas. It does not require much foresight to discover that he will receive a large majority of votes."

* * *

While Vaughn pounded the typewriter in the office of his printing shop, composing the short notation about Henry (allowed by the Republican patriarch), Alex Beaton pulled a heavy loaded wagon up through Turner Canyon on the way to the County Seat. As a resident of Sattley, I heard all the local gossip, and was privy to the intimate details of this incident.

Alex was a teamster, and had mastered the skill of handling a six-horse team. Slowly they moved upward, around the narrow winding road that led over Yuba Gap.

Suddenly an animal darted out of the woods in front of the horses. Some folks say he didn't see what it was—a coyote, a badger, or maybe even a small deer.

The front team reared, and then began a panicked gallop. Alex held the reigns firmly between his fingers, pulling back gently, as he yelled, "Whoa there!" But it was too late, one of the horses stumbled, and the wagon began to tip. As Alex sailed through the air his mind was on the horses. "Please, no . . . not the horses. . ." he whispered, as he saw two of them fall, crashing over the bank, against the rocks. Then Alex heard the thud of his own body landing on the ground, and saw for only an instant, the heavy wagon as it rolled on top of him.

* * *

Henry tucked the newspaper inside his coat, mounted his silky black mare, and rode the short distance to Alex Beaton's house.

Alex's wife, Elvira, graciously invited him inside.

"Is he awake?" Henry asked.

"Awake and driving us all crazy!" Elvira said. "I'm sure glad you came, Henry. He will be so happy to have the company."

Henry had removed his hat when he entered the house, and he flipped it gently against his leg as he walked to the bedroom where Alex lay propped up in bed. A bandage circled his forehead, and another was wrapped around his arm. Bruises and cuts covered his face—in fact, his entire body, as far as Henry could see.

Henry shook his head. "I hear you are one lucky man," he said.

Alex scowled. "I lost a horse. It's a crying shame, Henry. It was a good horse, too: Old Trooper!"

Henry smiled as he pulled the newspaper out of his coat and sat down in a chair by his friend's bed. It was just like Alex to be worried more about a horse, than about his own health.

The campaign trail beckoned. From the neighboring Plumas County, duty stretched its long neck, and pleaded with Henry. But instead, he spent as much time as he could seated beside the bed of a black and blue Alex Beaton. A small donation on a debt he would never be able to repay.

CHAPTER FORTY-TWO - 1888

And so it was that I crossed the line and voted for a danged Republican. How could I do otherwise?

* * *

"Will you sit down somewhere?" Hart peered up at me from the woodstove, where he knelt down and shoveled out ashes into an ash bucket. "You're going to wear out a hole in the floor."

I sat for a minute, picked up the paper, which I had grabbed off of the stage I flagged down, when it rumbled through on its way to Sierraville. The pages were already crumpled from my reading them over and over. "Sufficient returns have been received to indicate with tolerable accuracy, that all the Republican candidates for *county* offices, have been elected. . ."

I slammed the paper down, stood up, and paced the floor again.

Hart glared at me.

"Well, what more could I expect from a Republican newspaper?" I asked. "Why didn't they tell the results of the Assembly race?"

"The results weren't in when the paper went to press," Hart said. "I'm sure you read that too." He began stuffing kindling into the stove.

"Who cares if the Republicans won all the county seats? I don't care!"

Hart smiled. "I thought you'd care, Judge."

I walked back to my chair, and plucked myself down. "All right, I care. It doesn't make a bit of sense to me, why the people of our county would continue to vote Republican, year after year, when the Democratic Party has just as fine candidates—good men, and good policy."

Hart raised his eyebrows. "Is that true for the Assembly race also?"

"Of course not, you know that!" I growled.

We heard footsteps on the porch, and I jumped up from my chair like a man half my age, and quickly opened the front door.

Henry emerged from the porch, like a coroner bearing bad news.

I didn't know what to say. Even Hart kept his mouth shut.

This man, for whom our hopes rose high, walked slowly across the room, and dropped his body into a chair. Quietly he pulled out his pipe, and began to stuff it with sweet smelling leaves, which he picked with great deliberation from a tobacco pouch, that he slowly removed from another pocket.

Silently we watched as he stood again, and walked over to the fire, which Hart had been working on. He picked a small twig from the kindling box, and used it to light his pipe. He never spoke a word until the smoke was twirling upward, crisscrossing in the air. Then, watching the smoke, he said, "Well, the vote is in."

We knew the outcome. It was written all over his stern face.

Henry puffed on his pipe once more, and said, "Yep. Our county has chosen Schlesinger, 854 votes to 832."

I crossed the room, subtracting in my mind, and slumped into a chair. "Twenty-two votes . . . You lost by 22 votes?"

Hart crossed his arms, and shook his head. "I'm sorry Henry."

Henry raised one eyebrow, and cocked his head toward his brother. "I thought you would be happy, Hart. You didn't really want me to win, did you?"

Hart uncrossed his arms, and put his hands on his hips. His eyes narrowed into unreadable slits, as he glared at his brother.

Henry returned the stare—demanding an answer.

"I didn't *want* you to lose—not really," Hart said. "I've thought a lot about what the Judge said, and he is right, you know. You were meant to be in politics. That seems to be your purpose in life. I believed the Judge, when he said maybe God was giving you a second chance."

Henry removed the pipe from his mouth, and smiled, "Do you still believe that?"

"I guess so—but..." Hart shrugged.

Henry's eyes twinkled. "Well, what if I remind you two gentlemen that our Representative to the State Assembly is chosen by two counties."

I sat straight up in my chair.

"And," Henry continued, "I won Plumas County!"

The room was deadly silent as Henry's words soaked in.

"You mean you won?" I asked.

"You are looking at your new State Assemblyman."

Hart's mouth dropped open. "You won?"

"Yes Hart." Henry smiled. "I won."

* * *

Henry and his family returned to Sacramento. Rachel and I stayed on at the ranch, and helped Hart with the house and children. I kept up my law business, and as I was sorting through my books one day, I found a favorite of mine by Robert Louis Stevenson. I flipped through the pages until I found these words, which I read aloud to Hart: "'To be what we are, and to become what we are capable of becoming, is the only end of life.' I think that describes our Senator very well," I said. "He picked up his fears, faced the challenge of the election, and once again became who he was meant to be."

Hart ran his fingers through his thick, dusty hair. "Well, I don't know about that, Judge," he said. "I think it was the fever from the smallpox that made Henry go back into politics."

END

Fact or Fiction

CHAPTER ONE - 1888
- How James Galloway voted at any time in this story is speculation.

CHAPTER TWO – 1850
- Henry Turner's father, Tom Turner, and James Galloway were in the upper Yuba River area at the same time, but it is not known if they knew each other.
- Rachel Daugherty and James Galloway were both from Merced Co., Penn. Little is known about their trip west, if they traveled by wagon, or on the same wagon train; how well they knew each other; or if they were engaged when they arrived at the Forks.
- Downie's reference to Rachel as "Mrs. Galloway" infers that she was married when she arrived at the Forks in March 1850. This probably is a mistake in wording. He always knew her as Mrs. Galloway and mentions her in those terms. Franklin Hurd Turner states that his grandparents, James and Rachel went to Downieville in March 1850 and were married there on June 24, 1850.
- The purpose of Rachel's trip west is unknown, nor if she came alone, or lost family on the trail. The fact that she was the first white woman to come to that area is true.

CHAPTER THREE – 1850
- The location of the Galloway home is true.
- The location of James Galloway or Rachel Daugherty's claims are fictitious.
- William Downie states that he knew James Galloway from his first days at the Forks. They were apparently friends because Downie was invited to the Galloway home for dinner occasionally. Downie also stated dislike for Cut-Eye Foster, and the fact the he "watered down the gin". Downie and Galloway both had claims near the sawmill, and the information about Vineyard also came from Downie. It is

Downie who gives credit to James Galloway for the naming of the town. James Galloway's speech is taken from Downie's book, *Hunting For Gold*.

CHAPTER FOUR – 1850

- Downie summarized Galloway's performance as Justice of the Peace.

CHAPTER FIVE – 1850

- F. H. Turner gives the date of Galloway's wedding, but not who married them.
- 1851 – The year of Agnes's birth is known, but not the actual date. The month when they returned to Downieville is also a mystery, except that they did return that year, and were present on July 5, 1851. Agnes was the first baby in Downieville, although she was not born there.
- An early lithograph shows a magnificent tent in the center of town. The only information the author could find on this tent, is a few years later some miners purchased a large canvass tent that once was a gambling saloon.
- The gold stories are apparently all true, as related in Sinnott's book on Downieville. In the same book, a miner recollects that there were not a half-dozen women in town in 1850-51. In another place Sinnott states there were about 25 women, but he doesn't give the source.
- The population of Downieville, and the surrounding area, is true.

CHAPTER SIX –1851

- The Democratic County Convention was held on the Fourth, in Downieville. There is no information about Galloway taking any part in this convention. He was out of town on the Fourth, and liked to tell the story that he was on the way to Downieville at the time of the hanging.
- The hanging of Juanita is well covered by historians, and a favorite story in the history of the town. My main source for the details of the murder of Cannon, and the hanging of Juanita, was Sinnott's book on Downieville. Downie covers it well in his book also, and states that Cannon could speak

Spanish, and was actually conversing in Spanish with Jose, when stabbed.

CHAPTER SEVEN – 1860

- Agnes's ability in school is not known. She may have been an excellent student.
- James Galloway did run for State Senator, and lost. His political views are stated by Bill Copren.
- In 1860-61, many miners and businessmen left Downieville area for the silver strikes in Washoe County, Nevada, which was then the Utah Territory. Some left their entire business behind. (Sinnott, *Downieville* . . .)
- The Galloway Ridge Road, called Galloway Road, was one of the earliest traveled roads that led into Downieville (Ibid).
- The entire business section of Downieville burned down on February 21, 1864.
- Mr. Cocran was chief of one of the local hose companies.
- Listed among the few buildings saved was "the building which was later to become the J. W. Brown Hardware Store" (Ibid). Later Sinnott states that C. W. Gilbert owned it in the 1860's.
- The closeness of Agnes Galloway and Ottie Gilbert is only a guess. They were approximately the same age. They both attended school at Downieville, where the average attendance in 1860 was: primary department, 25; and grammar school, 31. Later when Ottie lived in Sierra Valley, she hired Agnes to be her housekeeper; this would indicate they knew each other.
- There is no indication that Agnes Galloway was ever known as "Aggie".
- 1867 – F. H. Turner states that H. K. Turner was trustee for the district where Ottie taught. Although there is no reference to who hired her, it could have been him.
- The name of the school where Ottie was hired to teach is unknown. It was at, or near, the George Hale Ranch, in Sierra Valley. There is no reference to there being a school in that area, at that time, but school records were not well

kept in those days. It seems coincidental that the Rocky Point School was established at approximately the same time that Ottie moved to the valley to teach, and that it was built a short distance inside the Sierra County line. This would indicate that it was a Sierra County School. It is also interesting to note, that the school was moved three times from its known location on Rocky Point, and two of those times it was located at Sattley, where the building still stood in 1980, on the south side of Sattley Hill. It seemed logical to the author that Rocky Point School's first location may not have been Rocky Point, although this is not historically documented. Because this school's history is more easily identified with the arrival of Ottie Gilbert, the author chose it as the school where she taught, and apologizes, if it causes confusion to local history buffs.

- Rev. I. B. Fish was both minister of Downieville's Methodist Church, and Sierra County's Superintendent of Schools.
- Garnosette is the true name of the man who owned the long mule train that ran to Sierra Valley.
- Ottie's experiences are based on the description of another young pioneer school teacher hired to teach in Sierra Valley, while I. B. Fish was Superintendent of Schools, and there were not roads into the valley (Alexander).

CHAPTER EIGHT – 1867-68

- Although the Turner's were Irish, George Hale's nationality is not known by the author.
- Isaac Church, who had been in business in Downieville area, went east and got his parents, two brothers, and a sister. They settled in the south west corner of Sierra Valley, in the area which became known as Church's Corners.
- F. H. Turner states that Ottie boarded with the Hales. Sierra County Assessment Rolls show that George Hale began to pay taxes on a hotel on his property in 1868, which would indicate that the hotel had been raised between 1867 and 1868.

- In 1862, George Hale had a hotel at another location in Church's Corners, which had a dining room, and meals were served by young widows. This was prior to the time he married Rachel Street. Whether or not they had widows as waitresses in this new hotel is not known.
- *The Mountain Messenger*, of May 23, 1868, refers to Garnosett and Darling opening the trail over Yuba Gap (Sinnott, *Sierra Valley . . .*).
- The marriage certificate of H. K. Turner and Ottie Gilbert, states they were married by George B. Hinkle. He was then the minister of the Methodist Episcopal Church in Sierraville.
- George Hale and Rachel Street were married Sept. 3, 1866.
- George Hale did own a hotel up near Sierra City, prior to moving to Church's Corners.
- Harriet Hale's nickname was "Hattie", and her father did leave her behind with an aunt, when she was a baby.

CHAPTER NINE – 1868

- On old maps, there are two individual towns, where Sierraville is today. At the junction of Highway 48 and 89, was the town of Sierraville. East of there, on 89 (heading toward Truckee) was the village of Randolph.
- When Frank Campbell became associated with the Turners is unclear. It may not have been until after he was married. Guinn states that Campbell came to Sierra Valley in 1863, joined the infantry in 1864, and was involved in the Indian War until 1866, when he moved back to Sierra Valley and began working in a mill. F. H. Turner states that this was Fletcher's Mill. Because Fletcher's was near Church's Corners, and the Fletchers were friends of the Turners, the author assumed the Turner-Campbell friendship began then.
- Ordell Howk wrote in the *Mountain Messenger*, Dec. 1859 (Sinnott, *Sierra Valley . . .*), about life in Sierra Valley. She lived in the vicinity of the Hot Springs, and she wrote, "Parties and sleigh riding are becoming both irksome and dangerous . . . the other night some jolly gallants tipped over three Pike County girls into a snow bank . . ." The

Pike County girls were most likely visiting the Hot Springs, which had already been developed into a resort in the 1850's. The *Sierra Democrat* of Oct. 4, 1862 (Ibid) reported about Fenstermaker's "famous hot springs", and said, "But, for one circumstance, we would *recommend* this house as a quiet place of 'Rest for the weary'." But, they do not explain the "circumstance". It may be jumping to a conclusion to say it was a party spot.

- In this chapter, and elsewhere, George Hale is referred to as a drinking man, which may not be true. There is no record of this, and it is a fictional attribute given to a character who came west with the 49ers.

CHAPTER TEN– 1868

- This chapter is total fiction, except for the fact that Ottie was pregnant.
- As mentioned before, the author has no facts about the relationship between James Galloway and his wife prior to their wedding.

CHAPTER ELEVEN – 1869

- When Agnes Galloway was 18 years old, she came to Sierra Valley as a housekeeper for Ottie Turner.
- Clara B. Nelson (*Sierra Valley News*), stated that Dr. Schubert built the Turner house, or the first two rooms of it, in 1877. I realize I am stretching the point to move the date back eight years, but the fact remains that Schubert did build a two room cabin on the Turner Ranch. In this same article, she tells about Dr. Schubert's drinking habit, and the fact that he would build a cabin, live there about two years. He would "commence drinking again", and "pull up stakes". She writes that he lived in Loyalton, Beckwirth, and Sierraville, besides the cabin in Sattley, and in another article she mentions that he lived in Long Valley.
- C. G. Church states that Mrs. Fletcher was "one of the old pioneer women and mothers that you read about", and also tells of her willingness to help the sick. It is the author's guess that she also played the role of midwife.

- H. K. and Ottie Turner's first child was named Franklin Hurd Turner. Throughout his life he was known as Frank Turner, as was his uncle "Hart", who as previously mentioned, was never called "Hart". Because of this, it is assumed that the second was named for the first, although the initials are reversed.
- What influenced H. K. Turner used to push toward getting the road built to Downieville is not known.
- Jared Strang did cut the first trail over Yuba Gap, and until then, the wagon trains traveled through Johnsville and Mohawk Valley (in Plumas County) to connect Sierra Valley with its county seat.
- The desire of many Sierra Valley people to have Truckee or Loyalton as the County Seat, because of the "inaccessibility of Downieville", is true.
- The names of people who attended the meeting in 1862, to discuss construction of a wagon road to Downieville, are true.
- Sinnott (*Downieville* . . .) In the summer of 1862, contractors by the name of Watson and Dunn, began to build the wagon road from Downieville to Sierra Valley. They employed about 100 men, but apparently did not supply sufficient food or collateral. The men went on strike in December of that year, and because of the fact that costs were higher than anticipated, the project was abandoned.
- Davis states that H. K. Turner was Senator for Nevada and Sierra Counties from 1869 through 1876.
- $16 per day, per diem, was established, for the senators, in 1849 (Driscoll). The author saw no change until 1879, when it was set at $8 mileage, not to exceed 10¢ per mile, and expenses not to exceed $25 for each session.
- It is merely a guess that Senator Turner left his wife at home that first year. For what other reason would Agnes have been allowed to stay at the ranch throughout the winter?

CHAPTER TWELVE – 1870

- The description of the "new" capitol building in Sacramento is from Reed's *History of Sacramento County*.

- The *Mountain Messenger,* Jan. 22, 1870, (Sinnott, *Sierra Valley* . . .), said that petitions for a new county, both pro and con, had been circulated and almost everyone had signed one or the other.
- The details of all the red tape involved in the construction of the Yuba Gap Wagon Road are true, and outlined in Sinnott's book on Downieville
- The Turner brothers had a sister Calista A. who married George Hale, and then later died, after giving birth to a girl. H. K. Turner's first daughter was named Mary Calista.

CHAPTER THIRTEEN – 1870

- The names of Sierra County supervisors are true.
- Charlie Church recalled going wild strawberry hunting with is brother and sister, near Sattley. He was born in 1863.
- Although the author is sure the Turner's had hired hands to help on the ranch, there are no facts to substantiate this, and the name Spuds is fictitious. It is true that local trappers worked on the farms in the summer.
- The petitions for a new county were circulated, but whether Henry used them or not, is not know.
- Beginning in the early 1860's many of Downieville's citizens left for the mines in Virginia City and Gold Hill.
- Campbell's biography (Guinn) states that he worked at a sawmill by the month, for three years, and then homesteaded a farm.
- The author does not know if there was clay on the Turner ranch; however Sinnott *(Sierra Valley* . . .*)* mentions H. K. Turner using bricks he made in his back yard in Sattley.
- The Turner's property originally belonged to George Hale, then to Merric Turner, at which time it may have been a ranch, because although it was a dairy farm when owned by Henry and Hart, all the references refer to it as Turner Ranch.

CHAPTER FOURTEEN – 1870

- The names of the men who worked on the road with H. K. Turner are listed in Sinnott's books *(Sierra Valley* . . . and

Downieville . . .); but their names were given as Mr. Spencer (who could be anyone), A. Sackett (for whom the author could find no information), and S. B. Davidson. There was a man by this latter name, who was District Attorney of Sierra County in 1862. If it was the same S. B. Davidson, it seems remarkable that the road may have been built by a California Senator, and ex-District Attorney.

- Isaac and Abram Church were brothers who each had their own ranch, and were neighbors of the Turners at Church's Corners.
- The information about the Sierra Buttes Quartz Mining Company is true, as are the other details about building the Yuba Pass Wagon Road.
- Jim Miller was a neighbor in Church's Corners, and was the first wagon up the road, with his load of butter and eggs.
- Once again, there is no information about H. K. Turner leaving his family behind, when he went to Sacramento, but the author can think of no other reason Galloways would have allowed Agnes to stay on the Turner Ranch.

CHAPTER FIFTEEN – 1870-71
- The details of the romance between Frank "Hart" Turner and Agnes Galloway are fictitious.
- Information about Alex Beaton and Elvira Colby is true.

CHAPTER SIXTEEN – 1871
- Prior to building of the wagon road, the mail contract to Sierra Valley had mail service only once a week. It was brought over the mountains by Garnosette and Darling's mule train, and it was often left at the Church's Ranch in Church's Corners. This means that the mail left Downieville every Monday, and returned every Wednesday. This would indicate that mail was not delivered when the trails were blocked with snow. Most likely there were some changes when the road was completed, but heavy snow did stop all traffic. The author always thought the mail was delivered on skis, but could find no mention of this until several years later.

- Although the letters mentioned in this chapter are fictitious, word must have been sent to Hattie from someone, because she finally came West during that year.
- The jovial sleigh rides and practice of surprise visits are recorded in Sinnott's *Sierra Valley* . . . I would imagine that Frank (Hart) Turner and his fiancée were among these large groups of young people. It is true they went to the Summit House. Robinson's Dance Hall and the Buxton Hotel were actual places in Randolph.
- The author does not know of Senator H. K. Turner's attendance record in the Senate during the 1870-71 session, but he was home on March 11, 1871, to help organize a new I. O. O. F. Lodge in Loyalton (Sinnott, *Sierra Valley* . . .).
- Information about the taxes is true (Sinnott, *Sierra Valley* . . .).
- One of the exhibits on display at the Loyalton Museum in Loyalton (in the 1980's) was the wedding gown worn by Jim Turner's grandmother in 1871. This would have been Agnes Galloway's dress. I do not know the details of the Turner-Galloway wedding, except they were married by Justice of the Peace, J. E. Beard.

CHAPTER SEVENTEEN – 1871

- Information regarding the Swamp Land Matter, was taken from Sinnott, *Sierra Valley* . . . , and *Land Titles in California* . . .
- The *Sierra Valley News*, Oct. 28, 1940, states that Hattie (Hale) Campbell was one of the first teachers in the old Rocky Point School District.
- Jokes about the Swamp Land problems, were used at every opportunity both in Sierra and Plumas County. Found in a gossip column in the *Plumas National Bulletin,* Oct. 28, 1871, is the comment: "Rumor ventures the prediction that… Frank C. meditates designs upon the individualhood of Hattie H . . . may their hopes never be swamped!"

CHAPTER EIGHTEEN – 1872

- In Sept. 1864, George Hale was one of the men who formed an Ecclesiastical Society to get a minister and church in Sierraville, and he was one of the first trustees.
- The information about the new Donner County is taken from Sinnott, *Sierra Valley* . . .

CHAPTER NINETEEN – 1872-1874

- Dates and facts in this chapter are true.
- Freda Turner, in a phone conversation, related that the family home was destroyed by fire several years ago, and along with it went most of the family records.

CHAPTER TWENTY – 1874

- Jack Campbell was sheriff of Sierra County from 1870 to 1873. He retired and bought the Hot Springs from Fenstermaker in 1874. C. G. Church states that "Jack was a little over-bearing." The author does not know H. K. Turner's true feelings about Jack Campbell, and what is related in this story is only a guess.
- B. F. Lemon and H. K. Turner build the large three story Inn at the new Campbell's Hot Springs.
- This story about Sam Berry (and the description of Sam) was written by Obediah Sattley Church, and published in the *Loyalton, Sierra Valley Times,* April 8, 1941, titled "A Bear Story, Tragedy in Hamlin's Canyon". The names of the people who took part in the event are true. All the information related here is from this article.
- Long board skis were used in the hunt for Sam Berry. Although they are called long board skis in this chapter, they actually were calling them snowshoes at that time. The author refers to them as long board skis for clarification.

CHAPTER TWENTY-ONE – 1875

- Doc Schubert did not live at the Turner Ranch, until 2 years later, so his part in the story is untrue. He was however, a factual doctor in the area, and the fact that he built a home on the Turner Ranch, his problem with liquor and "pulling

up stakes" is from Clara Nelson. Information about the "leetle pills" is from Charlie Church.
- The birth preparations for the mother, given in this chapter, are from Ruth Orzalli, "I Remember".
- The opinion of the *Mountain Messenger* is strictly from an opposing political point of view. The newspaper is still being published in Downieville, CA, and is a fine paper and an asset to the community.
- The date of James Turner's birth is true. It is only a guess that he is named for his maternal grandfather.
- William G. Copren refers to H. K. Turner as "Boss Turner", and his allies as the Republican courthouse gang. He states that they controlled county government without opposition until the early 1880's. Copren mentions Galloway's candidacy for State Senator in 1861, and the fact that he was editor of the *Downieville Democratic,* a newspaper that was published during the political campaign in 1871, where Galloway was very outspoken in his political views. Copren refers to him as "old fire-eater".
- The respect H. K. Turner and James Galloway had for one another was related in a letter to the editor of the *Mountain Messenger,* March 20, 1870. The letter comments on a complementary letter written by Galloway about Turner, and remarks that it is "interesting and pleasant" because it came from "so strong a Democrat and political opponent as Mr. Galloway".
- The author does not know if Frank Campbell belonged to the Debating Club, but because his wife taught at the school where the group met, and the Campbells lived in the vicinity of the school, and because Frank became involved in a political career of his own later in his life, it is reasonable to assume he was a member of this group. The topic of discussion on that date is correct (Sinnott, *Sierra Valley* . . .).
- The completion of Campbell's Hot Springs Inn and the purchase of new furniture is mentioned in Sinnott, *Sierra Valley* . . .
- The first winter snow storms usually come to this part of the Sierra Nevada Mountains in October. Because of the

- newspaper reports of huge forest fires in the mountains as late as Oct. 30 (Ibid), the author assumed that it was one of those years when the first snow fall came as late as November.
- Snow was over four feet on the level and the damage it caused in Sierra Valley is true (Ibid). The experience of the deep snow are the author's own childhood recollections of the winter of 1952, when the snow was over six feet deep a short distance from Sierra Valley, but not nearly as deep in the valley itself.
- It is true that George Hale sold his hotel to Ezra Church the spring after the big storm.

CHAPTER TWENTY-TWO – 1876
- Sierra County's Assessment Roll for 1875 declares that the Turner Brother's owned 12 cattle and 22 cows; while the Assessment Roll for 1876 shows they had 39 cattle and 35 cows.
- Conversations and feelings expressed are fictitious.

CHAPTER TWENTY-THREE – 1876
- The scourge of the grasshoppers attacking Sierra Valley in droves is true. (J. C. Lemmon, *Plumas National Bulletin*.)
- Apparently there were two stage lines which ran past the Turner Ranch in 1877-78. One ran from Truckee to Sierra City, via Sierra Valley, and the other ran from Truckee to Eureka Mills (Johnsville), via Sierraville. The later ran three times a week. The author does not know how often a stage was seen passing through the ranch, it is probably an exaggeration to say daily.
- Dr. Alemby Jump was a well known physician in Downieville, at one time the county coroner. He was one of the leaders of the Republican Party, and a close ally to H. K. Turner.
- The process of making bricks from clay is from "The Woodwright" TV show.
- The main source for information about the problems facing the state of California, The Workingmen's Party, and the

tactics used by the Republicans and Democrats, was Swisher.
- Sierra and Nevada counties formed the 24th District in 1874, which left Sierra County to share its Senatorial seat with Nevada County, and reduced their representation in the Assembly to one assemblyman (Fariss and Smith). H. K. Turner did not run for re-election after this change.
- The date is correct, for the election for Representatives to the Second Constitutional Convention. It is impossible to know who Galloway voted for in this election.
- Atwood's Store in Sierraville was the actual location of the polls.
- The result of the election is true.

CHAPTER TWENTY-FOUR – 1878-79
- September 28, 1878 is the birth date of Thomas Turner, but not necessarily the day the convention began. The Sierra County Supervisors minutes, Bk C, state this as the official date, but Swisher says they began on September 29th, and postponed until September 30th.
- The information about Henry Eagerton is from Woodridge, most of the other facts about convention proceedings are from Swisher.
- F. H. Turner states that H. K. was "much disappointed with the Constitutional Act, as adopted at the time. He and his associates were often in the minority, and considered the act as adopted very 'faulty', which is proved to be, as it was amended many times."
- The author does not know if H. K. Turner smoked a pipe. This is fictitious. If he smoked at all, it probably would have been cigars, which seemed to be the custom of local politicians of that era.
- The information related by Henry about the Constitutional Convention is from Swisher and Mason.
- The result of the election is accurate.

CHAPTER TWENTY-FIVE – 1882

- The facts about the Turner bid on the vault are from the Sierra County Supervisor's minutes.
- The Sierra County Supervisors were all Republicans (Copren), and Dan Cole was one of the members (Fariss & Smith).
- Sierra Valley still suffered from the grasshopper plague (Sinnott, *Sierra Valley* . . .)
- At age 62, Frances Campbell was one half inch short of six foot tall, had a light complexion and blue eyes (Great Register of sierra County – 1892)
- From a newspaper report of March 22, 1879, is the statement that Dr. Alemby Jump and D. T. Cole were well known in Forest City. It is reasonable to expect them to be known by Frances Campbell, who was active in his community. If anyone talked Campbell into running for political office, Cole and Jump would have been the men, but it is only a supposition (Sinnott, *Alleghany* . . .).
- The location of the Sierra Valley Frank Campbell's ranch is from the Plumas County Assessment Roll.
- Although Jack Campbell owned the Hot Springs for a few brief years 1874-77, it is still called Campbell's Hot Springs until the year 2000 and beyond.
- Details about Garfield's murder are from Ellis.
- The Republican Party had been in conflicts with reform groups prior to Garfield's death, but the murder (by a republican) only escalated the problem that already existed (Clark, ". . . Garfield", *Funk & Wagnallis*).

CHAPTER TWENTY-SIX - 1882

- Details of the proceedings of the Republican Central Committee are taken from a newspaper article in the *Sierra County Tribune*, September 6, 1882.
- Frances Campbell's involvement in his community is found in Sinnott, *Alleghany* . . . He was a deputy for Sheriff Fish (Supervisor's Minutes); and he did make a short political campaign in the north section of the county (*Sierra County Tribune*, July 13, 1882).

- Physical description of Sierra County, and names of towns are taken from Fariss & Smith
- August 17 was not the actual date of the convention, it was sometime during the previous week.
- The events that transpired at the Republican Convention in August, 1882, are taken from the *Sierra County Tribune,* August 17, 1882.
- In a letter to the editor of the *San Juan Times,* Judge Stidger of Sierra Valley names H. K. Turner and Dr. Jump, "notable among these mongrels who are engaged in the mud throwing—those who walked out of the convention." The names of the others, who left, are not known.
- The actual number of walk out votes, quoted in the *Sierra County Tribune,* was 22 ½.

CHAPTER TWENTY-SEVEN – 1882

- The quotes from newspapers are true, the meeting and discussions are fictitious.

CHAPTER TWENTY-EIGHT - 1882

- Ottie Turner's life style is not factual.
- Mr. Fish was a republican from the state of Maine (Fariss & Smith).
- Actual quotes from the *Sierra County Tribune* in reference to H. K. Turner and Dr. Jump in particular, were "men who bolted the convention", "*Messenger* and its bolting allies" (a reference to the reins Turner and Jump had on the *Mountain Messenger),* "bolting of the throng", "slanderous gang", "mongrels", and "yelping and hellish clan".
- Turner's allegations about Campbell and the liquor licenses is from "Back Action Argument", *Sierra County Tribune.*
- Dan Cole's participation in the mudslinging is unknown. He may have bowed out. Turner's and Jump's names came up in the news constantly.
- The only reference to Daisy Turner's age is in her mother's obituary. The author does not have her birth date.
- Sinnott, *Sierra Valley* . . . indicated that the grasshopper plague didn't begin to disappear until 1883.

- The *Sierra County Tribune,* May 10, 1883 (Sinnott, *Sierra Valley* . . .) states "H. K. Turner is contemplating the building of a sawmill . . . " Tom Turner (Wooldridge) states Hartwell Turner built the mill, and Harry Turner (Ibid) says that H. F. and Henry K. Turner became interested in sawmills and built the mill. Both accounts say the mill was built in 1882 (which the newspaper account does not validate). It is reasonable to believe that Hartwell was as much involved in the planning as his brother.

CHAPTER TWENTY-NINE – 1882

- The family reunion is fictitious.
- Hartwell's home was apparently larger than Henry's, because the Assessment Roll 1882, assessed the house on H. K.'s property at $150, while the house on H. F.'s property was assessed at $250.
- Guinn lists all of Campbell's children apparently in chronological order. The earliest birth date the author has found is for Charles, who was born in 1880 (Beckwourth Cemetery), and is third on Guinn's list.
- The remark about Maine loggers compared to those in the West is a fictitious idea taken from the point of view of someone raised in Maine
- Campbell may well have smoked cigars, as later in his life he ran for Supervisor of Plumas County (Candidates Statements), and spent $3 on a box of cigars as a campaign expense.
- Campbell's loss of a child in 1882 is correct.

CHAPTER THIRTY – 1882

- Both Alex Beaton and George Wood were subpoenaed as part of the people, which indicates that they were witnesses that day (Superior Court Minutes). What they witnessed is unknown to the author.
- When Sierraville burned, George Wood lost a drugstore and a harness shop. Most of the town was insured and they quickly rebuilt. (Sinnott, *Sierra Valley* . . .)

- Alex Beaton had a daughter Hattie, born June 19, 1874. (Farris & Smith) This would make her eight years old in 1882.
- The location of Cody's Saloon, the Buxton Hotel, and Dolley's store are mentioned in the *Mountain Messenger,* September 22, 1882.
- Sinnott, *Sierra Valley . . . ,* gives the location of the school and church.
- George Wood and Alex Beaton were the same age. (Sierraville Cemetery; Great Register of Sierra County)
- Campbell's maiden name was Maggie Turner, of Downieville. I can find no indication that she was related to H. K. Turner. The Campbell's adoption of the Williams children is true (*Sierra County Tribune,* September 21, 1882).
- The details of Campbell's murder are true, and a combination of the accounts found in the *Mountain Messenger,* September 22, 1882; *Plumas National Bulletin,* September 23, 1882; and C. G. Church.
- Buxton, Cody, and Dolley were all called as witnesses for the People (Superior Court Minutes.)
- At the printing of the article, "The Assassination…" (*Plumas National Bulletin,* September 23, 1882), Stubbs had not been captured, and it is stated, "Many theories are afloat and some think that politics had something to do with it." Because H. K. Turner had been accused of throwing mud at Campbell and his campaign, the author concluded that, if politics did have anything to do with it, Campbell's friends would be after Turner's neck.
- Information about George Wood's business investments and political history are true.
- The posse consisted of "a large party of men and Indians (who) started out and searched all night in the storm." ("Atrocious Murder")
- Alex Beaton may not have had a Scottish accent. However, he was born in Nova Socia, of Scottish parents. (Farris & Smith)
- H. K. Turner's reaction to Campbell's murder is fictitious.

CHAPTER THIRTY ONE – 1882

- Information about Stubbs, his capture, transport to Downieville and autopsy are true, and taken from "Atrocious Murder".
- It is true that Campbell had been a saloon keeper when not sheriff (*Sierra County Tribune*).
- Amelia Dolley had a son, Fred Dolley, born in Sierraville on December 14, 1882 (Wooldridge).
- Incredible as it may seem, Dr. Jump did perform the autopsy on the object of his mudslinging campaign—Jack Campbell ("Atrocious Murder").
- Randolph's efforts at building a reservoir are true and found in Sinnott's book on Sierra Valley.
- The black eyes and fights that followed Campbell's murder are true.
- "Jack Campbell Assassinated" emphasizes the charitable attributes of Jack Campbell.
- The information about Ferguson is from "The Assassination of Jack Campbell". The article reported that Ferguson and Stubbs had been in conversation the day before the murder, and money exchanged hands.
- Campbell was "never known to carry a weapon of any kind." ("Atrocious Murder")

CHAPTER THIRTY TWO – 1883

- The name Nicholson and Mead are true. An interesting side note (according to C. G. Church) is the fact that Campbell's niece Maggie Williams, who was raised by Campbells from an orphaned child, later married Mike Mead.
- C. G. Church called the murderer Dode Stubbs, the newspapers called him J. J. Stubbs.
- According to Bowdoin College, H. K. Turner attended for two years and did not graduate. Their catalog (1850) describes the requirements.
- The Turner's were raised by their Aunt Mary (Wooldridge).
- It is not known why H. K. Turner stayed behind and went to college when his father came west.

- It is not known where or how Thomas Turner died. He was buried at Snake Bar (Wooldridge).

CHAPTER THIRTY THREE – 1883

- All of the information about Aggie's illness, and birth of her baby are true, including her great faith. The newspaper account states that she was surrounded by those she loved and "exhorted all to so live as to meet her in Heaven". (*Mountain Messenger,* May 12, 1883)
- The treatment for Aggie's illness was from *Vitalogy*, which had current treatment for illnesses in 1899.
- I do not know if Dr. Schubert was Aggie's physician. The *Mountain Messenger* (Ibid) stated there was a physician. C. G. Church states that Doc Schubert was the only doctor for a good many years.
- Conversation and reactions of the family are fictitious.

CHAPTER THIRTY FOUR - 1884

- Reactions and comments by the characters in this chapter are purely fiction.

CHAPTER THIRTY FIVE – 1884

- According to C.G. Church the Turner's built their sawmill in 1883 or 1885, but the tax records show they paid taxes for their sawmill starting in 1884.
- Fletcher and Cole both owned sawmills.
- Sierra Co. Tax records of 1884, show that H. K. Turner house and property were mortgaged to Blatchley for $2500. It is only a guess that it was to pay for the building of the sawmill. The blacksmith shop and town hall in Church's Corners, was owned by Emy Blatchley (*Delinquent Assessment*).
- The technical description of the Turner mill, and the fact they got Tom Labrook's ox team that first year, are from a newspaper article written by C. G. Church, in Elizabeth Laffranchini's album. In this article Church thought the mill was "possibly built in 1883".

CHAPTER THIRTY SIX – 1884

- George Hale died on February 20, 1884 at age 69 ½, and he was living on the Turner Ranch at the time.
- What Rachel Hale did after her husband's death is unknown, except she later married Isaac Church.
- Name change from Church's Corners to Sattley is from Sinnott, *Sierra Valley*....
- The relationship between George Hale and his in-laws is fiction.
- Charlie Church tells of the Turner's purchasing four oxen from Ed Freeman, who is referred to as "the cattle king of Sierra Valley" by another source.
- The author does not know who the Turners talked to or where they went in search of a driver for their ox teams, but Charlie Church states that they finally got an old man from Tools Station, the name and description for the man also came from Charlie Church, who was the young man who "swamped" for Colonel Woods.
- The amount of lumber the Turners produced that year is from the Sierra County Assessment Roll.

CHAPTER THIRTY SEVEN – 1885-86

- The author is not sure if Galloway was a lawyer in Sierra Valley.
- The amount of money Turner's borrowed from A. D. Church is from Sierra County Assessment Roll.
- The author is not positive about where the Turner home stood in relationship to the mill.
- Some of the details of the lumber business came from Williams, *The Logger*.
- Charlie Church states that the Turners cut and yarded 700,000 ft, bunched out along timber roads, and brought in with sled teams in the winter.

CHAPTER THIRTY EIGHT - 1887

- Senator Turner's life accomplishments are true.
- The details of the Smallpox Epidemic in Sierra County are from Sinnott, *Sierra Valley*...

- The information about C. C. Darling is true.
- The yellow flag as an indication of quarantine is apparently true, as the author found several references to it.
- The Morrison brother's death from smallpox is recorded by Charlie Church.

CHAPTER THIRTY NINE

- The fact that Alex Beaton nursed Henry Turner during his bout with the dreaded disease is from Sinnott, *Sierra Valley*.
- The symptoms and care of smallpox is from Wood, *Vitalogy*.
- Burning sulfur is something told to the author by a maternal grandmother.
- The precautions H. K. Turner's family took to ward off Smallpox are fabricated.

CHAPTER FORTY - 1888

- The mechanic's lien against George Morrison is true.
- The storm that kept H. K. Turner in Downieville for a week is true. (*Mountain Messenger* March 10, 1888)
- The fact that Turner was the Republican nominee for State Assembly, is true, how he made this decision is speculation. His brother and Galloway's reaction are also speculation.

CHAPTER FORTY ONE - 1888

- The first part of this chapter, about the upcoming election, is pure speculation.
- The names and attendance of the delegates to the Republican Convention in Downieville, mentioned in this chapter are true.
- Vaughn was the name of the editor of the *Mountain Messenger*, and in the research for this book, the author hunted through the old newspapers and could find no mention of H. K. Turner running for State Assembly. The only mention of his name in the newspaper is the comment quoted in this chapter.
- Alex Beaton's accident is true.

CHAPTER FORTY TWO - 1888

- Of course, the author has no idea how James Galloway voted in this election. The truth in this chapter is that Henry won.

BIBLIOGRAPHY

BOOKS:

Bancroft, Hubert H. History of California 1860-1890. Vol. VII. San Francisco: History Co. Pub, 1890.

Bartlett, John. Bartlett's Familiar Quotations. Boston: Little Brown, 1968.

Carter, Allan M. American Universities and Colleges. Washington D.C.: American Council of Education, 1964.

Copren, William G. The Political History of Sierra County, California, 1849-1861. Reno: Unplubished thesis, University of Nevada, 1975.

Davis, Winfield J. History of Political Conventions in California, 1848-1892. Sacramento: California State Library, 1893.

Driscoll, Jack D. California Legislature. Sacrameno: California Legislative Assembly, 1978.

Ellis, Edward. The Youth's History of the United States. New York: Cassell Pub. Co., 1887.

Fariss and Smith. History of Plumas, Lassen, and Sierra Counties. Fariss and Smith, 1882.

Guinn, J. M. History of the State of California and Biographical Record of the Sierras. Chicago: Chapman, 1906.

Mason, Paul, comp. Constitution of the State of California and of the United States and Other Documents. Sacramento: California State Senate, 1949.

Reed, Walter G. History of Sacramento County. Los Angles: Historic Record Company, 1923.

Romans. The Bible.

Roosevelt, Theodore. Ranch Life and Hunting Trail. New York: Century Co., 1888.

Sinnott, James J. Alleghany and Forest City. Volcano: California Traveler, 1975.

Sinnott, James J. Downieville, Gold Town on the Yuba. Volcano: Travelers, Inc.

Sinnott, James J. Sierra City and Goodyears Bar. Volcano: California Travelers, 1973.

Sinnott, James J. Sierra Valley, Jewel of the Sierras. Pioneer: California Traveler, 1976.

Swisher, Carl B. Motivational and Political Technique in California Constitutional Convention 1878-79. New York: Da Campo P, 1969

Williams, Richard L. The Loggers. New York: Time Life Books, 1976

Wood, George P. and E. H. Ruddock. Vitalogy. New York: I. N. Reed, 1899.

Wooldridge, J. W. History of Sacramento Valley. Vol. III. Chicago: Pioneer Historical Pub. Co., 1931.

CATALOGUES:
Catalogue of the Officers and Students of Bowdoin College and the Medical School of Maine. Bruinswick, Maine: Bowdoin College, Spring Term, 1850. 19.

General Catalogue of Bowdoin College, 1794-1950. Brunswick, Maine: Bowdoin College, 1950. 102.

CEMETERIES:
Beckwourth, California.
Sattley, California.
Sierraville, California.

ENCYCLOPEDIA ARTICLES:
American Forest Institute, comp. "Lumber Industry." Funk & Wagnalls New Encyclopedia XV. 1975.

Clark, Norman H. "James Abram Garfield." Funk & Wagnalls New Encyclopedia 1975 XI. 1975.

Thompson, Douglass S. "Smallpox." Funk & Wagnalls New Encyclopedia. 1975.

GOVERNMENT RECORDS:
Candidates Statements of Receipts and Expenditures. Plumas County Archives. Plumas County Museum. Quincy.

Delinquent Assessment Roll. California. Sierra County Courthouse. Vol. 1897-1898.

Great Register of Sierra County. Sierra County Archives. Sierra County Courthouse. Downieville, 1892.

Index to Marriages. Siierra County Archives. Sierra County Courthouse. Downieville.

Original Assessment Roll. Plumas County Archives. Plumas County Museum. Quincy, 1876-77.

Original Assessment Roll. Sierra County Archives. Sierra County Courthouse. Downieville, 1871, 1875, 1876, 1882.

Sierra County Board of Supervisor's Minutes. Sierra County Board of Supervisor's. Vol. C. Downieville.

United States. Cong. 1st Cong., 3rd sess. 2443. Land Titles in California - Memorial of Settlers in Sierra Valley. 1870.

INTERVIEWS:
Turner, Freda. Telephone interview. 22 Nov. 1987. Interview conducted by the author.

MISCELLANEOUS ARTICLES:

Turner, Franklin Hurd. "An Acccount of the Turner Pioneers of Sierra County, with some mention of other families connected by marriage" 1954

NEWSPAPERS:

"The Assination of Jack Campbell." Plumas National Bulletin 23 Sept. 1882.
"Atrocious Murder." Mountain Messenger 22 Sept. 1882.
"Back Action Argument." Sierra County Tribune 31 Aug. 1882.
Church, C. G. "Charlie Church Says: Sketch of My Early Life." Loyalton Sierra Valley Times 2, 9 May 1941.
Church, C. G. "Early History of Sierra Valley." Sierra Valley News Feb.-Mar. 1940.
Church, C. G. "Earl History of Sierra Valley." Sierra Valley News 10 May 1940.
Church, Obediah S. "A Bear Story, Tragedy in Hamlin's Canyon." Loyalton Sierra Valley Times 18 Apr. 1941.
"Death of Agnes Turner." Plumas National Bulletin 12 May 1883.
"Jack Campbell and His Traducer." Sierra County Tribune 31 Aug. 1882.
"Jack Campbell Assassinated." Sierra County Tribune 21 Sept. 1882.
Lemmon, J. G. "The California Scourge, Chapter III." Plumas National Bulletin 12 Dec. 1879.
Miller, Bertha. "Sub Zero Terperature Complicates Life for Hardy Sierra Valley Ranch families." Sacramento Bee, Suppliment, Californai Country Life 31 Jan. 1960.
Mountain Messenger Oct. 1867, May 1883, Mar. 1888.
Nelson, Clara B. "Mrs. Nelson Writes Again." Sierra Valley News 23 Aug. 1940.
Orzalli, Ruth. "I Remember." Sierra Booster 2 Sept. 1977: 14.
Plumas National Bulletin Oct. 1871, Sept. 1882, May 1883.
"Proceedings of Republican Central Committee." Sierra County Tribune 6 Sept. 1882.
"Stick to Your Party." Sierra Valley News 17 Aug. 1882.

SCRAPBOOKS:

Church, C. G. "Thoughts of Early Days." Elizabeth Laffranchini's Scrapbook.
Nelson, Clara B. "Mrs. Nelson Writes Again." Elizabeth Laffranchini's Scrapbook.

THESIS:

Copren, William C. "The Political History of Sierra County, California, 1849-1861." Thesis. Reno: University of Nevada, 1975.

TV SHOWS:

Underhill, Ray, and Geary Morton. "The Woodwrite Shop." PBS. 1989.

About the Author

C. L. Neely is a native of Northern California and was raised a short distance from the beautiful Sierra Valley. Interest in the local history began at an early age. *Behind Every Hero* is an accumulation of fifteen years of research on the historical details of Sierra County. Neely's love for books led to the ownership of three bookstores, and the publication of a book on the history of Graeagle. Cartooning is another love of the author who has illustrated two cookbooks, a magazine article, designed dozens of greeting cards under the Chicken Scratch logo, and was a partner is a sweatshirt design company named 5th Sparrow. C. L. Neely is married with four children and ten grandchildren and is now retired and lives in Oregon.

Other works by this author:

Graeagle – History of Mohawk Valley
Including Clairville and Johnsville

Notes:

Made in the USA
Las Vegas, NV
07 June 2021